T0266935

JAILBREAK

James Durney is an award-winning author of over twenty books on Irish national and local history, including *Interned: The Curragh Internment Camps in the War of Independence* (2019). He works at Kildare County Archives and Local Studies.

JAILBREAK

GREAT IRISH REPUBLICAN ESCAPES
1865–1983

JAMES DURNEY

MERRION
PRESS

First published in 2024 by
Merrion Press
10 George's Street
Newbridge
Co. Kildare
Ireland
www.merrionpress.ie

© James Durney, 2024

978 1 78537 492 0 (Paper)
978 1 78537 493 7 (Ebook)

A CIP catalogue record for this book is
available from the British Library.

Typeset in Minion Pro 11/16 pt

Cover design by Padraig McCormack

Merrion Press is a member of Publishing Ireland

To my granddaughter
Autumn Ellen Reddy

ACKNOWLEDGEMENTS

My thanks to: Conor Graham, who believed in this project from the beginning; Tony Kelly and Dermot McNally for their insights on the escape from Long Kesh and Tony for use of the photograph of escapees; Joe Murphy; Mick Healy for use of the photograph of Frank Driver; Patrick O'Donoghue; Fergal McLoughlin; Co. Kildare archivist Karel Kiely; Gerard Shannon; Kildare Local Studies; Jim Maher; Monica Healy, my sister-in-law, whose search for the LP 'Irish Republican Jail Songs' was partly an inspiration for this book; Brian Crowley, Kilmainham Gaol Museum, for photograph credits and help in sourcing them; the editorial team, Síne Quinn, John Whelan and Wendy Logue, for the edits and additions to the book; James Doyle for the use of a photograph from the John Sweeney Collection. Thanks to my wife, Caroline, for her understanding when I again become engrossed in another publication deadline.

CONTENTS

INTRODUCTION

The blockbuster movie *The Great Escape* (1963) is considered one of the greatest war movies of all time, except it features no battles but an escape by Allied prisoners from Stalag Luft III during the Second World War. It is the tale of a well-known, though largely unsuccessful, escape from a German prisoner-of-war camp. While researching the escape of over fifty republican prisoners from the Rath Camp, on the Curragh Plains, during the Irish War of Independence, I noticed many similarities to *The Great Escape*. There was an escape committee in Stalag Luft III, which coordinated and approved breakouts, just like the one in the Rath Camp; both camps had a tunnel ventilation system, and the distribution of the tunnel soil around the camp was similar. The Rath Camp tunnel had also come up short just like Stalag Luft III's, hindering the escape. I wondered had the British studied the Rath Camp escape and similar republican ingenuity in building tunnels from jails and internment camps and passed on this information to their servicemen who might become POWs in a future conflict.

Irish republicans have been escaping from places of confinement since the foundation of the republican movement, but it was really with the escape of James Stephens in 1865 that the tradition of republican escapees began. The focus in most chapters in this book is one main event, but I have also provided some details of other escapes relating to the main breakout. I have left in the age of the escapees as reported in the newspapers of the day to give a sense of the profile of those engaged in republican activity; many were quite young at the time. Most, it can be assumed, grew up in a world of political violence. They did not go to war; the war came to them. Others came from traditional republican backgrounds, with 'credentials' stretching back many years through family involvement. With the passage of time not all names and addresses of escapees are remembered or even identified. It is still unknown exactly how many men absconded in the Great Escape from the Rath Camp in 1921. Where known I have provided all names and addresses of escapees. Some escapees might only have a first initial as reported at the time, but further research might provide full names. The files of the 1925 Mountjoy Prison escape were only released in February 2024, while this manuscript was in its editing stage, so luckily the Military Archives provided new information.

Some men were two-time escapees; as Piaras Béaslaí said, 'It is a theorem with prison-keepers that, while a man may serve twenty years in prison without once thinking of escaping, he who has once escaped is certain to attempt it again.'[1] This opinion was justified in Béaslaí's case, for he subsequently escaped five months after having been recaptured. He was not the only one. Tomás Ó Maoláin escaped through a tunnel from the Rath Camp in September 1921 and again got out through a tunnel from Tintown Camp in 1923. Patrick Bagnall escaped from Newbridge Barracks in October 1922 only to face a firing squad two months later when he was recaptured. Many other escapees returned to active service only to be killed in action. Paddy Carty and Michael McVerry escaped from the Military Detention Barracks in the Curragh in October 1972. Within a year both of them were dead – killed while engaging in operations against Crown forces.

Jailbreak: Great Irish Republican Escapes, 1865–1983 tells the stories of the many successful republican escapes, but also the elation and the heartbreak that followed. Some never got to enjoy their freedom; others lived among us as ordinary citizens, their time in jail and their life on the run forgotten now as time moves on and conflicts become a part of history.

James Durney
Naas, Co. Kildare

CHAPTER 1

'ALL THE WORK OF MONTHS IS UNDONE IN A MOMENT'

James Stephens's flight from Dublin's Richmond Prison concluded one of the shortest stays of detention in the history of Irish republican escapes. He was arrested on 11 November 1865 and within twelve days was a free man. The daring operation proved a propaganda coup for the fledgling separatist movement, the Irish Republican Brotherhood (IRB).

The 'Fenian Chief' James Stephens was born at Blackmill Street, Kilkenny, in 1825. In 1848 he joined William Smith O'Brien's revolutionary attempt and took part in the skirmish at Widow McCormack's house near Ballingarry, Co. Tipperary. After the failure of the 1848 Rising, Stephens escaped to France, where he worked as a translator and English tutor.[1] In 1856 Stephens returned to Ireland, and on St Patrick's Day, 17 March 1858, he founded the Irish Republican Brotherhood. On that national day of great importance, for the Irish at home and abroad, in a little room in Dublin, James Stephens and his comrades swore an oath pledging to bring about an independent Irish republic. Not long after, in New York City, a recent Irish immigrant, John O'Mahony, established an American counterpart to the IRB, the

Fenian Brotherhood, named after the legendary Fianna warriors. The Stephens–O'Mahony alliance began planning for a rising in Ireland to rid the country once and for all of British rule.[2] They declared 1865 the 'year of action'.

Following the end of the American Civil War in May 1865, scores of military veterans of Irish origin began to arrive in Ireland under the guise of returned emigrants. The authorities were aware of their ulterior motives in returning and that something was about to happen. They struck first and armed with information from an inside source, the informer Pierce Nagle, arrested 187 suspects, among them IRB executive leaders Charles Luby, John O'Leary and Jeremiah O'Donovan Rossa. However, they missed their most important target – the elusive mastermind, James Stephens.[3]

Finally, on 9 November 1865, after countless unsuccessful tips, a man walked into the detective office of G Division of the Dublin Metropolitan Police and announced that he knew the whereabouts of James Stephens. Two days later police swooped on Fairfield House, Sandymount, in the Dublin suburbs, and arrested Stephens, Charles J. Kickham, Edward Duffy and Hugh Brophy. Four loaded revolvers, ammunition, documents and money were also seized. The four men were accused of belonging to the Fenian conspiracy, 'having for its object the levying of war against the Queen in Ireland, subverting the Queen's authority in Ireland, separating it from the United Kingdom, and establishing a republic'. A newspaper report said the four men 'did not appear to be depressed, but on the contrary seemed to take the matter lightly'.[4]

The prisoners were conveyed to Richmond Prison, Grangegorman, and appeared before the chief magistrate on 14 November, where Stephens refused to defend himself and ridiculed the police for taking four months to find him. He insinuated that the police had misappropriated £500 found during the search of Fairfield

House.[5] His arrogance later raised the belief that he did not expect to remain in prison very long. Stephens encouraged this belief for propaganda purposes, but in fact was not aware that the organisation happened to have the means to rescue him. The staff of Richmond Prison included a night watchman, Daniel Byrne, a sworn Fenian, and John J. Breslin, the hospital steward, a strong sympathiser whose two brothers, Michael and Niall, were active members of the IRB.

John Breslin met Stephens at the prison the day after his arrest and was greatly impressed with the man known as 'The Captain'. A few days later Breslin found that his brother Niall was obsessed with the idea of rescuing Stephens, and through him he arranged an interview with IRB Captain Thomas J. Kelly. Breslin then agreed to undertake Stephen's rescue with the help of Daniel Byrne.

Meanwhile, Kelly appointed John Devoy to select nine men to serve as Stephens's escort outside the prison and wrote to America to inform O'Mahony about their plan. Very soon the scheme to rescue Stephens became an open secret inside the IRB, but the government did not receive the warning until it was too late. On 22 November two soldiers who had been approached by a Fenian agent declared that there were five Fenian warders in Richmond Prison who could let Stephens out at any time, but this report only reached the authorities on 24 November, when Stephens had already been rescued.[6]

The cell that was occupied by Stephens was on the third floor, close to Breslin's quarters at the prison hospital, in a section called Class no.9. This section consisted of a main corridor, called 'long range', and two shorter ones at a right angle to it. Stephens's cell was located at the end of one of the short corridors, which was connected to the inner sections of the prison by two successive doors. His cell door was composed of strong hammered iron and secured by a large double lock. The corridor on which the cell opened was guarded by another double-locked iron door. Escape from the iron-barred windows was impossible. No one was permitted to see the Fenian prisoners except the officials of the prison and their legal advisers. In case of a rescue attempt, some of the Metropolitan Police were kept constantly on duty in one of the prison's outer corridors.[7]

Stephens's cell had been previously occupied by a regular convict, John McLeod, who had been moved to an adjoining cell and placed between Stephens and Kickham to prevent them from communicating. As a further security measure, McLeod had been provided with a handbell and instructed to ring it if he should hear anything suspicious. The door separating the short corridor from the long range was also locked – to prevent the policemen from communicating with Stephens. This would prove to be a fatal mistake.

Breslin's plan to get Stephens out of prison was simple. Some time during his working hours Breslin took the chance to make wax impressions of the keys to Stephens's corridor and cell, both of which were locked in the governor's office at night. These wax impressions were conveyed to Michael Lambert, an optician and sworn Fenian, who made the corresponding false keys and sent them back to Breslin. As soon as he had the keys in his possession, Breslin informed Captain Kelly that everything was ready. On the night of 23 November Captain Kelly, John Devoy and ten other Fenians took up positions around Richmond Prison and prepared to receive Stephens as soon as he should appear over the wall.

The night watchman, Daniel Byrne, went on duty at 10 p.m., and later recalled that Stephens was secure in his cell. It was a wet and windy night, and this was a further benefit for the rescue party. Outside the prison the streets were deserted, while inside the banging of open windows helped to muffle any inappropriate noises. A police sentry, James Kennedy, placed at the end of the long range in Class no.9, was later to blame both the wind and the closed door leading to the short corridor for his failure to hear what had happened in the vicinity of Stephens's cell. At 1 a.m. on 24 November Breslin left the hospital ward, climbed the stairs and quietly opened the metal door leading into Stephens's corridor. Stephens was lying on top of his bed with his clothes on waiting for him. Breslin unlocked the door of Stephens's cell, handed him a revolver, and both proceeded along the corridor.[8]

Hearing no sound from McLeod, Breslin and Stephens went down the stairs and crossed several doors until they came out into the insulating area of the prison. Byrne had assured Breslin that the ladder used to light the lamps in the yard was long enough to reach the top of the wall, but on testing the ladder Breslin found it was much too short. At this point, Stephens's nerve broke and he thought it was all over. Breslin, however, rushed back inside, found Byrne, and with his help brought two tables from the asylum dining room, some eighty yards from the spot where Stephens was waiting. Breslin and Byrne piled up the tables, placed the ladder on top and held it while Stephens climbed over the wall onto a tool shed on the other side in an area called the governor's garden. Before climbing the ladder, Stephens handed Breslin his revolver. This hasty gesture soured Breslin's good impression of Stephens as a fearless leader.[9]

Beyond the first wall the prison was surrounded by the governor's garden. Stephens still had to climb another wall before he could complete his escape. He approached a pear tree close to the outer wall on the side facing the North Circular Road and threw over a handful of gravel as a signal to the men outside. They flung over a rope and gripped it while Stephens climbed about eighteen feet to the top of the wall. It was a high jump down and a member of the rescue party, John Ryan, told Stephens to drop down with his back to the wall and the men would catch him.

According to John Devoy, 'he did so, and Ryan caught his feet on his chest ... it staggered Ryan, and as Stephens was coming down, I caught him about the knees and let him slide to the ground.' Stephens was trembling from the tension and physical strain, and this shattered Devoy's belief in his leader's 'coolness and self-possession'.[10]

After the successful escape of the Fenian chief, the members of the rescue party went their separate ways. Capt. Kelly led Stephens to Mrs Boland's house, on Brown Street, in Dublin's Liberties area, which was to be his hiding place for the time being. Inside Richmond Prison, Breslin had quietly returned to his room, while Byrne went about his rounds as usual until 4.05 a.m., when he called the chief warder and notified him that something was wrong. Going through the insulating area, Byrne had seen two tables piled up against the wall, which he thought was suspicious. On examination, the prison officials discovered a trail of open doors leading straight to Stephens's cell, and Breslin's false key in the padlock on the floor. The alarm was quickly raised through the prison, and the governor, Dominick Marques, and all the officials were soon at their respective posts. The prison authorities sent special messengers in hot haste to inform the police at the nearest stations and at the detective office of the escape. When the governor and his assistants went to the section of the prison in which Stephens had been confined, they found the corridor doors and his cell door open. His bed looked as if it had not been slept in, Stephens's numerous books were spread about and it was evident from the general appearance of the articles in the cell that he had been preparing for his departure.

The investigation into Stephens's escape revealed a series of security failures in the management of Richmond Prison. Governor Dominick Marques was adjudged to be incompetent in his duties and was dismissed from his office. The Lord Lieutenant was so disgusted, he vowed that henceforth he would keep the appointments to the city jails in his own hands.[11] It was evident that Stephens was under the guidance of a person who knew the prison well, as they had traversed the winding and difficult route from one end of the prison to the other without a single blunder or without baulking at a lock or door.

Daniel Byrne was immediately arrested and put on trial. Two successive juries failed to agree a verdict – although Byrne had been found in possession of a copy of the Fenian oath and an identical padlock to that in Stephens's cell. The prisoner McLeod said the escape was assisted through a person inside the prison. He stated that while he was lying in bed awake, he heard the prison clock strike one o'clock, and immediately after he heard the footfall of a single person, who seemed to come up the stairs to the corridor to Stephens's cell. McLeod heard the corridor door being unlocked, then heard the lock on Stephens's door being opened; after this he heard someone come out of the cell, join the person in the corridor, and heard the footsteps of two people as they walked off together. The authorities assumed that this was Byrne and Stephens. McLeod declared he did not ring his bell, for fear that whoever was letting Stephens out might enter his cell and kill him.[12]

Stephens's escape boosted the republican movement's morale and attracted hundreds of new members and sympathisers to the Fenians' cause. A reward of £1,000 was offered for his recapture, but that was the last time the British authorities ever held The Captain a prisoner. Lord Lieutenant Wodehouse wrote in dismay, 'All the work of months is undone in a moment.'[13] But the newly liberated Stephens, now among the world's most wanted men, was not in a mood to capitalise on his sensational escape. He called a round of meetings in Dublin the following month, and declared that the planned rising was to be postponed. Stephens's continued reluctance to order the long-expected rising led to his overthrow by Thomas J. Kelly in December 1866 and his resulting exile in France. The result, however, was the failed Fenian Rising of 5–6 March 1867.

After his deposition, Stephens spent most of his remaining years in France, in dire virtual poverty, hoping to regain his position at the head of the republican movement. He never did. Stephens's repeated failure to order the rising destroyed his reputation, and he was shut out of republican politics. He returned to Ireland in 1891 to retirement and died ten years later on 29 March 1901. James Stephens was given a formal and dignified nationalist funeral and was interred in Dublin's Glasnevin Cemetery.[14]

John Breslin never attracted any suspicion, and he remained at his post in the prison for another year, until he took leave of absence and left for America. He lived in Boston for several years and joined the United Irish Brotherhood, a small Fenian group. John Devoy, also resident in America, had been impressed by Breslin's composure and decisiveness during Stephens's escape, and he asked him to organise another rescue of Fenians. This time from Fremantle Prison, in faraway Australia![15]

CHAPTER 2

THE *CATALPA* RESCUE

The daring rescue of the Fenian military prisoners from Australia was an incredible event for its time. It was organised more than 11,000 miles away on the east coast of America, a feat that would be hard to repeat today in an age of technology.

The escape took root with a series of pleading letters smuggled to John Devoy, the famed Irish rebel leader and exile. In January 1871, after a two-year campaign, which highlighted the ill-treatment of Irish political prisoners, Devoy and many other Fenians, jailed after the failed Fenian Rising of 1867, were released in a general amnesty. However, this pardon was not extended to the Fenian military prisoners, the largest group of whom were lodged in Fremantle Prison in Western Australia.[1] Nothing alarmed Britain more in connection with the revolutionary movement known as the Irish Republican Brotherhood (IRB), or Fenians, than the knowledge that undercover agents, many of whom wore the uniform of the Crown, had won over a considerable portion of the British Army to the Irish national cause.[2] Despite strong appeals, Prince George, Commander-in-Chief of the British Army, refused leniency to these men on the grounds that if they were granted release, discipline in the forces would suffer.[3]

On the other side of the world, a great sense of desertion overcame the military Fenians, as their comrades were released to begin new lives in America. The outside world seemed to have forgotten them, and they felt destined to rot in the dreaded Fremantle penal colony – half a world away. There was, however, an understanding that their former fellow prisoners would try and rescue them. Some of the civilian Fenian prisoners recently released in Australia had promised to help organise an escape of the remaining soldier Fenians. But one by one, the released men left the district. Time passed, and when there was no sign of release or rescue the military Fenians grew utterly despondent.[4]

Unknown to the soldier Fenians, Devoy was already working on a plan of escape, but he had an insurmountable task convincing the Clan na Gael (Family of Ireland) Executive in America that the rescue of these men could and should be achieved. Most Clan na Gael men considered that it was an impossible task and a waste of time and money to give a possible rescue any attention. Devoy, however, felt he had a special obligation to the men. They had been convicted mainly on evidence that related to their connection with him, and Devoy felt honour-bound to try to free them.[5] Two years after he arrived in America, Devoy received a smuggled communication in his New York office from James Wilson, a former British soldier and Fenian, who was imprisoned in Fremantle. Wilson, worn down by work and despairing of release, wrote in desperation to Devoy:

> What a death is staring us in the face, the death of a felon in a British dungeon, and a grave amongst Britain's ruffians. I am not ashamed to speak the truth, that it is a disgrace to have us in prison today.
>
> A little money judiciously expended would release every man that is now in West Australia. Think that we

have been nearly nine years in this living tomb since our first arrest and that it is impossible for mind or body to withstand the continual strain that is upon us. One or the other must give way.[6]

To underline this message Wilson added, 'Remember, this is a voice from the tomb. For is this not a living tomb? In the tomb, it is only a man's body that is good for worms, but in this living tomb the cankerworm of care enters the very soul.'[7]

When Wilson finished his letter with the words 'our faith in you is unbounded', Devoy decided that the rescue of these men would take place regardless of the risks, costs or obstacles. He felt guilty that the military recruits he and others had persuaded to join the Fenians were still languishing in horrific conditions while he was free in America. At the Clan na Gael Convention held in Baltimore in June 1874, a letter from another military Fenian, Martin Hogan, was read in the presence of 4,808 members. A printed copy of James Wilson's letter was also sent out to all branches of the Clan. The Baltimore convention entrusted a committee of ten with the duty of organising the military Fenians' rescue. John Devoy was appointed chairman of the rescue committee, and, as he found it difficult to coordinate the number on the committee, the real practical work fell on five men: Devoy, James Reynolds, John W. Goff, John C. Talbot and Patrick Mahon. In the following months, the organisation spared no effort to raise funds through public functions, lectures and entertainments. Proceeds flowed into the rescue fund, and soon Devoy had enough money to set his plans in motion.[8]

Devoy sought the advice of John Boyle O'Reilly, who had successfully escaped from Fremantle in February 1869 – the first prisoner ever to do so – and was picked up on a deserted beach by the whaling ship *Gazelle* with the assistance of the local Catholic priest, Father Patrick McCabe. O'Reilly settled in Boston and found work with *The Pilot* newspaper, eventually becoming editor. When he was rescued, O'Reilly had met Henry C. Hathaway, who was the *Gazelle's* third mate, and they became great friends. O'Reilly sent Devoy to Hathaway, who was then captain of the night police force in New Bedford, Massachusetts.[9]

Hathaway, a former whaler, signed up to Devoy's plans with enthusiasm, recommending that a ship could be bought, fitted out as a whaler, a trustworthy captain placed on board, and sent out to Western Australia. He explained how a ship like that could pay its own way and even make a profit if the whaling was good. Enlisting the help of whaling agent, John T. Richardson, Devoy and Hathaway searched for a suitable ship. They bought a three-masted barque, the *Catalpa*, as an elaborate cover for the escape plan. Devoy paid $5,250 for the *Catalpa* and spent another $10,400 on her before she was ready to sail.

Richardson hinted that his son-in-law George S. Anthony, a courageous and experienced whaleman, would be suitable as the captain of the ship. Anthony had recently married and retired from whaling, but still heard the call of the sea. A meeting was arranged and Devoy outlined his plan that this whaling ship was to pick up a small group of freedom fighters off the Australian coast and bring them to America. Devoy had a unique way with people, and Anthony willingly signed up for the mission. He did so, even though he had no Irish connections, but he did possess a love for the American ideals of freedom from oppression.[10]

The *Catalpa* set sail from New Bedford on 29 April 1875, carrying a crew of twenty-three, mainly Portuguese and African sailors, with Clan member Denis Duggan, the only Irishman on board, sailing as carpenter. Only Duggan and Capt. Anthony knew of the *Catalpa's* true mission. Having dispatched the first unit of the rescue team from America, Devoy had another momentous task in coordinating the escape on the ground in Australia. This task was as critical and potentially dangerous as that of Capt. Anthony's mission. John J. Breslin, who had planned and assisted the escape of the Fenian chief James Stephens from Richmond Prison, was sent to Australia to establish contact with the prisoners. His instructions were to organise the rescue of six named military prisoners, to use his own judgement as to the means and manner of the rescue, to expect the *Catalpa* in January 1876 and to complete the mission in cooperation with its captain. Breslin was accompanied by Thomas Desmond, another Clan member, and the two arrived in Sydney on 18 October 1875 after a month-long journey from California.

In Sydney, Breslin met several IRB and Clan na Gael men, letting them know of his plans. Funds collected from branches throughout the colonies and all the resources he would need were put at his disposal. He travelled to Melbourne and Perth, and then set up his headquarters in Fremantle at the Emerald Isle Hotel, which was run by Patrick Maloney, formerly of Co. Clare. Using the name of 'James Collins', Breslin posed as a businessman with large interests in mines in America. Desmond went to Perth, where he got employment in a carriage factory and became known as 'The Yankee'.[11]

The *Catalpa* carried out its whaling business in the North Atlantic for about six months. On 20 October she was in the Azores, having taken on 200 barrels of sperm oil, valued at $12,000, which were shipped to New Bedford to help pay some expenses. The *Catalpa* then proceeded to Tenerife where fresh water was taken on, after which she set course for the River Plate and then to the east, around the Cape of Good Hope, past St Paul's in the Indian Ocean, until at length the barque cast anchor at Bunbury, in Australia, to await instructions from John Breslin. There was no pretence of whaling now, and the first mate, Samuel

Smith, was let in on the real purpose of the voyage. He, too, joined the conspiracy with gusto.[12]

Within days of setting up his residence in Fremantle, Breslin met William Foley, a native of Waterford, who was on ticket of leave with a heart ailment from Fremantle Prison. Foley, a Fenian military prisoner, had access to the prison and his fellow prisoners, and he became the contact between James Wilson and Breslin. Wilson, whose real name was James McNally, was born in Newry, Co. Down. He served with the British Army in America, India and Syria, and on returning to Ireland became a member of the Fenian organisation. After swearing in many Irish soldiers to the Fenian Brotherhood, Wilson deserted with Martin Hogan in November 1865. He was arrested in Dublin on 10 February 1866, tried for desertion, mutiny and conspiracy to raise civil war in Ireland. He was found guilty, and sentenced to penal servitude for life.[13]

Fremantle Prison, Breslin concluded, was impregnable, so the escape would have to be when the prisoners were outside. Crucially, the prisoners were by now engaged in daily work projects outside the jail. All the Fenian prisoners were lodged in Fremantle; some were engaged in building a reservoir to supply water to the shipping in the harbour. Wilson, at the time, was training a horse for the prison doctor, which gave him an opportunity to go in and out of the prison and keep in touch with Breslin and Foley. By January 1876 Breslin and Wilson had determined the plan of escape.[14]

On the morning of 15 April 1876, after receiving a telegram from Breslin confirming the date and time for the rendezvous, Capt. Anthony announced to the custom house that he was ready to clear his ship for sea. As was the practice in the colonies, the customs officers checked every part of the ship for stowaways. They gave the all-clear, and the *Catalpa* sailed out of port. The *Catalpa* was to wait offshore outside the three-mile limit so as to keep the captain and the ship amenable to international law, and the escapees were to be taken out in a boat.

Capt. Anthony took the whaleboat and five of his best crewmen and landed on Rockingham Beach to await the escapees. Meanwhile, John Breslin had two hired horse-drawn traps ready and waiting at the Rockingham Road. Three other Fenians accompanied Breslin. They had hats and coats for the prisoners and were also armed with a rifle and pistols. All the prisoners designated for the escape had contrived to be working outside the prison walls that morning. Their good conduct and length of time served gave them trustworthy jobs outside the prison. Wilson and Michael Harrington (Macroom, Co. Cork) were working in the same party on a harbour-building scheme in Fremantle. Robert Cranston (Stewartstown, Co. Tyrone) had a job in a store nearby. They left their places of work together, and were first to arrive at the Rockingham Road, where they were driven away in a trap by Thomas Desmond.

Thomas Darragh (Broomhall, Co. Wicklow) was working as a clerk, and on the morning of the escape took Thomas Hassett (Doneraile, Co. Cork) with him to plant potatoes in the garden of the clerk of works. On their way to work they met up with Martin Hogan, a painter by trade, who was on his way to paint the house of Mr Fauntleroy outside the prison walls. The trio made their way to Rockingham Road, where they met Breslin and jumped into his trap. They made off for the beach rendezvous, with John King on horseback taking up the rear. The two traps raced twelve miles to the coast where the rowboat awaited, and they arrived at the beach simultaneously. The escapees and their rescuers quickly took their places in the whaleboat, where the astonished crewman alarmed at the swift approach of so many men thought it was an attack. The boat shoved off out towards the open sea; the traps and horses were abandoned on the beach.[15]

The escape was witnessed by an old British official named Bell, who out of curiosity had approached Capt. Anthony and asked him what he was doing on the beach. Anthony replied that he was going to Fremantle for a replacement anchor. Bell stood open-mouthed in shock as the traps arrived with the escapees and their rescuers, who jumped into the whaleboat. He asked what was to happen to the horses and traps and was told 'let them go to hell'. Bell spotted some convict caps in one of the traps, deduced the men were escapees and lost no time in mounting one of the abandoned horses, riding back to Fremantle to raise the alarm. When Bell reached Fremantle, he found that the prisoners had already been missed and the alarm raised.[16]

Meanwhile, the whaleboat sailed in a south-easterly direction in search of the *Catalpa*, but driving rain and squalls pushed them further away. After a vicious squall had broken the masthead and following a cold bleak night on the open ocean, the whaleboat carrying sixteen men – Capt. Anthony and his five crewmen; six escapees; and Breslin, Desmond, King and Brennan – spotted the *Catalpa* and headed towards it. However, looking behind, Breslin noticed the smoke of a steamer also heading towards the *Catalpa*. It was the *Georgette* with a complement of police under arms searching for the escapees and their rescuers. Capt. Anthony plied oar and sail to reach the *Catalpa* first, but the *Georgette* was travelling faster and, not seeing the whaleboat, was soon alongside the *Catalpa*. The *Catalpa* was flying the Stars and Stripes of the United States. The superintendent of police, John Stone, asked to speak to the captain and enquired if the *Catalpa* had seen a rowboat. First Mate Smith stated that his captain was at Fremantle and that no boat had been seen. When asked if the police could board and search the ship, Smith replied more sternly not 'by a damned sight'. The *Georgette* remained alongside for about ten minutes, but then headed shoreward. The whaleboat had taken down its makeshift sail and lay to, hoping that the *Georgette* would not see them. When the *Georgette* sailed away towards Bunbury Harbour, Capt. Anthony ordered the oarsmen to head for the *Catalpa* again, but their ship inadvertently sailed away from them.

It was hours later before the whaleboat came close to the *Catalpa*. At the same time, a coastguard cutter with armed police on board was also heading for the *Catalpa*, and it again became a race against time. The coastguard cutter tried to intercept the whaleboat, but Smith manoeuvred the *Catalpa* in between the two boats and quickly lowered the hoisting tackle. The sixteen men lost no time in scrambling on board the rescue boat as the others hoisted it and secured it at the davits. They hoisted the US Stars and Stripes again, and the *Catalpa* turned around and set on her course out to sea as the police cutter drew alongside. Breslin stepped to the rails and as he later said, 'kissed my hand to the gentleman who had lost the race'. Gallantly, the coastguard cutter captain called out, 'Good-bye, Captain, Good-bye.'

The men had been twenty-eight hours in the open boat, soaked with rain and sea spray. They were given a change of clothing, glasses of rum and hot mugs of coffee. John King described the scene on board the *Catalpa*: 'Then the prisoners felt that they were free at last and they gathered around Breslin and fell on the deck and kissed his feet in token of their gratitude. We were all overwhelmed with thanks and it certainly was a relief ...' But it was not all over. The *Georgette* had refuelled and once again gave chase to the *Catalpa*. The next day the *Georgette* caught up with the *Catalpa* off Rottnest Island, and Breslin said, 'they seemed quite eager and determined to capture us'. The Fenian soldiers were all in the cabin out of sight with rifles and revolvers ready, while Breslin and the other Fenians were on deck ready to fight to the last, too. Capt. Anthony asked the *Georgette* what they wanted. On board was a company of artillery with a field piece trained on the *Catalpa*. Superintendent Stone asked them to heave to and enquired were any convict prisoners aboard. Anthony replied in the negative. Stone said they would blow them out of the water, to which Anthony replied that they were under the protection of the American flag. 'If you fire on this ship you fire on the American flag,' he said.

The fifteen minutes allotted to comply elapsed, and the *Georgette's* captain asked the *Catalpa* 'to surrender to our government'. There was no response, and the two ships sailed side by side for another ten minutes until the *Georgette's* captain asked again to come on board. Capt. Anthony replied 'no', that he was bound for sea and could not stop. This was the last exchange, and while the *Georgette* continued to keep the *Catalpa* company, eventually she swung off and headed back to Fremantle. The Fenian soldiers were finally free.[17]

The *Catalpa* docked in New York Harbour on the morning of 19 August 1876. No provision had been made for the men's reception, as her arrival was totally unexpected, but soon a party representing Clan na Gael set out to welcome the rescued men. They were placed in carriages and driven to Jeremiah O'Donovan Rossa's hotel at Chatham Square, where hundreds had gathered to greet them. When he heard of their arrival, John Devoy left his sickbed in Philadelphia. He had known all the men, except Darragh, since the time of his Fenian activities in Ireland. The escapees greeted him heartily.[18]

On 25 August, the Irish-Americans of New Bedford gave Capt. Anthony and the crew of the *Catalpa* a grand reception. On the previous afternoon, when it was announced that the *Catalpa* was coming into the harbour, great crowds assembled on the wharfs, and an artillery salute was fired – one gun for every state in the Union and one for every county in Ireland. John J. Breslin later wrote a letter to the Governor of Western Australia:

This is to certify that I have released from the clemency of Her Most Gracious Majesty Victoria, Queen of Great Britain, etc., etc., six Irishmen condemned to imprisonment for life by the enlightened and magnanimous government of Great Britain for having been guilty of the atrocious and unpardonable crimes known to the enlightened portion of mankind as 'love of country' and 'hatred of tyranny'.[19]

The *Catalpa* rescue stands out as one of the most extraordinary and inspirational prison escapes ever. When word reached Ireland, Dublin erupted in celebration. The rejoicing populace held torchlight parades throughout the city and burned effigies of British Prime Minister Benjamin Disraeli, who had refused the Fenians a pardon. *The Times* blamed America and stated its government was responsible for a gross violation of international law.[20] Irish-America was delighted, too, and sang the praises of John Devoy, John Breslin and the hero of the hour – the Yankee captain, George S. Anthony.

CHAPTER 3

UP DE VALERA

The separatist party, Sinn Féin, was reorganised throughout 1917 and began a campaign of civil disobedience against the British government and its authority. In April 1918 Sinn Féin, along with the Irish Parliamentary Party (IPP) and the Catholic Church, united to resist any attempts to introduce military conscription to Ireland. During the summer of 1918, the British government, nervous of growing political unrest, undertook to quell the disorder. As Sinn Féin was publicly perceived to be the key instigator of anti-government and anti-conscription feeling, the Lord Lieutenant, Sir John French, claiming 'evidence of a treasonable plot between Sinn Féin and Germany', ordered the arrest of seventy-three prominent republicans. The 'German Plot' arrests were trumped-up allegations, designed to placate American opinion and turn anyone with nationalist sympathies against the republican movement. Nevertheless, the lack of evidence in the 'German Plot' was viewed with deep suspicion outside official and unionist circles.[1]

Eamon 'Ned' Broy, who worked as a confidential clerk in G Division, the intelligence section of the Dublin Metropolitan Police, tipped off Michael Collins about the impending raids. Most leaders evaded arrest, but some, like Éamon de Valera (Dev) and

Arthur Griffith, allowed themselves to be captured for the adverse publicity. They argued that the arrests would shock and arouse the country. Broy gave clear warning not only of who was on the list of those to be apprehended but of exactly when the arrests would be carried out. De Valera was told not to go home, but after a meeting of the Irish Volunteer Executive in Dublin on 17 May, he left Westland Row travelling on the prearranged train to the village of Greystones, Co. Wicklow. De Valera had been followed by two plainclothes policemen, and when he alighted at Greystones station a Royal Irish Constabulary (RIC) inspector was waiting for him on the platform. He was promptly arrested and handed over to the military. When Broy later questioned Collins, Michael replied that a 'few minutes before train time de Valera looked at his watch and announced that, notwithstanding the threatened arrests, he was going home'. Broy concluded, 'His own arrest ... might do the cause more good than harm. What else was there for him to do by way of action till the war in Europe ended.'[2]

De Valera joined another seventy-odd republicans, picked up in the day's swoops, on board a British warship in Kingstown (Dún Laoghaire) Harbour. The following evening the ship sailed for Holyhead, where the prisoners were divided into two groups – one group went to Usk Prison, in Wales, the others to Gloucester Jail. De Valera and Griffith were among the prisoners sent to Gloucester. After a brief spell there, de Valera was sent, with seven other prisoners, to Lincoln Jail in eastern England.[3]

The arrests of the 'politicals' of the revolution – de Valera, Arthur Griffith, Count Plunkett and William Cosgrave – left the more radical element in control of the republican movement. Militant men, like Michael Collins, Cathal Brugha and Richard Mulcahy, all evaded capture, and this made the resumption of violence more probable. De Valera's stature at the time resembled that of Charles Stewart Parnell in the 1880s: the uncrowned king of Ireland. Like Parnell in Kilmainham Gaol in 1881–2, Dev could play the role of imprisoned martyr before a national and international audience.[4]

Due to their exemplary behaviour, the terms of confinement for the Irish internees in Lincoln were lenient and they were allowed to associate together. De Valera spent much of his time reading and writing in his cell. He exercised regularly and served Mass. His imprisonment, however, meant he could not contribute to Sinn Féin's election strategy, despite being nominated to stand in four constituencies – East Clare, East Mayo, West Belfast and South Down. He did not issue an election address, because what he first wrote was blocked by the prison censor, and instead, Dev declared that 'silence is preferable to mutilated statements'. De Valera was elected in absentia to East Mayo and East Clare, but he suffered a defeat against Joe Devlin in West Belfast and he had withdrawn from South Down in favour of the Irish Party candidate rather than split the nationalist vote.[5]

In the dreary surroundings of Lincoln Jail, de Valera soon began to regret allowing himself to be arrested. He was not achieving much inside the walls of an English prison, and he was unable to make the first sitting of Dáil Éireann (Irish Assembly) called in Dublin on 21 January 1919, when Sinn Féin refused to take its seats in the Westminster parliament. Now, his imprisonment became intolerable. Dev needed to get out. 'It was tantalising to be in within prison walls when there was work to be done to inform American opinion … to the true state of Irish feeling. I made up my mind to try to escape.'[6]

One of the Dáil's first decisions was to appoint three envoys to the Paris Peace Conference (due to be held in January 1919) to present Ireland's claim to freedom before the world. 'Government with the consent of the governed' was US President Woodrow Wilson's principle of self-determination after the conclusion of the war to end all wars. Britain, inevitably, would do all in its power to block the presentation of Ireland's case. Ireland needed impressive credentials – the Dáil chose de Valera, Arthur Griffith and Count Plunkett, all of whom were in English prisons, to be the delegates. It became imperative that all, or some at least, be broken out of prison. The plan of escape was led by Michael Collins and Harry Boland, and they prepared to go to England.

Hopes for a successful escape in Britain were raised when four Irish prisoners, arrested as part of the 'German Plot', escaped from Usk Prison on 21 January 1919. Using a blank key and nail files smuggled into the prison in freshly baked bread loaves, George Geraghty, Frank Shouldice, Herbert (Barney) Mellows and Joe McGrath simply opened their cell doors and scaled the prison wall using a makeshift rope ladder. The escapees hid out in Liverpool. Within a week all of them had been smuggled back to Ireland by boat.[7]

On 22 January 1919 Seán Etchingham, Teachta Dála (TD) for East Wicklow, was released from Lincoln Jail on grounds of ill health, and on his arrival in Dublin was taken to a convalescent home in Rathmines. Interviewed from his sickbed by an *Irish Independent* journalist, Etchingham, also a journalist, gave an interesting account of his experiences in jail, and he conveyed a message from Sinn Féin President Éamon de Valera to the Irish people, urging them to remain calm and confident and not to give their enemies an excuse for further military aggression. He also had a private message for Michael Collins and Harry Boland, that de Valera was ready to leave his abode. Collins and Boland crossed the Irish Sea at once to organise a series of safe houses and a chain of transportation. When their names were called at Dáil sittings, other members answered for them, so that their absence would not be generally noticed.[8]

It was in the exercise yard of Lincoln that de Valera and his close friends Seán Milroy and Seán McGarry had seen the chance of an escape. They had an idea that if they could procure a key to their cells, they would be able to get to a door in the wall of the exercise yard which, they learned, opened to the outside. While serving Mass for the prison chaplain, de Valera was able to take a wax impression of the chaplain's key which had been carelessly left on a desk in the sacristy. He assumed this was a master key. However, they would have to get this impression out to make an actual key.

Prison guards scrutinised letters and mail coming in and out of the prison, so de Valera came up with a clever way of getting the message out. Milroy drew a cartoon on a Christmas postcard showing a drunken man with a huge key trying to open a locked door with a key that would not fit, saying, 'I can't get in'. On the other side of the card was the same man in jail looking through a carefully drawn keyhole saying, 'I can't get out'. Both key and keyhole were of the exact dimensions of the actual lock and key. To avoid suspicion, the card was sent out using Seán McGarry's name. The censors were deceived, and the postcard was sent to Dublin.

Once the coded message was deciphered in Dublin, a key was cut and smuggled into Lincoln inside a fruitcake. The key, however, would not work because the cartoon dimensions were slightly off.

De Valera sent out another postcard drawing, through Milroy, this time disguising the key design in the centre of a Celtic pattern and with the words: 'Eocair na Saoirse' – 'The key to freedom'. A matching key was made, and Kathleen Talty, an Irish girl living in the city, brought it into the prison in a cake. When the prisoners tried out the key, they found that it opened some of the doors only. It was then they realised that the chaplain's key was not a master key.

Another prisoner, Paddy de Loughrey, of Kilkenny, was a locksmith, and he dismantled a jail lock which was found to be a multiple lock. The key required to open this lock would serve as a master key, so he asked that blank keys, files and key-cutting tools be smuggled into the jail. These duly arrived inside a third cake. Paddy de Loughrey set to work to make the master key. It was, he said, 'trying and at times exasperating. I had to be as noiseless as I could ... With the file and two stout pen-knives I made a key.'[9]

In the meantime, Michael Collins had sent Frank Kelly, from Sinn Féin headquarters in Harcourt St, Dublin, over to liaise with Paddy O'Donoghue, who was in command of the Irish Republican Army (IRA) in Manchester, in spying out the topography surrounding the jail. They saw that the gate in the exercise yard did, in fact, lead out to the surrounding fields. They reported that it faced the main gate of a military hospital from which there were always some comings and goings by convalescent soldiers and others. The field adjacent to the prison was about 250 yards wide and was protected by single lines of barbed wire about 18 inches apart and rising to a height of 7 feet. Kelly continued his surveillance of the jail vicinity, and he was soon able to report that the presence of so many people near the main gate of the hospital would be a help rather than a hindrance. The fields around the jail were a popular place for convalescent soldiers courting their girlfriends, and strolling figures in the darkness on a winter's night might be thought to be no more than another courting couple.

When Collins and Boland arrived in Lincoln, they contacted Paddy O'Donoghue and went over the final details of the escape plan. On the evening of 3 February Collins, Boland and Frank Kelly arrived at the jail, which was situated in the north of the city. All three were armed, and Kelly carried a rope ladder. As there were many couples milling about near a stile that straddled the route of the escape, so Collins sent Kelly to find another way across the grass to O'Donoghue who had a taxi waiting at the lonely Wragby Road. Collins and Boland sat down on the grass. At about

7.30 p.m., Boland flashed a torch; seconds later he flashed it again and then gave another flash. He did not flash the light longer, in case an alert guard should notice it and become suspicious. As they anxiously awaited a return signal, it came suddenly from an upper-storey cell window when Milroy lit a box of matches to signal that the internees were coming out.[10]

Cautiously, Collins and Boland approached the gate in the wall of the exercise grounds. Inside the jail, de Valera, Milroy and McGarry were able to unlock every gate they came to without difficulty. They made their way across the prison yard to the door in the outer wall. Shortly after reaching the door, the rescuers heard the footsteps of the three escapees on the other side. Collins had brought a duplicate key. When he attempted to open the door from the outside, his key snapped in the lock.

According to Piaras Béaslaí, Collins said, in a distraught tone, 'I've broken a key in the lock, Dev.' For a moment, it looked as if the escape was going to end in disaster after all their meticulous planning. But de Valera, with his accurately filed key, and with an extraordinary piece of luck, managed to poke Collins's key out of the keyhole from the other side. The door creaked open, and the escapees stepped out into the field where they received a quick warm embrace. Briefly recounting his escape, de Valera said he paused for a moment after sneaking out of the prison door to lock it again behind him, but his entourage hurried him away, insisting that he be as quick as possible. 'Had I locked that door, nobody would ever have known how we had escaped,' he said.

Harry Boland wrapped a fur coat around the gangly de Valera, putting his arm around him as if they were a courting couple.[11] Without arousing suspicion, the 'couples' casually strolled past a number of off-duty British soldiers, who were loitering with their girlfriends outside, and, with a cheery 'goodnight' to the courting couples by the stile, they walked past the hospital gate and across to the taxi waiting at Wragby Road.[12] Kelly and the rope ladder were left behind; he knew what to do once he saw the car was gone. All five crowded into the taxi with Paddy O'Donoghue, who drove them to the city centre where Collins and Boland were dropped off to catch a London-bound train. The taxi then pulled up at the Adam and Eve tavern on Lindum Road, and, to throw anyone off the scent, the group crossed the road to where Fintan Murphy had another taxi waiting to bring them to Worksop in Nottinghamshire.

By the time their escape had been discovered, about two hours later, another car had moved them to Sheffield. When they arrived there, a third car, driven by Liam McMahon, was waiting to transport them to safe houses in Manchester. Milroy and McGarry were taken to McMahon's house, while de Valera was brought to Father Charles O'Mahony's house.

The alarm was raised about two hours after the three prisoners had escaped. Cars were stopped and searched; a watch was kept on ports and railway stations, and trains were searched; but the escapees were already in hiding. A prison-issue sock was found in Queen's Way near the jail. There was a gap in the wire almost opposite the prison door; this was large enough for a man to wriggle through and was made by forcing two lines of wire apart. Several sets of footprints were found at the spot, indicating the tracks of persons moving through the stubble towards the Wragby Road. Police began house-to-house visitations, and handbills were circulated giving descriptions of the three escapees together with an offer of a £5 reward for information leading to their capture. The London *Daily Express* even reported that 'the police at the House of Commons, of which De Valera is a member, kept a special lookout for him' in case he turned up to take his seat! It was also reported in the press that a man answering de Valera's description, 'who has relatives in Skibbereen, visited Bantry, but escaped over the hills while the police were telegraphing to Cork regarding him'.[13]

After several days Milroy and McGarry made their way to Liverpool and boarded a steamer to Dublin. De Valera stayed for a week with Fr O'Mahony, and then hid at a house in Fallowfield on the outskirts of Manchester. On 18 February, dressed as a priest and escorted by two Irish girls, Kathleen Talty and Mary Healy, he was taken to the house of Mrs McCarthy, who lived near the Liverpool docks. Collins wanted Dev's return to Ireland to be as spectacular as his escape, but he slipped into Dublin unobtrusively at 1 a.m. on 20 February after being smuggled on board the *Cambria*.[14] De Valera first hid out at Dr Robert Farnan's home at 5 Merrion Square, in the centre of Dublin. Farnan, a leading gynaecologist and physician from Moone, Co. Kildare, was an old friend, and his Dublin home later became de Valera's headquarters. He then moved to another safe house in Drumcondra.[15]

On 4 March the audience in the Mansion House Round Room were thrilled when, after the doors had been securely locked, Lincoln Jail escapee Seán McGarry appeared on the platform. McGarry delivered his lecture and disappeared to rapturous applause. Dublin Castle detectives, who had been locked out of the Mansion House and who had waited outside until the concert ended, did not learn of his appearance there until the following day when it was reported in the newspapers.[16]

Two days later, on 6 March, Pierce McCan, a Tipperary TD and another of the 'German Plot' prisoners, died of influenza in Gloucester Jail. His death caused great ill feeling in Ireland. Amongst others who contracted the dreaded flu were prominent men like Arthur Griffith and Art O'Connor, TD for South Kildare. The prison doctor at Gloucester Jail urged that the entire prison be evacuated. The British authorities had already been considering an amnesty for the 'German Plot' prisoners, and, coupled with de Valera's escape and McCan's death, they were forced to decide upon a general release of the jailed republicans. The first batch of liberated prisoners arrived in Ireland three days after McCan's death. De Valera was subsequently re-elected President of Sinn Féin, and on 1 April he was elected President of Dáil Éireann. Satisfied that Ireland would not be permitted to present her case for independence to the Paris Peace Conference, de Valera decided to set out on a bid to win over the American public to the Irish cause.[17]

On 2 June 1919 de Valera headed off to America – smuggled on board the SS *Lapland*. The government had revoked his passport in order to restrict his movements. The President of the Irish Republic passed the nine-day journey on a bunk hidden below in the ship's boiler room. He suffered bouts of seasickness, and occasionally breathed in fresh air when he was secretly brought up on deck. De Valera arrived in the city of his birth, New York, on 11 June and was smuggled down the gangway to meet Harry Boland and Joseph McGarrity.[18] On his eighteen-month tour of America, de Valera would meet James Wilson, an escapee from Fremantle Prison in Western Australia. More than a half century separated the two men in age but they had much in common, having served time for the republican cause in different jails and having both escaped from Crown custody. It showed the continuity of the struggle for freedom. Wilson, the last surviving member of 'the Catalpa Six', had settled in Rhode Island, where he married and lived out the rest of his life. He died aged eighty-one on 6 November 1921.[19]

CHAPTER 4

OVER THE WALL

Sinn Féin had swept the boards in the general election of December 1918, winning 73 out of 105 seats and destroying the Irish Parliamentary Party. On 21 January 1919 the newly elected Sinn Féin members of the British House of Commons met in the Mansion House, Dublin, and instituted the first Dáil Éireann. They refused to go to Westminster for the opening of Parliament, setting up a parliament of their own. Those Irish members of parliament (MPs) called themselves TDs, or representatives of the Dáil.[1]

Among those arrested and incarcerated in Dublin's Mountjoy Prison in the spring of 1919 for making seditious speeches were four Sinn Féin TDs: Robert Barton who was Sinn Féin TD for West Wicklow; Piaras Béaslaí, Kerry East; William Sears, Mayo South; and J.J. Walsh, Cork City. Because of their status as elected representatives, the four were put in the hospital, a detached building at the rear of the prison. Almost immediately a plan was hatched from both inside and outside the prison for them to escape. Barton was first to go, on 16 March. Barton was already working on his own plan to escape so General Headquarters (GHQ) decided that rather than complicate things he could go ahead with his escape bid. Having sawed through the bars of his cell in the Mountjoy infirmary, Barton got to the outer wall and threw over a bar of soap as a signal. A rope ladder was thrown back in return. Barton climbed the twenty-foot wall and jumped into an outspread blanket. The next morning, St Patrick's Day, warders found a note in Barton's cell addressed to the prison governor which said, 'I am about to make an escape from your hospitality. If I escape, well and good, if not I am prepared to suffer the consequences ... I hope that we may shortly turn your prison to a useful national purpose.'[2]

The next escape was a more ambitious venture – planned by Michael Collins on the outside and Piaras Béaslaí on the inside. It involved the escape of Piaras Béaslaí, J.J. Walsh and Padraig Fleming, a remarkable young volunteer from the Swan in Co. Laois. When he had been arrested in May 1918, Fleming refused to wear a prison uniform – which resulted in him being left naked and locked in his cell. After he destroyed his cell, Fleming was restrained with a strait jacket. Fleming continued his extraordinary fight for treatment as a political prisoner in Maryborough (Portlaoise) Prison, enduring hunger strike, torture and physical mistreatment for ten months until he was finally granted political status. He was transferred to Mountjoy in January 1919 where the republican prisoners speedily elected him as their Officer Commanding (OC). Fleming organised a prison strike against jail regulations in support of four prisoners who were not being afforded political status and were being treated as ordinary criminals. On 23 March the four prisoners being denied political status broke away from the warders and led them on a chase around a prison field before being recaptured. As a result, they had to take their exercise in an iron cage and were guarded by up to eleven warders. The presence of so many warders presented a serious obstacle to the budding escape plan. Fleming ordered the four prisoners not to cause any more problems, because an escape had a better chance of success with a calmer atmosphere in the prison. As a result, the prison authorities were lulled into a false sense of security.

Michael Collins began sending in coded messages to Béaslaí outlining his plans for an escape. It would involve Béaslaí, Fleming and the four prisoners being treated as common criminals. A further list of men with long sentences, including J.J. Walsh, was created. It was decided that men serving short sentences or who had sentences close to completion would not escape, but if they wanted to escape after the prisoners who were designated to go, they could. The original plan was for the IRA to blow a hole in the outside wall when the prisoners were exercising, but this was thought to be too risky as it would bring the military and warders rushing to the scene.[3]

Liverpool-born Béaslaí was a journalist and a veteran of Easter Week 1916, when he had been deputy commanding officer of the 1st Dublin Battalion under Commandant Ned Daly. As he was awaiting trial, Béaslaí was entitled to see his solicitor, Éamonn Duggan. A veteran of Easter Week 1916, Duggan was a practising solicitor and an elected Sinn Féin TD for Meath South. He was subsequently the IRA's Director of Intelligence until his arrest after the Bloody Sunday shootings in November 1920.[4] Béaslaí used this meeting with Duggan, his solicitor, as an opportunity to discuss the escape plans.

The escape was fixed for 3 p.m. on Saturday, 29 March, just thirteen days after Robert Barton's departure. On the afternoon of the escape, the prisoners were locked in their cells for their meal at 1 p.m. At 2.30 p.m. they were let out for exercise. On that day a snowstorm started, and for a while it looked like they might not get out for exercise. Béaslaí said, 'Fortunately, the storm cleared up about half-past two and we were all allowed out.' More luck was on the escapees' side, when the number of warders guarding the four prisoners in the cage was reduced from eleven to three. This meant that there were seven unarmed warders to deal with. The armed military and police guard were stationed in front of the jail, and it would take them some time to get around to the exercise yard. At 2.30 p.m. one of the prisoners sent a signal from a window to a volunteer stationed on Claude Road to let those waiting outside know that all was ready.

Prisoners exercised in three groups: Fleming, Béaslaí and Walsh were in front of the prison hospital; the bulk of the political prisoners were in a field just inside the wall; and the four prisoners being treated as ordinary criminals were in the iron cage. The different groups were not allowed to associate with one another, but the prison authorities had long given up all hope of compelling Fleming to submit to rules. Fleming had joined Walsh and Béaslaí at a position where they had a view of both the wall and the iron cage. Minutes before the escape commenced, the deputy governor came by and passed a comment to the three about being out of bounds. Fleming replied with a joke, and the deputy governor passed on, obviously having thought it wise to say no more. He was hardly out of sight when a whistle sounded from outside the prison, the signal that the escape was on. The prisoners rushed to the selected point on the wall at the rear of the hospital.

A Dublin prisoner, Paddy O'Daly, was placed in charge of the prisoners who elected to stay. O'Daly and five prisoners under his command went up to the warders with their hands in their pockets holding spoons which the guards thought were guns. The men ordered the guards not to speak or move. Seán Robbins described how a party of men under his command controlled the warders. He said, 'There was no resistance. The terrified warders, thinking another rising had broken out, threw up their hands and begged for mercy. They were quickly hustled together behind the prison hospital, and then, in broad daylight over the wall went twenty of us.' One of the warders asked O'Daly to rough him up a bit to make it look like he made a genuine effort to stop the escape. 'Tear my coat, at least, Paddy,' he said.[5]

Outside the jail on the canal bank, Peadar Clancy threw a weight with a rope attached over the wall, and a rope ladder was pulled up from inside. O'Daly took his place at the foot of the wall and called out the names of those designated to escape. Piaras Béaslaí was first, followed by Padraig Fleming and J.J. Walsh. In all, twenty men went over the twenty-foot wall, exceeding all expectations and leaving only seven prisoners under Paddy O'Daly's command inside. The breakout lasted about ten minutes. Just as the last man cleared the wall, the military guard rushed up with fixed bayonets. O'Daly lined up the remaining men, and they greeted the soldiers with a derisive cheer. Eyewitness accounts told of men sliding down a rope from the top of the jail wall to the canal bank outside Mountjoy. A number of men held the rope while the escapees were sliding to the ground and then directed them where to go. The cheers of those prisoners still detained could be heard outside the prison.

The escapees dashed off in various directions and were gone before the police arrived on the scene. Béaslaí, Fleming and Walsh ran along the canal bank and down an entry into Innisfallen Parade, where volunteers were waiting with bicycles for them.[6] Some of the men disappeared into a crowd which, had come to help them; some went in the direction of the North Circular Road; others crossed the canal to Whitworth Road. One prisoner asked onlookers, 'Who will lend me my tram fare?' His fare was not long in coming, and with a quick thanks the man ran off. Another of the escapees, after reaching the public road, made a short speech to onlookers, quoting poet Richard Lovelace: 'Stone walls do not a prison make.'

Rory O'Connor and Dick McKee of the Dublin Brigade had charge of the arrangements for the escapees. The twenty escapees were: Piaras Béaslaí, Padraig Fleming, J.J. Walsh, Seán Robbins, Dermot O'Shea, Seán Forde, T. Malone, P. Farrelly, Ben Hickey, William Finucane, Martin Fleming, Liam Tannam, Henry Morgan, John Sharry, Stephen O'Connor, John Irvine, Ed Lehane, P. McQuillian, E. Collins and P. McGee.[7]

The escapees had an estimated twenty minutes' headstart on the police, quite a number of whom had been on duty at the Phoenix Park races. All the men who escaped got away safely. Seán Robbins from Clara and Martin Fleming from Ballycumber, Co. Offaly, were making their way down Clonliffe Road when they were stopped by a police patrol. Word of the escape had not yet reached the patrol, and, as Martin Fleming looked as if he were injured, the police assumed he was an ex-serviceman and let them pass. The two men were brought to a safe house on the Quays in Dublin, and they got back to Rahan, Offaly, by canal on a Pullough-bound boat.[8]

The unionist press was furious. *The Irish Times* said, 'The fugitives included two members of Parliament; one of whom had been tried by court martial the previous day.' Perhaps they had reason to be furious, as it was the first time MPs had escaped from custody! According to the *Times* the escape 'w[ould] increase the prestige of the young men who control Sinn Féin' and 'that jail will be counted as a necessary condition of the glory of jail-breaking'. The Irish newspapers were ecstatic, reporting, 'Dublin absorbed them immediately and completely, and at a late hour on Sunday night not one of them had been recaptured.'[9]

In Dublin, a cartoon postcard called 'The Back Way' was published with an illustration of a small boy asking the guard at the gates of Mountjoy Prison if he knew 'there's a back way in your place' and an illustration of heavy artillery pointing at the closely guarded front gate, while a stream of IRA prisoners flooded over the back wall.[10]

Padraig Fleming would serve time in total in nine different prisons and would escape three times. Béaslaí did not remain free for long; he was rearrested on 31 May in Finglas, Co. Dublin, and was sentenced to two years' imprisonment. As an escapee, he was regarded as dangerous – it was observed by jailers that an escapee who has been recaptured is likely to try and escape again. An important consequence of the Mountjoy escape was that the government decided to transfer the more important republican prisoners from Irish to British jails. Béaslaí was moved to Strangeways Prison in Manchester, where he joined Austin Stack, TD for West Kerry, and Fionán Lynch, TD for Kerry South. In August 1919 Lynch was released, having completed his sentence, and he was then able to assist greatly in planning the escape of his comrades. Béaslaí was also able to provide valuable inside information to his colleagues about the mass escape from Mountjoy. The same tactics were to be used in an escape from Strangeways. Subsequently, more of the other Irish prisoners completed their sentences and were released. Messages were also sent out with them.

Paddy O'Donoghue and Liam McMahon, who been involved with de Valera's escape from Lincoln, set the plan in motion. Messages and maps were sent into the prison baked in cakes or hidden in butter and jam. Handcuffs given by a sympathetic Irish policeman in Manchester were also smuggled into the prison. Collins followed the plans closely, and he wrote to Béaslaí several times using coded messages. Rory O'Connor was sent over from Dublin to Manchester to examine the escape plans. O'Connor and Peadar Clancy were put in charge of the rescue operation. They enlisted two Dublin men and another eighteen volunteers living in Manchester and Liverpool. George Lodge had not been long in Manchester, so his home was considered a safe house.

The escape began a little after 5 p.m. on 25 October 1919 while the prisoners were guarded by a lone warder. As the men were political prisoners, they were allowed to congregate at intervals during the tea-hour. One of the prisoners jumped on the prison warder's back and dragged him to the ground. Three men – Con Connolly, Paddy McCarthy and John Doran – gagged and handcuffed him, and placed him in a cell. Béaslaí, Stack and Daniel Walsh then rushed into the prison yard, where a rope was thrown over the thirty-five-foot wall. The prisoners used it to drag over a rope ladder, and each, in turn, climbed up to the top of the wall. Stack was the first up the rope ladder, followed by Béaslaí and then Walsh. Their rescuers had another ladder which they leaned against the outside of the wall with three volunteers around it, allowing the escapees to climb down onto Sherbourne Street. As the prison was located in a well-populated area, a number of spectators gathered around, although most were held back at either end of the street by eight armed IRA volunteers.[11]

Some of the spectators initially thought the escape was a 'moving-picture performance'. One woman realised what was happening and attempted to raise an alarm, but she was immediately restrained by a man with a strong Irish accent who said, 'You can't pass this way.' A workman at the brickworks near the prison said, 'I then saw that two men were sliding down a ladder. Before I could make up my mind what to do, six men rushed up the incline and made off as hard as they could run.'[12]

The six escapees were Piaras Béaslaí, Austin Stack, John Doran (Loughinisland, Co. Down), Daniel Walsh (Fethard, Co. Tipperary), Paddy McCarthy (Freemount, Co. Cork) and Con Connolly (Clonakilty, Co. Cork). Stack and Béaslaí were taken by George Lodge to his residence in a remote suburb where they remained for a week. A few days later, they were taken to Liverpool and smuggled to Ireland on board a B&I steamer by a crew member, who put them up in staff quarters. Joe O'Reilly picked them up in Dublin at Sir John Rogerson's Quay and took them to a colleague's home.

This was the sixth successful escape by republican prisoners within a year, the most-high profile of these being that of de Valera from Lincoln Jail. In all, forty republican prisoners had escaped from jails in Ireland and England. Only two had been recaptured: Béaslaí and Liam Tannam. Tannam, a Dublin Corporation clerk, had been serving a nine-month sentence for illegal drilling when he escaped from Mountjoy in March 1919. He was rearrested on 24 July in Dublin and returned to Mountjoy, where he spent five weeks in solitary confinement. His defending solicitor said there were no witnesses to Tannam escaping. Warder Thomas Brachan said he had last seen Tannam at 3 o'clock but couldn't find him fifteen minutes later. Tannam was sentenced to a month with hard labour for escaping. His solicitor asked that he be fined instead, as he was a married man with three children. When Justice Gordon agreed to a fine of £10, Tannam opted to serve the month instead, replying, 'I won't pay a fine. Thank you very much all the same.'[13]

The following year, John Doran and Daniel Walsh were recaptured and brought back to Strangeways. Austin Stack and Piaras Béaslaí remained free, while Paddy McCarthy was killed in an attack on Millstreet RIC Barracks on 22 November 1920.[14]

CHAPTER 5

ESCAPE OR DIE!

Political violence intensified in the country with the arrival of British recruits to the RIC from March 1920. Unemployment was high in Britain, and the majority of recruits were ex-servicemen. A shortage of uniforms led to the new recruits being kitted out in army khaki and police bottle-green, earning them the nickname the 'Black and Tans'. They were joined by ex-officers, known as the 'Auxies', recruited to the RIC Auxiliary Division in late July 1920 . Both groups were responsible for many atrocities committed on the civilian population and republican insurgents. In Dublin city British intelligence operatives were hunting IRA leaders, resulting in several targeted killings of republicans. As a result of this, in November 1920 Michael Collins planned to eliminate British intelligence in the capital in one bold stroke.[1]

On 21 November 1920, a day forever known as 'Bloody Sunday', Frank Teeling was one of a group of IRA volunteers who entered 22 Lower Mount Street, Dublin. They were looking for Lieutenant Henry Angliss and Lieutenant Charles Peel, who had been involved in the shooting dead of republican John A. Lynch in a bedroom in the Exchange Hotel. Lt Angliss was shot dead in his bed, but Lt Peel, on hearing the shots, blocked his bedroom door and survived. Fianna Éireann youths (Nationalist youth organisation founded in 1909) on lookout reported that Auxiliary policemen were approaching the house, so the assassination squad split up into two groups. One left by the front door, the other by the laneway behind the house. In the gunfight that followed in the laneway, two Auxiliaries were killed. Teeling was wounded and captured as he covered his colleagues' retreat. One of the Auxiliaries held a cocked pistol to Teeling's head – he was giving him to the count of ten to name his accomplices or die, when Brigadier-General Crozier, Commander of the Auxiliaries, arrived on the scene. He told his men he had no objections to Teeling being executed, but it would have to be done legally. Teeling was court-martialled and sentenced to death in January 1921. He was held at Dublin's Kilmainham Gaol.[2]

IRA GHQ's principal concern was to free Frank Teeling and leading IRA officer Ernie O'Malley, who, once his identity was confirmed, would meet with the same violent death. Patrick Moran was also on the list of those to be rescued. Timing was crucial, as Teeling was due to be executed. Patrick Moran, who had been arrested and accused of killing intelligence officer Lt Peter Ames at his Mount Street address on the morning of Bloody Sunday, could also face the death penalty. On 9 December 1920, Auxiliaries had arrested Ernie O'Malley in possession of a loaded revolver and four maps at Inistioge, Co. Kilkenny. On his arrest, O'Malley gave his name as 'Bernard Stewart'. He was brought to Dublin Castle where he was brutally tortured, but he did not reveal his true identity. At the time, O'Malley was operating with flying columns which were involved in a wave of large-scale attacks on RIC barracks in Tipperary and Kilkenny. He was subsequently taken to Kilmainham Gaol, where he was placed in a cell next to Patrick Moran.[3]

Simon Donnelly, Vice-Commandant, 3rd Battalion, Dublin Brigade, was arrested and taken to Kilmainham Gaol on 10

February 1921. He was placed in an old and long-disused part of the jail that had been reopened to cope with the increasing number of political prisoners being detained in the wake of mounting violence. Donnelly, too, was facing a murder charge, as the British suspected he had been involved in the Bloody Sunday killings. He said, 'So many of us were charged with murder – for the British did not recognise us as prisoners of war although a state of war was in existence – that we used to talk about our part of the jail as "Murderers' Gallery".'[4] Fortunately for the prisoners, the old wing of the prison had not been fitted with the modern lock-and-key systems, and the older bolt-and-padlock method was still in use. The wing also had the older peephole, four inches square, while the newer portion of the jail had been fitted with the new-sized peephole, an inch-and-a-half square. These two factors would prove invaluable when the time came for an attempted breakout.[5]

A rescue attempt from outside was contemplated, but Kilmainham was not an easy place to penetrate with its high surrounding walls, barbed-wire entanglements and machine guns mounted at each strategic position. At the end of January 1921 two British soldiers inside the prison – Privates Ernest Roper, a Welshman, and J. Holland from Belfast, members of the Welsh Regiment – appeared at the Grafton Bar at the corner of Grafton Street and St Stephen's Green which was owned by IRA volunteer Seán Farrelly. They had a letter from a prisoner, James McNamara, as an introduction, and they offered to help free Frank Teeling. When asked why, they said they were very fond of Teeling and that 'he was a great bit of a nut'. Farrelly reported this to his superior, Martin Conroy, who went to Oscar Traynor, OC Dublin Brigade, and suggested to him that, with the help of the two sympathetic soldiers, an escape from the jail might be successful.[6]

The plan was, once the escapees had left their cells, they would quietly walk down two flights of stairs to a distant yard in the jail. The yard had a gate that was only secured with a thick bolt which could be cut with heavy bolt cutters. Martin Conroy contacted Michael Smyth, a garage worker, who proposed that a simple bolt cutter could be used to cut the jail bolt. Smyth obtained a bolt cutter and sawed off its wooden handles, so that one of the soldiers could bring it into the prison concealed under his uniform. Without its handles the bolt cutter would not have the necessary leverage to cut bolts, so detachable handles of tubular steel had also to be smuggled in to replace the original wooden handles. The two soldiers managed to smuggle in the bolt cutter, the handles and a fully loaded Smith & Wesson .38 revolver. As a backup, the outside rescue party had a rope ladder and a rope tied to it. The bolt cutters and revolver were hidden in a disused cell. At one stage, the jail authorities decided they were going to clean up the cells on Murderers' Gallery. Discovery of the hidden items would end any chance of escape, so a precedent was established where by the republican prisoners volunteered to do fatigue duty and clean the cells themselves. The authorities fell for the ruse, and the prisoners were able to prevent the discovery of the escape material.[7]

Newspapers were forbidden in jail, but someone who knew O'Malley's real identity secretly gave him a copy of a newspaper article. It referred to a recent raid on a flat in Dawson Street, Dublin, during which many papers had been taken away and the female occupant of the flat arrested. Michael Collins had used that flat, and some of his papers were seized, as were other documents which O'Malley had in a separate room. The seizure of O'Malley's papers led to a new name of interest to the British. By late January a letter from Dublin Castle to senior British military authorities referred to an IRA officer, a 'notorious rebel' called 'E. Malley', whom they were most anxious to arrest in connection with a wave of attacks on police barracks. One morning O'Malley received a visit from a plainclothes RIC man, who told him he was going to be hanged for his involvement in the Macroom ambush in which eighteen Auxiliaries had been killed. O'Malley pleaded his innocence, but he was determined to escape: 'I had no intention of being hanged. I was going to escape, dead or alive.'[8]

On Murderers' Gallery, because the cell doors were fitted with the old-style bolts and padlocks, one of the friendly military guards opened the padlocks but left them to look as if they were still locked. On a dry run the designated escapees were able, with little difficulty, to put their hand out through the peephole and ease back the bolt from its socket. Confident that no one could scale the thirty-foot wall that surrounded the jail, the prison warders seldom locked the door leading out of the yard from the jail building. The men were easily able to get from their cells to a disused gate in the outer wall through which they hoped to escape.[9]

The breakout was fixed for Sunday night, 13 February 1921. At the appointed time, volunteers from F Company, 4th Battalion outside the jail came upon four British soldiers and their three girlfriends, whom they rounded up at gunpoint. To ensure no alarm was raised, they marched them about 200 yards up the road to a large house in Crumlin, where they were held until Tuesday, 15 February, and then released. The captives were well treated, and the girls were allowed to write letters to their relatives assuring them they were safe. A young man on a bicycle delivered the letters.[10]

As planned, Teeling, O'Malley and Patrick Moran left their cells and made the long walk to the gate. However, they could not cut the outside bolt with the cutters, and O'Malley rapped on the gate and asked those on the outside to throw over a rope. The rescuers duly threw a weighted rope over the wall – but it snagged on the roof. As O'Malley pulled on the rope, it snapped, and he was left with a useless length of rope and a weight. The three hid the bolt cutters in the nearby lumber shed and returned to their cells.

The following night, 14 February, Teeling went into O'Malley's cell and excitedly reported that he and one of the British guards, working together, had just managed to cut the bolt on the outer gate. They had put the handles on the bolt cutter the wrong way the night before! The escape was back on. O'Malley and Teeling continued on to Patrick Moran's cell. 'Come on, Paddy,' O'Malley said, 'Teeling's cut the bolt.' Moran was writing a letter. He stood up. 'God, that's great,' he said, 'but I'm not going.'

Moran said he would not let down the witnesses who gave evidence for him. He said he was not guilty and was convinced he would be found innocent.

'To hell with the witnesses,' O'Malley said, 'come on.'

'Oh, come on,' Teeling pleaded, 'come on.'

Moran shook his head slowly, smiling. 'God, keep you,' he said. O'Malley went to Simon Donnelly's cell. 'Hop it, Simon, we're escaping now.' Donnelly, conscious that he too could soon be facing the death penalty, decided to join O'Malley and Teeling. Before leaving the corridor, O'Malley went to Desmond Fitzgerald's cell. Fitzgerald, the IRA director of publicity, gave him six pence for a tram fare.[11] Donnelly also tried to persuade Moran to join the escape, but he replied that any attempt by him to escape would be interpreted by the British as an admission of guilt. Patrick Moran would pay for this decision with his life: he was executed on 14 March 1921.

One of the sympathetic soldiers accompanied Teeling and O'Malley to the gate. Donnelly joined them, but the way to freedom was not so easy. The bolt securing the gate was rusted. They greased the bolt with butter saved from their rations. Then, following some minutes of hard work and extreme anxiety, they eventually succeeded in working back the rusted bolt from its socket. Slowly they opened the gate while keeping a sharp eye out for anyone hanging around outside. The soldier slipped back inside to his duty while the three prisoners walked out to freedom. He had informed the escapees that he had been prepared to join in the fight if they had been discovered. O'Malley went out first, the revolver in his hand. He saw figures in the darkness who turned out to be soldiers courting with their girls. They had other things on their minds, which were certainly not escaped prisoners.

The three escapees walked casually out of Kilmainham and down a back road. O'Malley said, 'The wind was cold, it blew clean and sweet in our faces. Gas lamps beamed out of the blackness; front porches shone on to small evergreen shrubs in tiny gardens and the stars winked at us in a friendly way.'[12] Donnelly suggested that they dump the revolver, because if they were held up in the streets by an armed patrol their escape would end violently and probably not in their favour. Reluctantly, O'Malley hid the revolver in the garden of a private house. The three walked past Richmond Military Barracks and along the banks of the Grand Canal. As they were about to cross the canal at Rialto Bridge, an armoured car came careening around the corner. They flung themselves down on the grass as a searchlight flashed out from the car. The armoured car passed on its way, and the trio picked themselves up from the grass and boarded a tram to the city. Donnelly got off the tram at Camden Street; O'Malley and Teeling got off at Heytesbury Street and headed to Brigid Malone's home. Brigid, a Cumann na mBan (founded in 1914 as a women's auxiliary to the Irish Volunteers) member who had married Dan Breen on 12 June 1921, greeted the pair enthusiastically. But later that night, Brigid, fearing the house might be raided, linked arms with Teeling and O'Malley and brought them to another safe house near Mount Street Bridge.[13]

There was great consternation when the prison gate was found open at Kilmainham. Armoured cars and lorries scoured the area for hours, and several houses in the vicinity were searched. The Commander-in-Chief of British forces in Ireland, General Nevil Macready's reaction summed up the escape. 'We have had a real disaster. The man Teeling and two other important men escaped last night from Kilmainham Prison and got clear away. It is about the worst blow I have had for a very long time, and I am naturally furious.'[14]

There was mention that a soldier was seen at the gates, and newspapers reported that the military, or someone disguised as military, had helped the escapees. Several soldiers on duty were arrested, and Privates Roper and Holland, who had been on duty together at the prison for at least a month before the escape, came under suspicion. Following a court martial, Pte Roper was imprisoned for eight years on the Isle of Wight for his involvement in the escape. A few days later, Pte Holland deserted and made his way to the home of republican John Tallan at Seville Place, Dublin, where he burned his uniform and went into hiding.[15]

After his escape, Donnelly returned to duty and was appointed chief of the Irish Republican Police in mid-1921 as part of an attempt to enforce law and order in those areas of the country where the RIC had been forced out. Donnelly took the anti-Treaty side in the Civil War.[16] In an attempt to mend some of the rifts in the republican movement, he subsequently founded the National Association of the Old IRA.

Tragically, Frank Teeling suffered severe post-traumatic stress disorder, and while he was commissioned as a lieutenant in the newly founded National Army, his erratic behaviour and descent into alcoholism became a cause for concern. Teeling was later wounded in the fighting in Limerick. In October 1922, he accidentally shot dead a sergeant major in Gormanstown Camp, Co. Meath. The subsequent investigation cleared him of any malice in the case. However, several months later, Teeling, in a drunken altercation, shot and killed William Johnson, a member of the Citizens' Defence Force. At his trial, Teeling claimed he had acted in self-defence, citing the fact that Johnson had also drawn a gun. The jury found him guilty of manslaughter and recommended clemency 'on account of the state of his mind'. Teeling was jailed for eighteen months. When he died in January 1976, only three national newspapers reported his death.[17]

A month after he escaped, Ernie O'Malley was placed in command of the IRA's 2nd Southern Division, the second-largest division in the IRA's new military structure. On 19 June 1921, O'Malley's men captured three British Army officers. In retaliation for the execution of IRA prisoners in Cork, O'Malley ordered the three officers to be shot the next day. O'Malley took the anti-Treaty side in the Civil War, and, after a shoot-out with National soldiers, he was captured at his secret headquarters, the home of Nell Humphreys at Ailesbury Road in Donnybrook, Dublin, on 4 November 1922. As troops broke down the panelling concealing his room, O'Malley shot four National soldiers, killing one. O'Malley was shot nine times, five times in the back, but survived. 'Anno' also known as 'Anna' O'Rahilly, who lived in the house, was accidentally wounded by O'Malley as he fired at the soldiers. His severe wounds saved him from execution, although he claimed one of the soldiers wanted to finish him off as he lay on the ground but was restrained by another. O'Malley joined the mass hunger strike in October–November 1923, in which 8,000 prisoners were involved, and was the last anti-Treaty prisoner to be released from custody. Ernie O'Malley left the Curragh Camp, along with Seán Russell, on 17 July 1924, over a year after the end of the Civil War.[18]

CHAPTER 6

PRISON 'BREAKS'

In the immediate aftermath of Bloody Sunday, 21 November 1920, the British government decided to open internment camps in Ireland. Facilitating a record use of imprisonment without trial, these camps, rather than jails, quickly became the largest holding centres of political prisoners. By late June 1921, 3,311 men were interned in the camps, constituting just over half of all those then jailed because of the War of Independence.

As conditions in the country became more militarised, the circumstances of the imprisoned men began to resemble those of prisoners of war – a status the British authorities did not want to concede to them. From the start of the conflict the British government had refused to recognise that there was a war in Ireland, as claimed by republicans, and by strengthening the police rather than the military, it could justify the conflict as mere 'civil disorder'. However, the opening of internment centres and the use of regular soldiers as camp guards helped to dispel this belief.[1]

Rory O'Connor is known as the man who destroyed many of Ireland's national records when the Four Courts in Dublin was blown up at the beginning of the Civil War in June 1922. However, he has an impeccable War of Independence record. O'Connor was an Easter Week veteran and was wounded by sniper fire during reconnaissance at Dublin's Royal College of Surgeons. On his recuperation from his wounds, O'Connor was prominent in the successful Sinn Féin parliamentary by-election campaign in Co. Roscommon. He was appointed to the Irish Volunteers' GHQ staff as Director of Engineering in March 1918, a post he held throughout the War of Independence. O'Connor was also involved in the planning and execution of prison escapes in both Ireland and Britain, most notably the daring daylight escape at Mountjoy Prison in March 1919 and the escape of Piaras Béaslaí, Austin Stack and four others from Strangeways Prison in Manchester later that year. Because of this he bore the unofficial, and jocular, titles of 'OC of escapes' and 'director of jail deliveries'. Not long after arriving in the 'escape-proof' Rath Camp, Rory O'Connor made his own successful escape.[2]

On 28 January 1921 O'Connor was arrested by Auxiliary police at his home in Monkstown, Co. Dublin, and was taken to Dublin Castle. Three days later, he was transferred to Kilmainham Gaol and was there when Frank Teeling, Ernie O'Malley and Simon Donnelly made their sensational escape. O'Connor was moved from Kilmainham to Mountjoy Prison and then transferred to Arbour Hill, a military prison on Dublin's north side. At Arbour Hill, he came into conflict with Joseph Lawless, an officer commanding republican prisoners. On 6 March O'Connor was conveyed to the Rath Camp, at the Curragh. The Rath Internment Camp opened for business on 1 March 1921. Situated on the Curragh Plains adjacent to the biggest military installation in Ireland, the Rath Camp was named after the Gibbet Rath, scene of a massacre of 350 rebels who had surrendered to Crown forces in May 1798.[3]

Joseph Lawless, as Dublin Brigade engineering officer, was involved in the production of bombs and other ordnance for the volunteer companies in north Co. Dublin. Republican prisoners were routinely transferred from Arbour Hill to Ballykinlar Camp, in Co. Down, and other areas of detention. At the end of January 1921, when Con O'Donovan, the prisoners' OC, was moved to Ballykinlar Camp, Joseph Lawless was elected the Rath prisoners' OC in his place. Rory O'Connor, as a member of IRA GHQ staff, maintained that he was the senior officer and should, by rank, automatically be OC. However, according to Lawless, O'Connor was not popular with the men and so was passed over. Lawless soothed O'Connor's wounded pride by telling him it would not do to elect him OC, as to do so would alert the enemy to his prominent position. In accordance with the practice, the name of the prisoners' OC was forwarded to the British governor of the prison, and the two would iron out any difficulties that arose. However, this was not the end of the affair. When the Rath Camp opened to receive prisoners from Arbour Hill, both Lawless and O'Connor were in the first batch of 150 men to be transferred. O'Connor, who had been involved in the escapes of republican prisoners from several prisons, asked Lawless if he had made plans for a mass escape during the move to the Curragh. Lawless replied that he had not and explained that as they were certain to be heavily guarded, it was not possible to make any prearranged plans.

In his witness statement to the Bureau of Military History Lawless said:

> I assured him that, of course, if any opportunity showed itself on the way we would do what we could about it when the chance arose. He [O'Connor] then took up the heavy attitude with me and, speaking as a member of the General Staff, warned me that it was my duty as the prisoners' commandant to organise an escape. Poor Rory was evidently still suffering from the snub to his dignity of my election as commandant against his candidature, and I

regretted the necessity for a further snub when I replied that the matter rested safely in my hands. It was clear, however, that Rory was likely to cause trouble and I discussed this quietly with Peadar McMahon and a few others while we waited. We concluded that nothing was likely to happen until we arrived at the Curragh, but then we would be in a position of a new community and Rory would most likely try to gain an ascendency and have himself elected as camp commandant. We agreed that we would not allow this to happen, but I said that I would not stand as a candidate for election and suggested Peadar McMahon as more suitable. Peadar tried to persuade me to accept election to the appointment, and only agreed to accept it himself on condition that I would act as his vice-commandant or second in command.

The position was that the general body of prisoners would accept any reasonable rule of leadership provided that there were no divided councils. If opposing factions were allowed to arise, then the men would be unable to decide what was the right thing to do. A division in the ranks would be exploited by the camp authorities. It was up to the senior IRA officers to make the decision and present this to the general body of prisoners – for rectification in the form of an election.[4]

Lieutenant Daniel Ryan, F Company, 2nd Battalion, Dublin Brigade, was arrested near St Stephen's Green, Dublin, on 28 January 1921, the day after he had taken part in a gun and bomb attack on a military lorry in which one soldier was injured. After interrogation – and the customary beating for volunteers caught with arms – he was transferred from Dublin Castle to Arbour Hill and subsequently to the Curragh. In his witness statement to the Bureau of Military History Ryan described how, on a bitterly cold March morning, he arrived at the Rath Camp (although he referred to it as Hare Park Camp, an adjacent holding centre) in a convoy of military trucks, with two British Army aeroplanes patrolling overhead:

> As we proceeded on our journey, we amused ourselves by singing national songs, and the soldiers of the escort laughed when an officer put a gun up to one of our boys and told him to stop singing rebel songs. To the great delight of the soldiers, our party sang a parody of 'Rule Brittania' [*sic*] which infuriated the officer still more. We arrived at our destination about 5.30 p.m., weary and hungry. We were duly searched and allotted our places in the huts. A crowd of us who were old members of the Dublin Brigade had no desire to be separated, and we luckily succeeded in remaining together. We were about the first batch of prisoners to arrive at Hare Park Camp. For the first week, on account of our changed addresses, we received none of the usual parcels from our friends outside, and to say that we were often hungry during that week would be putting it mildly. A friend in the enemy's camp invariably proves a valuable possession. In our case he turned out to be an exceptionally valuable one.[5]

While strolling around the camp one morning after breakfast, Ryan accidentally opened the door of a hut which appeared to be in the course of construction. To his great surprise and delight, Jerry Gaffney rushed over to him. Unknown to the British, Gaffney was an active member of E Company, 2nd Battalion, Dublin Brigade, and was employed as a civilian carpenter at the Curragh Camp.

After a warm handshake, Gaffney produced a packet of cigarettes, and they discussed the question of getting into communication with IRA GHQ as early as possible. Gaffney arranged to bring in loaves of bread and some cigarettes daily, and letters that the censor had not had the pleasure of reading. After a few days, the two friends discussed the question that was uppermost in Ryan's mind, that of escape. He said, 'With Gaffney's assistance there was a sporting chance of getting out.'

The next question for Ryan was, who was to go with him; so he approached one of the senior officers he knew in the camp, Rory O'Connor of GHQ. Ryan said, O'Connor was using an assumed name and, like many other important men, had kept his identity a secret from the enemy. Ryan continued:

> He [O'Connor] had often planned escapes for others. Now he was to have the pleasure of planning his own. I told him that I saw a possible chance of escape, but I would not disclose my plans until one condition was entered into – i.e. that I should be one of the two or three to escape. That was the greatest number I estimated could hope to get out without arousing suspicion. To this he smiled and said: "That's the spirit; you can do more outside than here. There are too many locked up." He added that he had been thinking of a possible way of escape since his arrival. I immediately revealed my plans to him. I told him about my meetings with Jerry Gaffney and to what extent the latter was prepared to go to help us.[6]

The two would-be escapers met Gaffney the following day in a disused hut at the end of the compound and discussed in detail the proposed escape. A pass system controlled the workmen's entry and exit, and guards supervised their work. It was arranged that Gaffney would stay away from work on the given day.[7] Internee Christopher Kenny of Rathangan, Co. Kildare, was brought into the plan. He persuaded another carpenter, Harry Rose, to stay away from work on the day selected. Ryan and O'Connor would escape in the guise of the two workmen. The plan was put for approval to Peadar McMahon and Joseph Lawless, and they gave the go-ahead.[8]

Over the following days, Gaffney smuggled in workmen's dungarees and various articles of tradesmen's tools, along with fake discs and passes to get through the military security at the gate. They decided that Friday, being the workmen's payday, would be the best time to chance their luck, and that 5.30 p.m. was the ideal time to escape because the workmen left at that time. At about 3.30 p.m., O'Connor approached Ryan while he was strolling around and told him, to his great disappointment, that the escape was off because the roll would be called in the camp at 6.30 p.m. and they would be missed within an hour of their departure. Later that evening, Ryan and O'Connor had a quick meeting in the old hut and arranged to make the attempt the following day, Saturday, 12 March. That morning, Ryan and O'Connor answered roll call at 6.30 a.m. and had breakfast at 8.15 a.m. Saturday was a half-day for the workmen.

Ryan described the incident in his witness statement:

> Saturday came, and after breakfast Rory and I had a long discussion. About 12.30 p.m. we both rambled away from the general body of the prisoners and made our way to the hut in which all our requisites were hidden. We dressed in the dungarees, smeared our faces with dust to make ourselves look like workmen, got our discs and passes ready, and after putting the finishing touches to our personal appearance we silently opened the door of the hut and, with a saw and tools under our arms, followed in the train of about a dozen workmen to the exit gates. We had to pass through two gates, with a full guard on each, and the majority of the workmen were well known to the guards on each gate. As we

approached the gate, I could feel my heart beating quickly, my breathing became jerky and my senses began to weaken. At the exit I brazened myself up, produced my pass and disc, which were examined and found to be in order by the sentry at the first gate. We next approached the second gate and, to my horror, I recognised the sentry on duty. This particular soldier was always sympathetic and when passing me in the camp invariably greeted me with the remark, 'Hard lines, old man.' I could feel myself sagging when he looked at the card and disc and then looked at me. Fortunately, I had a cap pulled down on the right-hand side of my face. He again looked at the disc and at me – these few seconds seemed like an eternity – and then he said, 'All right, pass on.' I have often wondered since if he did really recognise me. The gate was opened, and we passed out through it.[9]

The two escapees walked down the road, keeping a distance from the workmen. When they got out of sight of the camp, the two made their way across fields in the direction of Kildare Railway Station. They discarded the dungarees and tools in an old cowhouse, and endeavoured to make themselves look a little presentable. After about thirty minutes walking across the fields, they arrived at Kildare Railway Station in time to catch a train to Dublin. At the booking office, O'Connor purchased two first-class return tickets for Dublin. 'Not that we intended to return,' Ryan said, 'but in case we were missed before roll call, and inquiries were made at the station, this would help to turn the enemy off the scent.'

Ryan and O'Connor got off the train at Lucan village and walked about a mile to the old steam tram that ran from Lucan to Parkgate Street on the edge of Dublin's Phoenix Park. When they were about halfway along the road, they saw a Crossley tender with a group of Auxiliaries coming towards them. O'Connor said with dread, 'I'm afraid it's all up, but walk on.' They casually walked on, and as the tender drew near it pulled up. One of the Auxiliaries asked if they were on the right road for Newbridge, Co. Kildare, to which O'Connor replied, 'Yes'. The tender continued on its way.

O'Connor and Ryan arrived in Dublin at about 3 p.m., and after a warm handshake and arranging to meet later, parted company at Parkgate Street. Ryan said:

> I went to my digs, no doubt a risky thing to do, and when my landlady opened the door she nearly collapsed. However, the welcome was splendid. That night, with Rory I had the pleasure of meeting and being congratulated by Michael Collins, Gearóid O'Sullivan and other members of the GHQ staff, all of whom were delighted to get a first-hand account of the first escape of prisoners from an internment camp in Ireland.[10]

The two prisoners' escape was discovered at roll call that evening, and from then on there was a considerable tightening of security measures, so that no similar attempt was possible for a long time. Details of the escape remained secret for some time; the newspapers knowing nothing of the facts, commenting that it was a 'mysterious affair'. The facts were simple enough: Daniel Ryan and Rory O'Connor had arrived at the Rath Camp on 6 March and had walked out through the main gate six days later. Their escape within two weeks of the camp opening firmly established that it was not escape-proof and was a great morale boost to the prisoners – as well as a huge propaganda coup for the republican movement.[11]

Joseph Lawless made his own successful escape some months later, going out the front gate as his adversary Rory O'Connor had done. Lawless and Tom Glennon (Belfast), having observed the method of removal of the swill from the camp, formulated a separate plan of escape. The swill from the cookhouse was removed daily by two young boys using a donkey and cart. On arrival at the gate, the boys would hand over the cart to a member of the military guard. The cart was then taken to the cookhouse, loaded by prisoners, returned to the gate and handed back to the boys. Tom Glennon had ascertained the willingness of one of the soldiers to accept a bribe for his help. Joseph Lawless asked the prisoners' chaplain, Fr Paddy Smith, who held some money which was available for escape projects, to 'loan' him £10 to bribe the soldier. The duo then set their plans in motion, and they appropriated two large canvas mail sacks from the post office censor's hut.

On 2 October 1921, after Sunday Mass, Lawless spent the time disposing of his spare clothing and other belongings. He then waited anxiously for the swill cart to arrive after the prisoners had eaten dinner, which was about 6 p.m. Glennon had arranged that two other prisoners, who were members of the cookhouse staff, would conduct the financial arrangements with the soldier. They gave the soldier, £5 and the remaining £5 was to be paid to him when the prisoners were safely outside the gate. The arrangement with the soldier took only a few minutes while he was having a tea break inside the cookhouse. The loading of the cart was delayed by the shovelling of swill from one container to another until the prearranged signal was given from inside the cookhouse.

Lawless and Glennon were nervous that something would go wrong at the last minute. Meanwhile, a large group of prisoners collected around the cookhouse door to watch and give what help they could by concealing the movements around the swill cart with their bodies. The two escapees got into the mail sacks and curled up on the floor of the cart while their comrades began to empty barrels of swill on top of them. While the thick canvas sacks kept the slush from their clothes and allowed them to breathe, the limited air supply and weight of the swill pressing down on them began to take their toll.

Lawless said:

> I began to wonder if we would be able to survive long enough to get through the gate. Glennon apparently had the same thought. I heard him groaning once or twice and, though I was feeling no better myself, I mumbled to him to be quiet. He said that he could not stand it, and was about to get out of the cart when it at last began to move as the soldier took the donkey by the head. The slight movement of the cart improved our air supply somewhat, and with a last appeal to Glennon to be quiet and stick it out...[12]

After the cart passed through the camp gates one of the boys became suspicious of noise behind him, but when Lawless poked his head up through the waste and ordered the driver to keep going, the boys were only too glad to help in the escape. Exiting the cart at a safe distance from the camp and thanking their two willing helpers, the two escapees walked to the Central Hotel in Newbridge, to which they had been directed before they left the camp by a fellow prisoner. A car provided by local republicans brought Lawless and Glennon on to Dublin, arriving there by 10 p.m.

Lawless said, 'The feelings of joy in regaining my freedom; of reunion with my loved one, and the rejoicing of my friends was, in itself, overwhelming, so that my memory of those first days of freedom is confused and sketchy.' Despite the fact that the Truce had come into in effect, both escapees returned to their IRA units.[13]

CHAPTER 7

THE FERRETS OF KILDARE

The Rath Camp was designed to hold 1,000 men, and by June 1921 was deemed full with 1,007 prisoners.[1] Nevertheless, further batches of prisoners continued to arrive, which meant an overflow camp had to be built on the west side of the existing camp and adjoining it. Outside the camp peace overtures were being negotiated, which resulted in the signing of a truce between the IRA and Crown forces on 9 July 1921. Behind the barbed wire, internees expected an immediate release of prisoners to coincide with peace talks. However, many senior republicans felt the truce was only a respite, and when negotiations inevitably broke down the war would begin again, with both sides redoubling their efforts.[2]

When there was no general release of prisoners after the signing of the Anglo-Irish Truce, a group of internees at the Rath facility, on the Curragh Plains, began digging a tunnel. As a result of the discovery of an earlier escape tunnel that had been dug towards the outskirts of the wire entanglement, military engineers sank a four-foot-deep and four-foot-wide trench on three sides of the camp to deter any further escape attempts. No trench was necessary on the fourth (north) side of the camp, as it adjoined the quarters of the British officers.

The new tunnel was known as the 'Dublin Brigade Tunnel', because it was dug mainly by men of the Dublin Brigade who were all quartered in the same hut. They excavated the tunnel on the east side of the camp, beginning with a pit under the floor of one of the huts, intending it to run at a depth of eight to ten feet. The tunnel was to emerge about 100 yards clear of the outside wire in a clump of furze bushes and clear of the ring of lights that surrounded the camp at night. The soil was of a sandy nature, and bed boards and floorboards were used at intervals as props to prevent a cave-in. It was a big and ambitious project, and to get the maximum number of men out the tunnellers decided to make the tunnel wider than earlier attempts.

At the same time, another group of prisoners had decided to dig their own tunnel. Joe Galvin (Co. Mayo), who had been involved in the first tunnel attempt, had never given up on the idea of tunnelling. He again approached Jim Brady, a miner from Co. Cavan, and they agreed to try again. They had propped up the first tunnel with sticks and boards, which had proved too slow. They decided to dig without losing time on safety measures and in the same way as the first one – a hole two feet square and four feet deep, and then expanding outwards and downwards.

The select half-dozen internees involved in the escape plans held daily and nightly meetings in which the major problems were tackled. They decided that the tunnel entrance would be under the hut, as the huts rested on concrete blocks, leaving a one- to two-foot crawl space beneath the floor. The huts were seventy feet from the barbed wire, so the tunnel would have to go about twenty feet beyond that. Because of the many plants and spies in the camp, secrecy would be a priority – but all the men in the hut were considered trustworthy.

Tents were erected between the huts because of the arrival of a new batch of prisoners. As part of the escape plans John J. Martin, camp quartermaster, asked his British counterpart for a marquee tent to enable him to discharge his 'heavy duties'. The marquee was delivered and was set up beside the escapers' hut; the escape committee made it their headquarters. The space under the hut was boarded almost to the ground, and all that was necessary was for the tunnellers to lift the canvas wall of the marquee and crawl under the adjoining hut. A guard was always around to make sure that the passage from the tent to underneath the hut was unobserved.[3]

One late August night, Joe Galvin and Jim Brady slipped quietly out of their beds and crept under their hut. With a screwdriver, a crowbar and spoons from the cookhouse, the two men started the job of opening a shaft for a new tunnel, which was fifty feet away from the Dublin Brigade tunnel. They lay flat on the earth beneath the hut and scooped away the first sod over the proposed shaft – making a circular hole some thirty inches in diameter. Shortly before dawn, they cautiously returned to their beds, tired but contented with the results of their work. Their new tunnel became known variously as 'Brady's Tunnel', or the 'Rabbit Burrow', as it was quite narrow and resembled a rabbit hole.[4]

The shaft was about ten to twelve feet across, and a makeshift ladder was provided to enable the workers to get up and down the shaft. They hauled excavated clay back to the entrance in strong canvas mailbags supplied by the camp postman, Andy Harrold, and pulled the bags up with ropes that belonged to the marquee. When the space under the floor had been filled, they carried the bags of earth up into the hut and stored them temporarily in fire buckets, suitcases and anything else available. The soil was eventually spirited away in jacket pockets or paper bags supplied by the huts' occupants. The men subsequently carefully and unobtrusively distributed the soil in handfuls all over the camp, so that no one would notice it on the surface of the compound.

When the shaft was completed, two major problems confronted the tunnellers: direction and lighting. The tunnel was to be driven eastward for about 80–90 yards to a spot covered by a clump of furze bushes. In this way it was hoped that the exit among the furze would be most likely to escape observation by the sentries in the elevated posts. There was no compass available, so the tunnellers had to rely on home-made right-angled contrivances made from strips of timber. These were held vertically in the shaft to enable them to strike off approximately in the desired direction.[5]

Tunnelling was done entirely at night after roll call, when it was unlikely that the occupants of the hut would be disturbed without warning. The organisers drew up a set timetable to cope with the camp routine – such as meals, parades and counts – as well as precautions against sudden swoops and raids. One factor that greatly assisted the tunnelling was the type of soil, which, being of a gravelly nature, was favourable to the enterprise. There were comparatively few large stones. Initially, the tunnel was about thirty inches square, barely enough to permit a man to crawl through on hands and knees. In time, the tunnellers learned to round off the roof into a rough arch, but only after several cave-ins, which fortunately didn't cause any casualties. Jim Brady did most of the tunnelling, lying on his back or his side as he struck out over his shoulder at the tunnel face. Only one man at a time could work on the tunnel face and get the earth back to the end of the shaft. Brady's rapid and skilful tunnelling expertise earned him the title of 'the human ferret'. He worked tirelessly in the tunnel and oversaw the work of others.

Brady was helped mainly by Joe Galvin, and they endured the fetid smell of damp earth and their own sweat for the most part of eleven days, until they were almost completely exhausted. As the work proceeded, every prisoner in the hut who could do so lent a willing hand, though only a few were able to manage working in the tunnel. The task was exhausting, with extreme restriction of movement. Light was supplied by candles, which were scrounged, bartered for and plundered. When candles were not available, they were made up for by makeshift candles made of grease and string. Candles gave necessary light, but they also devoured the limited supply of oxygen. The air in the tunnel was foul, and a stage was reached when a lighted candle at the face of the shaft would not remain alight because of the lack of oxygen. The only ventilation was through the entrance, and consequently the air at the shaft face was rank.

When Brady had excavated about 50 feet, he found he could go no further without an air shaft. He went into the tunnel again with the crowbar and dug an outlet upwards to the surface eight feet overhead in the shape of a cone, so the poisonous gases could escape. Outside, anxious watchers waited to see where the crowbar would come through the surface. It came through – but right in no-man's land! This necessitated placing the air shaft back a few feet, safely under the barbed wire out of sight of the guards. The air quality in the tunnel then became tolerable. As Brady continued his excavations, he added several more air holes.[6]

Despite the difficulties, work on the tunnels proceeded at an amazingly rapid pace. Inside a fortnight, Brady and his comrades had arrived below the inner barbed-wire entanglements, and after they had tunnelled about 75 feet Brady began to dig upwards. While the two groups of tunnellers were unaware of each other's schemes, both tunnels were designed to come up under the outer barbed-wire entanglements at a point parallel with Row D of the huts. When they had reached the outside wire, Brady reported to Liam Murphy that the job was completed and, except for the outer barbed-wire barrier, the escape was ready to go. For that barrier, he had secured a wire cutters stolen from a British work party repairing the wire. However, a major problem then arose.

On 5 September British troops began unloading baulks of timber and barbed wire outside the outer entanglements along the side of the camp where both tunnels were to break the surface. Engineers then began to erect a new compound for prisoners on the spot where the tunnel exit was planned. Sappers also began deepening the trench which they had dug after finding the earlier escape tunnel, and it was probable that in a short time they would unearth the new tunnel. The decision to escape became paramount.[7]

It also became apparent that there were two rival tunnels heading towards the wire at the same time. Internees also saw that Brady's tunnel was a better proposition than the Dublin tunnel, as that route was shorter, the course easier and the tunnellers were nearer the goal. Tom Byrne, Dublin Brigade, said, 'We joined forces and a council of war was held at which it was agreed that all the workers on the other tunnel should abandon their own and get a chance to escape the Brady way. The Brady tunnel was chosen because it was the more advanced.'[8] It was, due to Brady's skill and tenacity, the more probable way for a successful escape.

On 7 September, eighteen days after the work had started, Brady and Galvin calculated that they had reached a point clear of the outer entanglements. They were ready to go that night, but, as an extra precaution, Brady was asked to push a marker upwards to make sure the tunnel went far enough. However, when they tentatively pushed a fencing foil with a piece of white paper on its tip through the topsoil, observers were dismayed to see that it appeared in the strip of land between the two entanglements. With renewed energy, the tunnellers pressed on with their work, though progress was slow. Despite this, the decision was taken that the escape should be made at night on 9 September.

They also decided that certain officers were to be given priority in the escape attempt. Despite the Truce and ongoing peace negotiations, the IRA was preparing for the worst, and the escape of experienced men from the Curragh was important. Tom Byrne, Commandant, 1st Battalion, Dublin Brigade, was one of those earmarked to escape. He asked that Joe Vize, GHQ staff, be allowed to escape too, and the escape committee agreed. The Brady tunnel was a small-escape project, so it was clear that many men would have to remain in the camp. Fifty escapees were selected, and there was disappointment all around.

The plan was that they were to go in two batches of twenty-five, with a two-hour interval between each batch. In that way, if anything went wrong, at least some men would have a chance to get away. The grandstand of the Curragh Racecourse was the rendezvous point to meet and strike out in select groups in different directions. The strategy was to get onto the railway line behind the racecourse and follow it until daylight.

It was a foggy night as the first twenty-five prisoners arrived, while the other twenty-five men chosen to escape quietly occupied the marquee tent next to the escape hut to await their turn. As they were waiting, all the lights in the new camp were turned on, but, after some anxious moments, to the delight of the escapees they were turned off. The British were only testing. Jim Brady and Joe Galvin went first. Their work was not complete; they still had important jobs to accomplish, as they were to open the tunnel into the outer entanglements and then lead the way. At 11.30 p.m. they slid into the tunnel to open the outer end and to cut the wire. Scurrying on hands and knees as fast as they could along the narrow passage, within minutes they were at the end of the tunnel that had taken days of hard labour to complete.

As loose earth rained down on them, they hacked anxiously at the roof, quickly opening a hole large enough to get through comfortably. Helped by Brady, Galvin got his head and shoulders above ground. After the black darkness of the tunnel, he was nearly blinded by the glare of the searchlight that shone straight into his face. On regaining his composure, Galvin was immediately filled with despair. They had seriously miscalculated the opening; the new shaft opened in the corridor between the two lines of entanglements in the newly constructed No. 2 Internment Camp, about twenty yards short of the objective. However, the point reached was outside the area covered by the arc of light surrounding the barbed-wire fence, and, in the darkness, the sentries in the elevated posts could not easily observe it. Brady and Galvin quickly recovered from this serious discovery and crawled towards the outer entanglement, flattening themselves against the grass of the corridor as apprehensive eyes watched from the darkened interior of the internees' huts.

Suddenly, a chilling challenge ripped the silence of the night: 'Halt! Who goes there?' The challenge was immediately followed by the more ominous metallic sound of a weapon being cocked in the nearest of the observation towers. A tense few seconds passed as Brady and Galvin lay motionless, hoping that the sentry had not seen them. The two escapers knew that the guards had orders to shoot anyone seen approaching close to the barbed wire. They steadied themselves for the worst but were greatly relieved when they heard the answer to the guard's challenge: 'Visiting rounds', which came from the side of the tower from where they lay. Suspecting nothing, the patrol moved on.[9]

Outside the barbed wire, No. 2 Internment Camp was now complete but not occupied. A very thick barbed-wire entanglement ran right through the centre of this camp, and a way had to be cut through this before the escapers could get to the camp gate, which was also heavily wired. Brady and Galvin had taken a ball of twine and wooden pegs with them. Brady had tied one end of the twine to one of the pegs. When he reached the exit, he drove the peg into the ground and trailed the twine along until he reached the first wire barrier, which he managed to cut through unnoticed. Still trailing the twine, he reached the second wire barrier fifteen yards further away and cut a gap in that. Using the twine as a guide in the dark, he made his way back and gave the all-clear. Brady turned, and, with Galvin, headed for the plains of the Curragh. A thick fog had come down but their sense of direction was good, and, within minutes, they found themselves on the road to Newbridge.

By following the guide twine that Brady had laid down, the escaping prisoners had no difficulty in locating the gap in the barriers. The escapers then started to leave at intervals of minutes to prevent congestion in the tunnel. They did not wear boots or shoes so as to avoid making any noise and churning up the tunnel floor. Each man had instructions to wait at the exit until he heard the sentry pass.

It was well after midnight when the first of the remaining internees got clear of the camp. Once they were outside the barbed wire, they set off in small groups towards the racecourse, but the thick ground fog enveloping the Curragh made a rendezvous impossible. Selected Dublin prisoners were the first group out, followed by internees from the west. At the tunnel entrance, Liam Murphy and Hugh Byrne directed their batch of twenty-five escapers in the order of their arrival. When they were finished, they handed over to the other party led by Walter O'Brien, and advised him of the procedure.

Tom Byrne and Joe Vize found some fifteen men lying under the ground, head to toe in the tunnel. Byrne described the scene:

> For about 7 or 8 feet we went at an angle of about 45 degrees, and then made a complete dive as we knew we were about to go under the trench. The tunnel then gradually worked up … Brady's tunnel was indeed a narrow one, each man had to fight his way through, panting and wrestling with

the walls. The hole was round and Vize and I, being big men, had to lever ourselves along on our elbows. The whole length of the tunnel was full of men, all screwing themselves onward in the darkness. Sometimes all movement would stop like a traffic block and we'd lie there wondering what was happening at the front. We couldn't go forward and we couldn't go back.

Just when we'd begun to think we were stuck there forever – or until we were caught and hauled out ignominiously – the movement would start again and we'd all wriggle forward another few yards. It was only later I learned the reason for the numerous halts. The lads at the exit couldn't go out until the sentry had passed on in the other direction to No Man's Land. Every time the sentry would turn his back a fresh batch would dodge out and away.[10]

One of the escapees, C.S. 'Todd' Andrews, did not know what towns, villages or landmarks lay between the Curragh and Dublin. He said, 'This was a measure of the ignorance of Dubliners of our time about rural Ireland or indeed of the geography of Ireland in general.'[11] He hung his boots around his neck while his two companions, Myles Ford and Jack Noud, unfortunately did not. They walked along a railway track, but soon Andrews' companions' feet were in a mess, and they had to proceed on the main road through Newbridge, a garrison town. They made it safely to Sallins Railway Station, where the porter, an IRA volunteer, gave them a half-crown and put them on a goods train to Dublin.[12]

Some of the men found the tunnel quite daunting and became pronounced 'nerve cases' underground. Tomás Ó Maoláin (Raemore, Co. Mayo), Seán Barry and Seán Doody (Tullamore, Co. Offaly) got lost in the fog. They wandered around until they found themselves back at the wire of the camp and heard a sentry muttering a challenge. In panic, they turned and headed back the way they came. Lost again, Doody theorised that the cold and clammy wind was coming from the east, and if they felt the icy sensation on their right cheek they should be heading off in a northerly direction, which would bring them away from the camp. This observation was correct, as the trio then crashed into a railing of the racecourse. Ducking under the railing, they soon arrived at the grandstand and subsequently the railway line. At daybreak, they reached a friendly cottage in the Bog of Allen, several miles from the Curragh Camp.

Several escaped prisoners wandered around for hours in the fog. Like Ó Maoláin, Barry and Doody, some, having lost their bearings, found themselves back at the outer barbed-wire entanglements, where the searchlights and arc lamps glowed away through the fog. They quickly altered their direction of travel, and in a short time were entirely outside the vicinity of the camp and the green lands of the Curragh were soon left far behind.

Tom Moran, brother of Patrick Moran who had been executed in Kilmainham Gaol, was with a group of eleven Roscommon men, but the heavy fog was nearly the undoing of them. When they thought they were well clear of the camp, they also found themselves back at the wire. They turned and walked in the opposite direction; soon they accepted they were lost. In desperation, they knelt and recited the Rosary. As they finished praying, they heard rooks cawing in trees nearby. Knowing that the only trees near the camp were at the back of the grandstand of the Curragh Racecourse, they used the rooks' cawing to guide them. The men decided to take a chance when they reached a group of houses near the Hill of Allen, about ten miles from the Curragh Camp. More luck was on the side of the escapers. The house where they called was that of a friendly family who fed them and then took them across fields to Fr Smith's home in Rathangan. He was the local curate and a republican sympathiser. The group of Roscommon men found two other escapers also enjoying the priest's hospitality. They all rested there during the day, and that evening local Volunteers brought fresh clothes and footwear along with horses and traps to Fr Smith's house. From there, they conveyed the escapers to Carbury, where the proprietor of Weyme's Hotel put his car at their disposal and asked the driver to take them to Athlone. There, a friend of one of the escapees provided them with a small lorry that brought them back to Roscommon.[13]

The network of friendly houses around the area was widespread; there were only a few places where a man wanted by the British would not be sheltered gladly. Michael and Elizabeth Cunningham of Tower House, Kildare, were responsible for the smuggling of maps and other equipment to potential escapers in the Rath and Hare Park Camps. They also supplied clothing to an escapee and transported him to Dublin.

Most of the designated men had escaped by 4 a.m., but not all the men who intended to escape did break out. John J. Gavigan, a member of Coole District Council, was only told about the tunnel on the morning of the escape. He had only been in the camp for nine days and was one of the last four men appointed to go. He said:

> When I came to the mouth of the tunnel, I remarked there were boots in the tunnel. There was a sentry 2½ yards from me. He could hear the noise and saw the last four going out. I was waiting to give the fellow before me a chance. The next thing I heard as a call of 'Halt there', and a shot was fired. The sentry shouted for the guard to come out, but they did not believe there was anything the matter and did not come out. The sentry went down and we heard him shout, 'If you don't come quick, there won't be a "Shinner" in the camp,

they are going out like rabbits.' And so they were, but I was fated not to succeed on this occasion and had to go back.[14]

The exact number of prisoners who escaped from the Rath Camp on that night has never been verified, but the accepted figure was between fifty and sixty.[15] It was at morning roll call that most prisoners in the Rath Camp learned of the mass breakout, when armed troops poured into the camp and surrounded the huts. The prisoners were held within the huts for two or three hours, while they were counted, re-counted and names checked. The camp authorities carried out a more detailed check of the names and identities of the prisoners who had escaped later that day. Every prisoner left in camp, except those confined to hospital beds, was paraded on the football field and held there for some hours, while the identity of each man was checked against a list. Those who knew of the escape had great pleasure in answering the roll call with 'Gone through the tunnel' when an escaped prisoner's name was called out. The prisoners were also informed that privileges in the way of letters and parcels would be curtailed or withdrawn on account of the escape, but they didn't care.

On the following day, a party of sappers began the digging of a ten-foot-deep trench around the camp inside the wire, to cut through any undiscovered tunnels and to discourage any further tunnelling effort. The military spent four days in an effort to check the number and names of prisoners who had escaped. However, the prisoners added to the confusion by giving wrong names and moving around from place to place. The result was that the military could not arrive at a full count at any attempt.[16]

At an Aeridheacht, or open-air gathering, at St Enda's, Rathfarnham, held a few days after the breakout, Michael Collins congratulated the escapees from the Rath Camp on gaining their freedom. He stated that the prisoners had escaped with no outside help, which would have been a breach of the Truce.[17] None of the men was ever recaptured, and all of them reported back for duty to the republican movement. This was the largest prison escape to date during the War of Independence period. However, it was not the last tunnel escape. When would-be Rath Camp escapees were sent to Kilkenny Jail as punishment, they brought their tunnelling experience with them!

CHAPTER 8

HEARTS NEVER WAVER

A rrests climbed in response to the increase in political violence. The numbers committed to prisons by courts martial rose from 137 in 1919 to 520, and to 1,343 in 1921. A further 4,454 men were interned between November 1920 and the Truce of July 1921. During the War of Independence (1919–1921), only around fifty female activists were jailed compared with over 5,000 males. Forty were still in jail at the cessation of hostilities in July 1921.[1] Few women prisoners escaped from jails during the revolutionary period. On 31 October 1921, in what was described as one of the most sensational events in the annals of Irish prison history, four female prisoners escaped from Dublin's Mountjoy Prison. The escapees were Linda Kearns, Eithne Coyle, Mae Burke and Eileen Keogh.

On 20 November 1920, Auxiliary police and the British military intercepted a car driven by Linda Kearns in Sligo Town and discovered 10 rifles, 4 revolvers and 500 rounds of ammunition. Linda Kearns, along with three local volunteers – Jim Devins, Eugene Gilbride and Andy Conway – also with her in the car, were brought to nearby Strand Military Barracks, in Barrack Street. Two rifles, one revolver and part of the equipment were identified as the property of a police patrol which had been ambushed at Moneygold,

Grange, Co. Sligo, on 25 October 1920. Three policemen had been killed and three others wounded and their equipment taken in the ambush. Linda Kearns recalled that she had collected the arms from a volunteer 'called Feeney and handed them over to another I.R.A. man'. At the barracks, the police were incensed, and Kearns and the three volunteers were brutally assaulted.

Kearns said that while they were being held in Sligo Barracks, 'the Auxiliaries adopted a devilish plan, probably to wear down my nerves. They took the boys out one by one and we heard a shot each time and we thought it was the end. I did not see the three again during the night.'[2] The Auxiliaries kept asking Kearns where she was going when they met them. She kept to the same answer, that she was going to meet 'boys' at an agreed place but that they were not the ones who were in the car with her when she was stopped. She said in her witness statement to the Bureau of Military History:

> Eventually, an officer came in to me with an overcoat over his pyjamas – he may have been an Auxiliary – and spoke very nicely to me. He said if I told where I was going and whom I was to meet I would be allowed to go home and nobody would ever hear about the episode, adding that I was damned unlucky to have got myself into such a stew. I still refused to give any information. When he left, the R.I.C. took me on again and one of them, a notorious fellow nicknamed Spud Murphy, gave me a bad time. He beat me about the head and chest and broke one of my front teeth. A real Cockney Black and Tan who was among them protested against this conduct.[3]

Kearns was locked up in the only place available – the mortuary, although there were no bodies present. They took her out to the square the next morning, and, to her great relief, she saw that her comrades had not been executed and that it was only a ruse. The Auxiliaries stole her watch and gold ring, and confiscated her car, which was never returned. She was brought to Sligo Jail and, after a week, the military took her along with her male comrades to Mullaghmore, Co. Sligo, and placed them on a destroyer. There was no pier in Mullaghmore and the prisoners were lowered by rope one by one from a cliff into a rowboat, which brought them out to the *Destroyer*. The prisoners were taken off at Buncrana, Co. Donegal, and were marched from Buncrana towards Derry city. After marching handcuffed to an army officer for several hours, a lorry picked them up and brought them the rest of the way to Derry Jail. Kearns said, 'We had been well-treated on the destroyer. The sailor boys provided me with towel, soap, nail file ...'[4] She was held for a week in Derry Jail where she was the only female prisoner. There was no suitable accommodation there for women, so she was held in the jail hospital. There were no patients in the hospital, and Kearns was guarded by a solitary prison officer – a kind, elderly man who brought her in a clothes iron.

After ten days in Derry, Kearns was brought with the other Sligo prisoners to Crumlin Road Gaol in Belfast. The male prisoners were taken in, but the governor refused to take Kearns because it was not a female prison. He shut the door on her and the young British officer who had her in his charge. The officer, who was considerably embarrassed, said, 'What shall I do with you?' Kearns said, 'Let me go home.' He replied, 'I wish to God I could.' Kearns was still handcuffed to him, so he took her to nearby Victoria Barracks, from where she was sent the following day to Armagh Jail. The female governor said to Kearns, 'You can do what you like as long as you don't escape. It is my duty to prevent that.' She asked Kearns for her word of honour that she would not attempt to escape, which Kearns refused to give. 'All this time, no matter where I was, my sole thought was to escape,' Kearns later wrote.

Linda Kearns's father, Thomas, died in February 1921. She recalled, 'I asked for parole to go to the funeral, but was refused. I felt very bitter about that.' At the end of February, Kearns was brought back to Victoria Barracks in Belfast for trial by court martial, where she was sentenced to ten years' penal servitude for possession of arms and ammunition. Devins, Gilbride and Conway were each given fourteen years' penal servitude. Unlike many republican defendants, she recognised the court and was defended by a solicitor and counsel. Kearns's sister, Mrs O'Connell, described the sentence as harsh and terrible. 'Ten years' penal servitude and the confiscation of the motor car in view of the evidence given at the trial is a sentence that really carries its own comment,' she told a representative of the *Irish Independent*. 'I know that my sister will not worry about the sentence … Linda will take her punishment as other innocent boys took a much harder sentence.' Mrs O'Connell referred to the fact that her sister had volunteered her services to the matron of Dublin Castle Hospital during the Great War.[5]

On 26 April, Wednesday of Easter Week, 1916 Nurse Linda Kearns had opened a Red Cross field hospital for casualties in an empty house in North Great George's Street, Dublin. She treated several republican volunteers, some civilian women and a wounded British soldier. The following day she received an ultimatum from a British officer to reserve the hospital for Crown forces casualties only or close it. Kearns closed the hospital and turned to nursing and dispatch carrying for the republican forces. She continued as a republican dispatch carrier until her capture in 1920.

Back in Armagh Jail, after she was sentenced, a plan was hatched to spring Kearns from custody. She wrote:

One Sunday after Mass the curate sent for me to the sacristy. He told me that the following Wednesday would be a fair day in Armagh. He told me to remain in the grounds all day except at meal times when I would have to go in. At a certain point of the surrounding wall, which he indicated to me, a rope would be thrown over. I was to hold on to it and I would be pulled up. I agreed. On Tuesday afternoon, however, an escort of twenty police and a sergeant came and took me in a lorry to Belfast where they put me on board a boat for Liverpool ...

Her destination was Walton Women's Prison in Liverpool – Walton held both male and female prisoners.

After her transfer to Walton Prison, Kearns's health deteriorated, and she spent much of the next five months in the prison hospital. Her ill health resulted in her transfer to Mountjoy Prison on 15 September 1921. 'We travelled by Holyhead and Dun Laoghaire,' She recalled:

I have very little recollection of the journey, except the joy I felt on coming in to Dun Laoghaire. I arrived in Mountjoy where I was given a great welcome. I was given a lovely tea, the first decent one I had had for a long time. I was very sick and was put into the hospital. Eileen McGrane, and K. Brady were in the hospital too. Altogether there were nine women political prisoners; the three of us, Eithne Coyle, Miss Keogh, who was Father Sweetman's housekeeper, Miss Burke, a post office worker from Limerick, who had been sentenced for giving information contained in telegrams to the I.R.A. There were three young girls from Cork whose names I can't remember. They had been working thinning turnips in a field near where an ambush took place and they were arrested, although they had nothing to do with the ambush. I don't think they were even in Cumann na mBan.

Political prisoners in Mountjoy were allowed more freedom than in any other of the prisons Kearns had been in. 'We were permitted to have our cells open from 6 to 7 p.m. every evening, and I decided to plan an escape to be attempted at this hour of the day,' she said. 'I suggested to Eileen McGrane that I would try to organise an escape and asked would she come too. She said she wouldn't and so did K. Brady. Eileen also asked me not to take the three Cork girls as she considered them too young and the plan too dangerous.'[6]

Kearns received a visit from a friend, Nurse Josie O'Connor, who brought an unusual visitor, a young man named Burke, who had just been released from an English prison. An ordinary criminal, he had served time with Fr Dominic, a patriotic Capuchin friar from Church Street, Dublin, and he brought a letter of recommendation from Fr Dominic. Burke had called to Kearns's Dublin address, 29 Gardiner Place, to see Nurse O'Connor, and suggested that he could help Kearns to escape. The ex-prisoner was able to contact one of the male warders, who brought Kearns notes from Burke. At the time, she was in the hospital, which was over the male prison hospital.

Kearns was still in poor health; Nurse O'Connor brought her in a food parcel and a thermos flask of hot beef broth for nourishment. More importantly, inside the flask was a piece of dental wax. She was to use the wax to get the impression of the key of her cell and the key of the door leading from the corridor to the grounds. The wax had to be kept in the thermos flask to be soft and ready to use. In order to proceed with the escape, Kearns needed to be transferred from the hospital to a cell, so she promptly got well enough to be discharged from the hospital. Kearns asked

Eithne Coyle to help, and she said she would cooperate in every possible way. She had been there the longest and knew which of the sympathetic female warders to approach.[7]

Eithne Coyle, a Cumann na mBan activist from Falcarragh, Co. Donegal, was charged in January 1921 with possession of documents and a plan of Beechwood RIC Barracks in Co. Roscommon. She had been sentenced to one-year's imprisonment.[8] During exercise, when Wardress Waters was on duty with them, Coyle chatted to her while Kearns took the impression of a skeleton key that was conveniently left on a nearby table. That key opened all the cells on their landing. The key to the door leading from the corridor to the grounds was more difficult, and Kearns got the impression of it by bribing Wardress Dunne. A cake duly arrived with a plan of the back of the jail and the wall, along with a note suggesting that a rope ladder would be thrown over the wall when the escapees got out to the grounds.

One of Kearns's facilities at Mountjoy was permission to send out some clothes to be laundered. Sewed up in her returned laundry was her plan of escape and the wax impressions she had made of the keys. She noted that the escape group would be in the grounds at 6.20 p.m., and she marked the spot – between the wall and the laundry – with an 'X' on the drawing she had received earlier. When the keys were sent back in, to their disappointment the cell door key would not work. As it turned out they never had to use it, because at the time arranged for the escape the cell doors were open. They did not need the second key, as one of the friendly wardresses said she would leave the door open.[9]

Eithne Coyle had agreed to escape with Linda Kearns, and Mae Burke and Eileen Keogh also decided to go with them. Burke, a Cumann na mBan activist from Knockanevin, Kildorrery, Co. Cork, was serving two years for giving copies of military telegrams to the IRA; Eileen Keogh, from Clonmore, Co. Carlow, was serving two years for possession of explosives.[10] Between 6 and 7 p.m., the prisoners were allowed to socialise in the corridor, and a football match was organised for the evening of the escape. The escapees had already found out that the more noise was made, the more the wardresses relaxed their vigilance. While playing football on the appointed evening, the escapees pushed their ball down towards the door. Eileen McGrane made sure to keep up the noise, as Linda Kearns opened the landing door quietly. The four slipped out and hurried towards the appointed spot at the wall. They hid in the laundry doorway until the military sentry on duty had passed to the other side of his round, which left them sufficient time to get to the wall.

Kearns threw a stone over the wall as a signal, and a strong string with a piece of lead attached was thrown over to her. She quietly called the other three women, and they started to pull a rope ladder that was attached to the string on the other side. However, it was too heavy and the women pulled too close to the wall, with the result that the string was cut by the sharp stones. The ladder fell back on the other side leaving Kearns standing with the piece of lead in her hand. They all ran back to the laundry doorway and waited until the sentry had passed again. Kearns went back to the wall and threw another stone over. The string came back again, this time with a penknife attached. The women pulled more carefully and well out from the wall for safety, and the ladder came over the wall safely. They had already agreed to climb up according to the length of their sentences, and Linda Kearns, who had been sentenced to ten years, went first. Next was Mae Burke, followed by Eileen Keogh and finally Eithne Coyle, whose sentence had been reduced to a year. The women never spoke during the escape attempt, because they were so tense. The ladder was so close to the wall, although the others did their best to keep it out as far as possible, that Kearns's knuckles were skinned and bleeding. When she got to the top of the twenty-foot wall, Kearns then had to slither down a rope that skinned and flayed the inside of her hands. The others had the same experience.

Tim Ryan, Dublin Brigade, IRA, a young Fianna Éireann member named Donnelly, and Nurse O'Connor were at the lower end of the rope. Tim Ryan, who was Fr Dominic's brother, took Linda Kearns across the canal to the bridge at Doyle's Corner, where Dr Oliver St John Gogarty was waiting in a car. They waited until Mae Burke arrived, and then Gogarty drove off to a safe house at Earlsfort Terrace. Eithne Coyle and Eileen Keogh were taken away in another car to Dr Robert MacLaverty's home at Howth, Co. Dublin.

Just days before her escape, Kearns had told her sister that if the authorities did not permit her to receive proper medical attention, the prison would not hold her much longer. She kept that promise. At Miss O'Rourke's Earlsfort Terrace home, she recalled the luxury of the hospitable reception: 'We had coffee, baths and she put us to bed in the most lovely bedroom. I never realised before what a lovely feel a satin eiderdown has, and how restful and soothing ironed linen sheets are.'[11]

Sir Alfred Cope, the Assistant Under-Secretary for Ireland, boasted the escapees would soon be recaptured. 'They'll be caught in Grafton Street in a few days; they won't be able to resist the shop windows.'[12] Kearns and Burke remained for several days at Earlsfort Terrace, and then, with Eithne Coyle, the three were moved to a convent in Kilcullen, Co. Kildare. Eileen Keogh went to Gorey, Co. Wexford. After a few days at the convent, the three women were moved for safety reasons to Duckett's Grove, Carlow.[13] Duckett's Grove was an IRA training camp, where someone took a famous photograph of the three escapees armed, wearing full-length belted coats and standing on the Union Jack. On 10 November 1921 *The Freeman's Journal* announced that two wardresses in Mountjoy Prison had been arrested in connection with the escape of the four prisoners, and an inquiry was to be held in due course. Less than a month later, on 6 December, the Anglo-Irish Treaty was signed. Linda Kearns and Eithne Coyle would later take the anti-Treaty side in the Civil War. Kearns was one of only three women allowed to remain in the Hammam Hotel during the Battle of Dublin in the Civil War. She treated the wounded Cathal Brugha, attempting to staunch his bleeding by holding his severed artery closed with her fingers. Brugha, however, died of blood loss. Coyle was jailed for fifteen months during the Civil War. Cumann na mBan voted overwhelmingly to reject the Anglo-Irish Treaty.

CHAPTER 9

TUNNEL FROM KILKENNY JAIL

Although 4,454 men were interned in 1920–21, only 3,300 remained in internment camps at the cessation of hostilities in July 1921.[1] The wholesale release of internees did not happen, and it was only mostly sick, infirm and elderly internees that were released. A system of parole had been introduced after the Truce, but when John Grehan, interned in the Rath Camp at the Curragh, applied for parole on the death of his father, John, he was refused. John Grehan jr, an elected member of Naas Urban District Council and an IRA activist, decided to escape. He had been arrested in January 1921 and had previously served a two-month sentence in Belfast Jail for illegal drilling.[2]

A plan of escape was forwarded to and sanctioned by the camp OC. On the night of 18 October 1921, Grehan and ten other internees made an unsuccessful attempt to cut through the barbed wire of the Rath Camp, and for their efforts were sentenced by court martial to twelve months' imprisonment. They were transferred to Kilkenny Jail. Among the would-be escapees were Michael Murney (Killowen, Co. Down), Joe O'Connor (Dublin), Daniel Gibbons (Armagh city), James Kelly (Tullamore, Co. Offaly), Bill Donoghue (Hacketstown, Co. Carlow), Tom Hyland (Portarlington, Co. Laois), John Grehan (Naas, Co.

Kildare), Tommy McCarrick (Tubbercurry, Co. Sligo), and Tom Leonard (Athlone, Co. Westmeath).[3]

At the end of February 1921, Tommy McCarrick was court-martialled in Derry for having been in possession of a revolver and ammunition, and documents relating to the IRA. He said, 'that as a soldier of the Irish Republic' he refused to recognise the court. McCarrick approached the OC of the republican prisoners in Kilkenny Jail, Martin Kealy, and suggested that they should tunnel out of the prison as the Curragh internees had done.

Kealy wholeheartedly accepted the suggestion, as many prisoners were frustrated at still being held in jail months after the signing of the Truce in July 1921. Prison numbers had swelled due to the influx of Grehan and the ten other internees from the Curragh,[4] as Kilkenny was deemed more secure. 'Conditions in Kilkenny were very bad,' William McNamara said, 'The military guards there were a bad lot and gave us a tough time.'[5] However, the republicans' OC, Martin Kealy, and the prison governor, John Boland, had come to an informal arrangement that, once there were no disturbances and hunger strikes, the latter would recognise the special status of the republican prisoners. Kealy, formerly OC 4th Battalion, Kilkenny Brigade, said, 'A number of prison warders were sympathetic towards us and were very helpful, with the result that we were able to procure from outside sources, messages and articles which would not be allowed through regular channels.' Kealy's brother, John, had been arrested after the Easter Rising and died of a heart attack when he was being marched to the railway station for deportation to England.[6]

Most of the thirty republican prisoners were held in A Wing. Access to an unused solitary-confinement cell below them was out of bounds, as there were rows of barbed wire across the stairway blocking off entrance to the lower cells. To gain access to the cell below, prisoners prised up the floorboards of the cell immediately overhead. They carefully cut a manhole in the floor with a hacksaw given to them by a sympathetic warder, so that the boards could be placed back in position and covered with a piece of matting. The prisoners then gained access to the cell by dropping down through the hole.[7]

Martin Kealy said:

> The bars of the window of the underground cell were next removed by sawing them through at the top and the bottom with the hack-saw. As this window was only about two feet below the ground level it was necessary to burrow downwards first for a further few feet so as to ensure that sufficient earth was overhead to withstand any traffic that might pass over the tunnel.[8]

The confinement cell provided the perfect place to start digging, as it was about fifty yards to the perimeter wall. Initially, the most challenging obstacle was to break the keystone of the prison block wall with fire pokers, to enable the prisoners to commence digging a tunnel six feet underneath the yard. They used a trowel, pokers, knives and sharpened spoons to dig the tunnel. They dumped earth from the tunnel into pillowcases and blankets used as bags tied to a rope and pulled up to the punishment cell. It was then disposed of in adjoining cells that were rarely entered. They removed eight tons of earth in total. A friendly prison officer, Tom Power, turned a blind eye to the digging and the disposal of the earth.[9]

Tunnellers dug by candlelight, in three shifts, largely at night, when the friendly warder, Tom Power, was on duty. Conditions were far from ideal. The tunnel, three-feet high by two-feet wide, was not ventilated, and the cramped conditions made it unbearably hot. There was also a constant stink of perspiration. The tunnel had to be shored up with bed boards to prevent collapse, and the tunnel opening was cleverly concealed with a carpet mat.

For security reasons, not everyone was privy to the escape tunnel. A republican priest, Fr Patrick H. Delahunty, who had been arrested in Callan, Co. Kilkenny, the previous year for the possession of 'seditious literature', attempted his own escape bid. Fr Delahunty, who was halfway through a two-year sentence, got himself transferred to the hospital wing of the jail. While there, he received a present from outside – a loaf of bread, which contained some hacksaw blades. The energetic curate proceeded to saw through the iron bars of his cell window, but his hard labour was discovered by a vigilant warder just before he could escape.

Luckily, Governor Boland did not assign Fr Delahunty to the punishment cells, nor did he increase security in the jail. He simply sent Fr Delahunty back to his cell on the short-term wing, just in time for the tunnel escape.[10]

On 18 November, just a few days before the expected completion of the tunnel, seventy-five prisoners arrived at Kilkenny Jail from the infamous Spike Island prison. Twelve of the Spike Island prisoners were placed in A Wing, as the long-term wing of the prison was overcrowded. Security was considerably increased because of the extra prisoners, and British troops were drafted in to strengthen the prison warden staff. In addition, a number of Black and Tans were assigned to patrol outside the perimeter wall of the jail. This would most likely foil the planned escape once the men got outside the walls. Kealy appealed to the Mayor of Kilkenny, Peter DeLoughry, a personal friend. He pointed out that the placing of the dreaded Black and Tans outside the walls of the prison was a serious breach of the Truce between the IRA and Crown forces. The mayor in turn complained to the military authorities, and the military guard and Black and Tans were removed the next day.[11]

After nearly a month of digging, on 21 November, the tunnel was purportedly ten feet from the wall. The tunnellers reported to Kealy, who fixed the escape for 6 p.m. the next day, on Warden Power's watch. Those serving the longest and those facing the death sentence were allowed out first. Edward Punch and Tim Murphy, of Limerick, were facing the death penalty and had nothing to lose. Martin Kealy, the prison OC, along with Fr Delahunty; James Hanrahan, who had been OC 5th Kilkenny Battalion; and Joe O'Connor, OC 3rd Dublin Battalion were also on the escape list. Michael Burke had survived a hunger strike in Cork Jail that had lasted ninety days and taken the lives of three hunger strikers. He was also picked to escape.[12]

Earlier in the day Ally Luttrell, a member of Cumann na mBan, received a dispatch to go into Kilkenny, where she would receive an important message. She collected a letter attached to a stone that a prisoner threw over the wall. The letter stated that there would be an escape at 6.30 p.m. the next day. Denis Tracey, of Dunnamaggin, arranged for six of his men to be in Patrick Street with six ponies and traps to receive the escapees.[13]

On the morning of the escape, John Boland was replaced as Governor of Kilkenny prison by Captain Hubert Burke, former Governor of Waterford Jail. It was feared that the new governor would change the daily routine, while, furthermore, prison warders would probably be more alert, eager to impress their new boss. At 6 p.m., the time scheduled for the escape, Burke made an impromptu inspection of the prison. He thoroughly examined the cells, but, luckily for the prisoners, he did not discover the entrance to the underground cell that led to the tunnel. The tunnel, on completion, exited along the foundation of the outer prison wall with the three-foot wide exit coming out in the centre of a public thoroughfare in St Rioch's Street.

Warder Tom Power, however, became suspicious when he noticed several men entering the cell that accessed the tunnel. He went to investigate, and when he saw what was happening complained that they should have picked another time to escape and not when he was on duty. The prisoners 'invited' Power to play draughts in a cell, and they then gagged and bound him, to conceal his collusion. In the meantime, dozens of prisoners had entered the tunnel and made their escape. They had laid lengths of wood along the base of the tunnel to assist them in crawling through, and some of the prisoners held lighted candles to show the way through the pitch darkness. Larry Condon was in command of the escape party. In keeping with respect for the clergy at that time, Fr Delahunty was offered to be the second prisoner to escape after Larry Condon. However, he replied, 'I'll go with you lads, but only after the men who are sentenced to death and the other men who are serving life sentences.'[14]

Condon entered the tunnel at 6.40 p.m. and was to remain outside the tunnel entrance until all the men were safely away. When he exited the tunnel, Condon went immediately to a house facing the jail, informed the occupants what was happening and asked for their cooperation. A member of the household accompanied Condon to the exit of the tunnel and helped the next prisoner through. Small groups of people were beginning to concentrate around the tunnel at this stage, and Condon ordered them into an adjoining house, asking them to remain quiet. As the going was laborious and difficult, the other prisoners came through the tunnel slowly. The escape took an hour and forty minutes in total. Many of the prisoners were scantily dressed while some were fully outfitted, and two carried hand baggage with their belongings. Denis Tracey had his volunteers from Dunmaggin Company at the ready with the ponies and traps waiting to pick up some prisoners. Groups of men in threes and fours jumped into each trap and lay down on the floor as the driver headed away, out the Waterford Road and towards south Kilkenny as fast as he could. Many of the escapees were dropped off in the Hugginstown district and made their way out of the city on foot to their destinations.

It was a dark winter night, as more escapees emerged from the tunnel and dispersed through the streets and lanes of the city. As confused prisoners emerged from the tunnel, two local men in St Rioch's Street, Paddy Donoghue and Matty Power, both later Kilkenny hurling stars, helped them get their bearings. They directed some of them up Kennyswell Road and out the Ballycallan Road. Among the prisoners they guided out was Edward Punch, who was under sentence of death. They brought their group of escapees to William Walsh, a prominent republican in Ballycallan, who fed the men and then brought them to safety.[15]

Power's colleagues noticed that something was obviously wrong when the warder was discovered trussed up at around 8 p.m. They blew whistles to sound the alarm, and the military guard rushed to the entrance of the tunnel. Before the last three escapees had exited, they heard the loud whistles in the prison announcing the alarm.

Martin Kealy said, 'About 27 or 28 prisoners, including myself, succeeded in getting safely away. Probably a considerably greater number would have got away, were it not for the fact that the tunnel got blocked by falling debris from overhead.'[16] There was another story that one of the prisoners had brought his suitcase with him and that this got stuck in the tunnel, preventing any more escapees getting out. However, this is an oft-repeated story about one of the many tunnel escapes in Irish prison history. There were so many prisoners passing through the tunnel that it was probably damaged by the sheer volume of men. As the last escapee crawled through the tunnel a portion of it collapsed in front of him, leaving him trapped. The last man into the tunnel was a young Limerick prisoner, eighteen-year-old Maurice Walsh. Unluckily for Walsh, the tunnel collapsed ahead of him, forcing him back. On his return to the tunnel entrance, armed soldiers and warders met him and took him back to his cell.[17] Initially, it was thought that up to twenty-eight men escaped, but others later calculated the number at forty-three escapees; twelve of them were recent transfers from Spike Island. None were recaptured. They were: Martin Kealy (Gowran), Fr Patrick H. Delahunty (Moincoin), James J. Hanrahan (Inistioge), Thomas Brennan (Co. Kilkenny), Tommy McCarrick (Tubercurry, Co. Sligo), John Grehan (Naas), Edward Balfe and Michael Kirwan (Enniscorthy), Thomas Barry (Co. Wexford), Michael Burke, (Glengoole), Frank Byrne (Ballyporeen), Jeremiah Ryan (Thurles), Patrick Power (Carrick-on-Suir), Patrick O'Halloran (Co. Tipperary), Larry Condon (Fermoy), Cornelius Conroy, James Pollock and James Thompson (Cork city), Gerald Kenneally (Youghal), John Tobin (Carrigtouhill), Timothy Murphy (Co. Cork), David Connolly and William O'Leary (Clonee), John Keogh (Kells, Co. Meath), Bill Donoghue (Co. Carlow), Daniel Gibbons (Armagh city), Thomas Hyland (Portarlington, Co. Laois), James Kelly (Geashill, Co. Offaly), Thomas Leonard (Athlone, Co. Westmeath), William McNamara (Ennis, Co. Clare), Michael Murney (Co. Down), Edward O'Dwyer, Henry Meaney and Edward Punch (Limerick city), Thomas Kearns and Tim Murphy (Co. Limerick), Patrick O'Neill (Chapelizod), Joseph Kelly (Lusk), Joseph O'Connor (Dublin), John Power (Waterford city), James Power (Kilmacthomas), Lawrence Fraher (Dungarvan, Co. Waterford), and Seán Quilter (Ardfert, Co. Kerry). The failed Curragh escapees – Murney, McCarrick, Hyland, Leonard, Gibbons, Grehan and O'Connor – were among the successful Kilkenny escapees.[18]

Fr Delahunty's escape was the first time a member of the clergy had escaped from custody. The priest headed back towards the Mullinahone district and was given refuge in a safe house at Ballyvoneen, where he stayed until the Treaty was signed in December 1921. He took the anti-Treaty side in the Civil War. When his mother died in 1924, Fr Delahunty was unable to take part in the funeral obsequies because of his republican stance. He emigrated two years later and served as a priest in America, including seventeen years as chaplain of Leavenworth State Penitentiary. In 1955 Fr Delahunty died in Kansas, and in 1957 Kilkenny Corporation named a new housing scheme near the former prison Delahunty Terrace in his honour.[19]

After an arduous journey through fields and dykes, Edward Balfe and his group of four escapees reached Ballymurphy, Co. Carlow, about twenty-two miles from Kilkenny. Here they located friends and were driven the rest of the journey to Enniscorthy, Co. Wexford. Tom McCarrick's group of escapees took the risk of asking for food and water at a farmhouse some miles west from Kilkenny City. In a stroke of luck, it was the home of Kitty Teehan, a Cumann na mBan activist, whose brothers were also members of the local IRA. She arranged safe houses for the men, who were subsequently transported to their home areas. Another group of eleven exhausted escapees from the midlands, including Bill Donoghue, arrived at Duckett's Grove, Co. Carlow, after walking about twenty-eight miles from Kilkenny Jail. They too, were in luck. An IRA training camp had been established there after the Truce. The escapees, after a short rest, were ably assisted in their journeys home. Larry Condon and a large number of escapees from Munster ended up on a farm near Cuffesgrange, eight miles from the city, where they were taken in. They were later smuggled by pony and trap to their individual home counties.[20]

Despite the huge manhunt, all escapees successfully returned to their units. The IRA was still on alert and continued training in the event the peace negotiations failed. Martin Kealy said:

> I returned to my Battalion area which, during the period of my imprisonment, was under the command of the Vice Commandant, William Carrigan. I inspected the various Companies, renewed old acquaintances, familiarised myself with the position of the Battalion generally, and assured myself that organisation, training and discipline were kept up, so as to be in a position to renew the struggle should the necessity arise.[21]

There was no need. Two weeks later the Irish plenipotentiaries and Lloyd George's government signed the Anglo-Irish Treaty in London, thereby ending the War of Independence. The remaining republican prisoners in Kilkenny Jail were transferred to Limerick and Waterford prisons. Kilkenny Jail was officially closed on 10 December 1921. Governor John Boland, who had initially been transferred to Dundalk Jail, was suspended from duty for his management of Kilkenny Jail prior to the breakout. He was later forced to retire.[22]

Martin Kealy enlisted in the National Army at Kilkenny Military Barracks in February 1922. He was wounded in both legs during an engagement with the anti-Treaty forces at Kilmoganny, Co. Kilkenny, on 10 August 1922 and was discharged from the National Army as medically unfit on 31 January 1924.[23] Tommy McCarrick joined An Garda Síochána and served as a detective sergeant at Ennis, Co. Clare. Laurence Condon took the anti-Treaty side in the Civil War and was captured in July 1923. He was interned in Cork Jail, Mountjoy Prison, Newbridge Barracks and in Hare Park Camp, the Curragh, where he took part in a forty-day hunger strike. Condon was finally freed with the last batch of anti-Treaty fighters to be released, in June 1924.[24]

Kilkenny Jail was temporarily used as a holding centre during the Civil War and was the scene of another escape in November 1922 when twenty-five men exited the jail through a tunnel.[25] The Jail finally closed in 1929, but it remained on the city landscape until 1948, when it was demolished and the rubble from it used in the construction of a stand at the county Gaelic Athletic Association (GAA) ground, Nowlan Park.

CHAPTER 10

THE HOLE IN THE WALL

When the Civil War broke out in June 1922, Commandant General Frank Aiken had tried to keep his 4th Northern Division neutral in the developing struggle between the pro- and anti-Treaty sides. Aiken decided to adopt a neutral position, to make every effort to secure a cessation of hostilities and to call off attacks on the Six Counties.[1] Although not overly supportive of the Anglo-Irish Treaty, Aiken enjoyed the support of both opposing sides. He had intervened in Limerick earlier in the year when pro- and anti-Treaty sides nearly came to blows. Aiken told General Richard Mulcahy, National Army Chief of Staff, that civil war could 'only ruin the country without gaining any ground for the Republic'.[2]

Aiken's 4th Northern Division had taken over control of Dundalk Military Barracks from the British Army on the morning of 13 April 1922. However, in mid-July, General Dan Hogan and his 5th Northern Division, more solidly aligned with the National Army high command – and apparently on his own initiative – occupied Dundalk, taking Aiken and his men prisoner. According to Volunteer Edward Fullerton, 'it is well-known that some of the officers in the military barracks at the time had associated themselves with this invasion and had been a party to the opening of the gates for Hogan's men.'[3]

Gen. Aiken was blunter: 'At 5:30 on the morning of the 16th, I awoke with two Thompsons at my nose. An officer who had been reduced for inefficiency, some men who were under arrest for drunkenness, opened the gates and – brilliant victory of the National Army! 300 Irregulars arrested! Not a shot fired!'[4]

His men were given the option of pledging loyalty to the provisional government or be imprisoned. When they didn't pledge loyalty, over a hundred of them were marched off to the town jail at The Crescent on the Ardee Road. Aiken was furious. He demanded a parole to enable him to go to Dublin to speak to Richard Mulcahy. Aiken naively believed that he could influence Mulcahy and members of the provisional government to allow him to continue his neutral status. Some members of the government, mainly Eoin O'Duffy, were unsure of Aiken's loyalty. Aiken was granted parole, but the interview with Mulcahy was wasted. Mulcahy said that Aiken's men were government forces whose loyalty was now in question. He would only release them if they signed a document recognising the provisional government. Aiken would not accept the condition, but he was told his men would be treated as prisoners of war. Upon his return to Dundalk, Aiken's parole was terminated, and he joined his men in Dundalk Jail. At a hastily convened meeting, Aiken and his men decided to abandon their previous neutral stance and join the anti-Treaty side.[5]

Eleven days later, on 27 July, a contingent of men were noticed concentrating in the vicinity of the jail at around 7 p.m. This was not an unusual sight on a road over which hundreds of railwaymen passed every day. But these were not railwaymen. About 200 men, who had not been taken in Dundalk and he were under the command of Acting Divisional Commander John McCoy, had filtered quietly into the town. Volunteers Malachi Quinn and Eiver Monaghan, using planks of wood, placed a mine on the ground along the jail wall, just midway between the gate on the

Ardee Road and the end of the prison. The republican prisoners were in the exercise yard for morning drill. They had been alerted that a breakout attempt was going to occur that evening, and they were ready to move. At 7.15 p.m., on a signal blown on a whistle by Aiken from within the jail, the mine was detonated with a terrific noise.[6] The explosion left a twenty-six-foot hole in the wall. It shook the town and smashed the glass in the windows of the Crescent dwelling houses, the windows of the County Infirmary and some of those in St Malachy's Priory. Large stones flew into the air and injured a warder's knee. Fortunately, no civilians were injured by the flying fragments, but the blast frightened hundreds of women and children to the verge of hysterics.[7]

The would-be escapees had to pull back some stones to make a hole big enough for men to get through. Andrew Lynch, Knockbride, Co. Cavan, asked a fellow prisoner to come with them, who replied, 'Well, I'll be out in a week, while you'll be back in in a week.' He was just about right! Andrew Lynch (22) was quickly recaptured in Co. Cavan and interned on the prison ship *Arvonia* in Dublin Bay. Andrew Lynch's older brother, Michael (30), and his younger brother, Philip (19), also escaped.[8]

Several hand grenades were thrown over the wall to distract attention. In the confusion, 105 prisoners, including Frank Aiken, escaped. However, a further 36 men could not get out because a guard threw the warder's keys over a security fence. The twenty warders on duty, armed only with batons, later complained that the military guard failed to turn out until the prisoners had gone.[9] Escaped prisoners ran through the streets nearby and made for the surrounding countryside. Street barriers suddenly appeared; every road around the prison was blocked. In one instance, an old engine was used as a barricade at Quay Street. Pursuing National troops were ambushed at Castletown Cross and Barrack Street Bridge. Two soldiers were wounded in these attacks, one of whom,

Volunteer J.F. McCaffrey, died the next morning. Comdt Mason was wounded in the foot. About half of the escapees were from the 4th Northern Division, the remainder being from Co. Meath and the midlands, with a handful from Dublin.[10]

There was great military activity in the town following the escape. Troops arrived on motors, and a guard was immediately placed along the breach. Passersby were stopped and searched. There were photographers anxious to get a photograph of the hole in the jail wall, but the soldiers on guard refused them permission. The place where the hole was blown in the wall can still be seen to this day.

Shots were heard at several points round the town, and a pursuit of the escaped prisoners ensued throughout the country. Over the following days around sixty escapees were recaptured and interned in the jail once again. Some of them had managed to get a considerable distance from the jail, with reports of arrests in Drogheda and other parts of south Louth. Among those recaptured were prominent republicans Andrew O'Hare, Newry, and Gerald Davis, Roscommon, who were picked up the day after the escape. Around twenty people alleged to have been involved in the jail release or in the ambushes of the National troops were also arrested. Among those arrested was John McCoy, second in command to Aiken, who had led the rescue. McCoy was captured as he struggled with motor cars that were reserved for the rescue.[11]

Following on the successful events in Dundalk the republicans in the area regrouped. Aiken reorganised his command, and he returned to recapture Dundalk and its military barracks on 14 August. At around 4 a.m. that morning a sentry in the barracks, suspicious of a noise near the main gate, called out to the guard. While inspecting the area, a young officer discovered a cable linked to a home-made mine. As he went to cut the cable, the officer was wounded by a burst of Thompson submachine-gun fire. Four mines exploded simultaneously around the barracks: at the barrack gate, the barrack hospital, the officers' quarters and the headquarters office building. Another mine at the main gate failed to go off. Three soldiers were killed instantly and fifteen were wounded, some buried underneath the debris caused by the mines. Dozens of Aiken's men stormed through the wreckage of the barrack gate, and within a short time the entire barracks had changed hands again.

Todd Andrews, a young officer from anti-Treaty headquarters in Dublin, took part in the attack, and he described it thus: 'As a guerrilla operation, his [Aiken's] recapture of Dundalk was by far the most spectacularly efficient carried out by the IRA.'[12] The well-coordinated assault resulted in the capture of the entire town and its garrison of 300 men in fifteen minutes. Around 350 republican prisoners were released from the military barracks and the town jail. In total, five National soldiers and two republicans – killed by their own mine – died in the fighting. Aiken's men also captured about 400 rifles, two 18-pounder guns and a huge amount of ammunition and stores.[13]

After a hasty breakfast at the barracks, the released prisoners set out for their home areas. However, most of them, were recaptured near the village of Skreen, Co. Meath, by a strong force of National troops. Jim Dunne, from Kill, Co. Kildare, took command of about sixty men from Kildare, and they set out for their home county. Michael O'Neill, of Weston Park, Leixlip, led another group of twenty men back to north Kildare. The two groups separated at Skreen, and very shortly afterwards each was in trouble, only a mile or so apart. Crossing a main road, one party was surprised by several armoured cars. A third of the men were on one side of the road and the OC with the remainder was on the other. The smaller group, about ten men, ran for the high ground under a hail of bullets, while the OC and his group withdrew to what cover was to be had in the middle of a field. 'We couldn't stick our heads up,' he said, 'the cars kept patrolling the road in opposite directions. That was bad enough but a plane came over and directed them. We just had to wait for darkness and hope for the best.' Eventually they made their escape at nightfall.[14]

Jim Dunne, who was a nephew of the Fenian leader John Devoy, had been captured with a column of men near Kill, Co. Kildare, and was held in Dundalk Jail at the beginning of August. Dunne said:

> I took charge of 60 men from Kildare. We were armed with 30 rifles and some explosives, etc. We then entrained with about 150 men from other areas to Dunleer, Co. Louth, and were instructed to blow up the railway bridge. This was carried out by P. Magee. Todd Andrews from Dublin H.Q. was in charge at Dunleer. He instructed me to cut across country for Kildare as best I could. Mick O'Neill of Celbridge, North Kildare Battalion, 1st Meath Brigade, had charge of another column of 20 men from that area and took another direction home. After travelling two days, mostly without food or sleep, we were surrounded by 500 Free State troops at Skreen, Co. Meath. After a fight lasting from 6 p.m. to 10.30 p.m., I managed to break through the enemy ring with 20 men and rifles, and after travelling about five miles we put up at a farmhouse owned by two brothers named Duffy who lived near Fairyhouse Racecourse. We had our clothes dried, as it had rained all night and we were wet through. They also provided us with hot drinks and food. When we had got through the enemy ring, I had left a rearguard of ten men to hold back enemy troops. Those men were under the command of Patk. Magee, our engineer and officer of Kill Company. Other men I can remember

with him were Peter Mills, Kill, Jim Collins, Kilcullen, Jim O'Keeffe, Kilcock. I can't remember the names of the others. Each man of the rearguard had been provided with 250 rounds of ammunition and was armed with a rifle. When they surrendered at 10.30 p.m. they had only 7 rounds of ammunition left and the rifles were jammed and red hot. The Dublin Guards who had been attacking them had lost three men killed and several wounded. None of our men was wounded. The prisoners were lined up by the Dublin Guards to be shot, when the officer in charge of the Guards, Comdt. Stapleton, arrived on the scene. He congratulated our men on the fight they had put up and accorded them good treatment. My column, after two days forced march, arrived back in Kill area, where we had to rest for a week. I got in touch with the Brigade O/C, P. Brennan, and reformed the column.[15]

John McCoy, Mullaghbawn, Co. Armagh, the man who had led the earlier rescue, was one of those freed, and he returned to active duty with his commander, Aiken. Fifty-six-year-old Domhnall Ua Buachalla, the former TD for North Kildare, was too old to go trekking across country, even though six years earlier he had walked fifteen miles from Maynooth to Dublin to take part in the Easter Rising. Ua Buachalla took a train to Dublin and hid at his brother's home. He was only rearrested in August 1923, when he put his name forward for the General Election.[16]

Escapee Frank Purcell should not have been in Dundalk Jail but took the opportunity to be freed. A pre-Truce Officer Commanding 1st Kildare Battalion, Purcell was on the office staff of the Irish Transport and General Workers' Union (ITGWU) and had remained neutral after the signing of the Anglo-Irish Treaty. However, he was arrested in Lucan, Co. Dublin, on 11 July 1922, after leaving Dublin to visit his fiancée in Carbury, Co. Kildare. Purcell claimed to have taken no part in the recent fighting but refused to sign a document recognising the provisional government. He was subsequently interned in Dundalk Jail, but took his case to court, where a judge served a motion of *habeas corpus* on the Governor of Dundalk Jail. However, he was freed on 14 August when the jail was attacked. His solicitor lodged a decree claiming that Purcell should have been released anyway, as he had satisfied the military that he was not an active republican, and the signing of the declaration should not be a condition of release. Purcell was not rearrested, and he continued his work with the ITGWU and as manager of the *Voice of Labour*, the official organ of the transport union.[17]

After the capture of Dundalk, Frank Aiken held a public meeting in the town's Market Square demanding an immediate truce, and, on the summoning of the prorogued Dáil Éireann, a resolution to reaffirm Irish sovereignty was passed. Aiken's troops remained in Dundalk for three days, only evacuating the town as National Army columns converged on it. The republicans left in two columns. One escaped under cover of darkness, while the other column fought a hard battle before surrendering. Aiken's men continued a guerrilla campaign, while many freed prisoners made their way back to their home areas to take up the fight again.[18]

On the death of Liam Lynch in April 1923, Frank Aiken became Chief of Staff of the Irish Republican Army. In the following month, Aiken issued the dump-arms order that ended the Civil War. He was a founder member of Fianna Fáil in Co. Louth, and as a TD from 1923 to 1973, he was one of the longest-serving members of Dáil Éireann and the longest-serving cabinet minister. The military barracks in Dundalk was later re-named Aiken Barracks.[19]

CHAPTER 11

THE GREATEST ESCAPE

As the Civil War entered a new phase, more space was needed to house the growing number of republican prisoners. On 12 August 1922, the *Kildare Observer* announced that the former British cavalry barracks at Newbridge was to be evacuated by the Civic Guard and was to be used as an internment camp. Seán Hayes, a pro-Treaty TD from Cork, was appointed Military Governor of Newbridge Internment Camp with Comdt Seán Kavanagh as Deputy Military Governor.[1]

Newbridge was originally designed as a British Army cavalry barracks in 1819, with the capacity to hold up to 1,000 horses and 700 men. It later became the central detention centre for the Free State. The IRA prisoners were housed in two three-storey buildings, known as the 'Cupola' block in the centre of the barracks. There was also a very large recreation area, including a hockey pitch, on the east side. The hockey pitch was turned into a Gaelic football pitch, and some guards and internees state that the fine football matches played in Newbridge Barracks were their fondest memory of the Civil War. After the large-scale fighting in Munster, Newbridge was soon overcrowded with prisoners and their guards. The large number of prisoners in the barracks worked in their favour, as the camp authorities found it hard to keep track of numbers. By the middle of September there were 1,120 prisoners in the barracks. Governor Hayes wrote in his notebook on 7 October, 'we cannot take any more prisoners ...'[2]

However, many of the prisoners held in Newbridge had no intention of staying. As soon as some of them arrived, they began plotting to leave by any means possible. Patrick O'Keefe and his brother Jim arrived in Newbridge from the prison ship *Arvonia*. Patrick said, 'An escape plan got under way, to tunnel from the room to the sewer. It took a few weeks to complete, from the old Barracks into the sewer and then under the field to the Liffey.'[3]

They were not the only prisoner's intent on escaping. Neil Plunkett O'Boyle, from Leac Eineach, Burtonport, Co. Donegal, wasted no time in starting work on a tunnel from G Block. This 'project' was abandoned when one of the group was given a Board of Works map of the sewerage system by a friendly National soldier. Nellie Kearns, of Eyre Street, Newbridge, Officer Commanding Newbridge branch Cumann na mBan, provided the map that made the escape possible. She said:

> I had Free State soldiers taking messages to and from prisoners in Newbridge barracks. Dr. Liam Clark and Dr. Bracken from Dublin and T.J. Williams, Naas, received messages from me and sent a request for a plan of the sewage system of the barracks which I obtained from Dublin and which they received. On this plan was marked the manholes which were no longer used for sewage and through which they could and did escape several days after.[4]

O'Boyle, with the help of another Donegal man who was an experienced miner, constructed a tunnel from R Block into the sewerage drain.

Veteran escape artists noticed that the sewer traps ran in a line across the quadrangle by the married quarters in the direction of the Liffey, which flowed near the barracks. They noted a disused sawmill on the bank of the Liffey in a direct line with the sewer traps, and they thought this would be likely to afford cover to potential escapees. The prisoners' building was about 500 yards from the river, so the magnitude of the task to be undertaken can be well realised. A remarkable feature of the escape was that it constituted the longest subterranean effort ever made by Irish prisoners seeking liberty.

The O'Boyle group made a start on the ground floor of a block near the clock tower. Direct descent into the sewer was not possible, and it was found that a tunnel of around thirty feet in length would have to be cut to connect with the sewer. They cut a square of flooring from beneath one of the trestle beds with a saw manufactured from a dinner knife. Carefully trimmed and with the marks of cutting erased, the square fitted into place and defied detection. Using a fire shovel and a pointed poker as a pick, they quickly got the work under way, as lookouts kept a careful watch on the guards' movements. The loose earth was disposed of beneath the floor of the room by lifting the floorboards, and it was also secreted in the top floor of another disused building in the camp. It was a good hiding place – the soil in this building would not be discovered until the structure was demolished in the 1960s. It was then thought to be peat from the Bord na Mona factory that occupied part of the barracks site in 1939–40. Progress was made day after day, with many narrow escapes from discovery when some of the guards arrived in the room while the tunnellers were at work beneath the floor.[5]

At the same time, another group, led by Seamus O'Connor, from Meenahila, Co. Kerry, was working on their tunnel. O'Connor had made several escape bids since his capture. He, along with his comrades, had smuggled tools into Newbridge – screwdrivers, knives and odd bits of iron – that they had used digging a tunnel in Limerick Prison before they were transferred. He said, 'We immediately set to work on a tunnel. Underneath the floorboards there was a high air space – perhaps two feet – an ideal place to hide the excavated earth. Everything had to be done neatly. There were periodic inspections for tunnels. All operations were kept as secret as possible for fear of spying.'[6] The achievement was all the more remarkable as the prison authorities had adopted the usual precaution of placing spies amongst the prisoners, and there were no security leaks.

> After a while, there were four separate tunnels being made by four different gangs. We came together and agreed that whichever tunnel came through first would be made available to the other teams, so that all could escape at the same time … There was a large manhole in the barrack square. This was the manhole of the main sewer, which ran right through the centre of the building into the Liffey, perhaps 300 yards away. The authorities had shown nervousness about the manhole previously, thus drawing attention to its possibilities. Now the gang in this centre block had only to sink a shaft in the appropriate room on the ground floor and run a short tunnel to connect with the sewer which passed underneath.[7]

When the sewer was located and penetrated, the escapees' troubles were far from over. As the tunnellers entered the sewer, they found the air was so foul it was impossible to explore for a few days. One man who got into the sewer was violently ill for some time. Then there arose the difficulty of finding the correct route in a network of sewers, with one of the explorers getting lost for several hours in his attempt to find his way back. Ultimately, the dedication of men intent on escaping overcame all these difficulties. Local republicans, who would be ready to help the escapees when they broke free, cut an escape exit to the sewer through the floor of the sawmill on the banks of the Liffey.[8]

On the night of Saturday, 14 October 1922 there was a swift exodus, as over seventy prisoners made a successful escape. Neil Plunkett O'Boyle was among them, as well as thirty-four men from Co. Kildare under the command of Tom Harris. The escapees climbed out of the sewer proper, up through the sawmill floor and out the back door. Rolling down a slope and moving noiselessly into the cold, rapidly flowing water of the Liffey, they waded carefully to the other side, mindful of the sentries on the bridge. The river was only about four feet deep at this point, but currents were treacherous. Moving swiftly onto the bank, they were out into open country and heading towards Kilcullen. The following day was one of high tension, as those in the know endeavoured to cover their comrades' absence. As it was Sunday, there was no roll call, and this covered the absence of so many men. Many inquiries had been made for prisoners who were amongst the absentees, and it was obvious towards evening that suspicions were aroused. That evening it was decided to rush another batch for freedom as soon as darkness descended.

Seamus O'Connor said:

We were ready for escape that night … There were four rooms, twenty men in each room and each block was self-contained. At 8 o'clock each night the guards blew a whistle. This was the signal for all prisoners to get into their block for the night. Once you were in your own block you could not enter any other block, except by coming out in the square, which was all lit up and under surveillance of the sentries, who were all around, in raised sentry posts. This meant that all those who were to escape should move into the four rooms of the escape block, instead of their own, when the whistle blew. After this, there was never any inspection of these rooms each night, because there was nowhere else the prisoners could go, once the square was vacated.[9]

On the Saturday night, O'Connor and his group of a half-dozen men had got ready to move into the escape block, but a few minutes before the whistle went they received word that the escape was called off until the following night. The following morning, O'Connor was told that the escape had taken place and that over seventy men had got away. He said it was a mix-up of information which had held his group back. A military search party had entered the barrack square, too, and this had unnerved the men preparing to escape.

O'Connor said:

> Ours were the only tunnel-diggers left. We moved into the escape block, which was mostly empty, and took over possession and control of the tunnel. The authorities knew nothing of the escape. It was in our favour that this day was Sunday ... the prisoners here looked after themselves and on Sundays especially, the soldiers never made their appearance amongst us, except to man the sentry posts. As far as I know, the news spread inside, and everybody must have known of the escape.
>
> We knew nothing of the working of the tunnel or where it led – all who did were gone. A wiry diminutive lad – [William] Hussey from Killarney – was selected to go and make an inspection. He did so, and came back. He found that the Free Staters had blocked the entrance into

the Liffey with inch-thick iron bars, but that the tunnellers had struck upwards and made their exit into the inside of a disused sawmill. They knew their geography because some were local fellows. The mill, however, was on the wrong side of the river for us, and between the mill and the river any escape would be under view of the sentries; this made a successful day escape unlikely, so we decided to take the chance and wait until night.[10]

An unnamed Dublin Brigade officer approached O'Connor's group and claimed that, because of his position, he was in command of the escape attempt. He insisted that some important Dublin men should escape first, and O'Connor's group would be in the second batch. The O'Connor group reluctantly agreed. When the whistle blew at 8 p.m. for all prisoners to go to their blocks, about 200 moved into the escape block. The first group to go into the tunnel were the key volunteers from the Dublin Brigade – about ten men. The cover of the shaft leading into the tunnel was under a bed, and the O'Connor group were next gathered around the bed. However, after the sighting of an armoured car on patrol duty outside the walls of the barracks, the escape was postponed. The Dublin group had already left, and, after an anxious hour, O'Connor decided his group were going out. He said:

> I bent over and lifted the neat square board that covered the hole and placed it aside – the bed underneath which it was hidden had already been pushed aside. I signalled to Hussey, who jumped in first, and each of us who wished to come followed him. After about a dozen feet of tunnel we got into the sewer proper. We were able to crawl without difficulty on our hands and knees. The distance seemed long. I think it took over half an hour. The noise made by

crawling seemed very loud. We knew we had to pass under
a sentry-box outside. It seemed incredible that the sentry
could not hear us.[11]

The disused sawmill, underneath which the sewer passed, was on
the bank of the river, and the architects of the tunnel knew the
location well, for they bored right up into the mill house. When
the first few escapees got out of the sewer into the mill room, they
waited to give a helping hand until all those following were pulled
up.

O'Connor said, 'About twenty-five had elected to follow us.
Anyone who wished was free to follow or otherwise ... We decided
that five of us should make the first attempt to leave the mill and
cross the river; the others to wait until they were sure everything
was all right and then come as they wished.'[12]

Emerging from the tunnel was a simple enough matter, because
the prisoners were concealed from the view of the sentries and the
lookout posts erected high over the corners of the barrack wall.
On coming up in the sawmill, the escapees left by the back door
leading to the river. To avoid the military guard on the approaches
of the bridge at Newbridge, escapees headed into the river and
continued northeast north-east towards the village of Kilcullen:[13]

We crawled out in single file. All was quiet. When outside
we turned to the right, along the river bank for perhaps a
hundred yards, in order to avoid going too close to where
we knew there was an outpost on our left, and then struck
straight across the river. The river was not deep and was
quite fordable at the point, and helped to cleanse us after
the sewer.

On the other side of the river was a steep bank. We
climbed it and into a large field. Then we were free. Never

have I experienced such delight which that sense of freedom gave me when going up that field.

There were six others with O'Connor, including William O'Sullivan, a fifteen-year-old Fianna scout from Tralee.

> I picked out the North Polar Star, O'Connor said, and from it selected one bright star which I calculated should lie directly over Dublin, and we struck neither to right nor left but straight towards the star ... After about half an hour we heard continuous bursts of gunfire from the direction of the Camp. We knew then that the escape had been discovered. We learned later that a party of escapees – not the one which came with us – had been caught under fire ... One wounded man was swept down the river, got into a friendly house and escaped. Some went back through the sewer again. One going through went astray in a smaller offshoot and got stuck there.[14]

The escape was discovered around midnight when sentries spotted movement on the bank and opened fire, wounding at least one prisoner. The sawmill was quickly surrounded, and a number of men who were on the point of leaving, or were still in the sewer, were captured – thirty-seven would-be escapees were returned to the barracks. When the discovery was made, sporadic firing by nervous military guards kept the inhabitants of the town in a state of panic for some time. Over forty men had successfully escaped that night, including the ten men from the Dublin group.[15]

Dr Joseph Roantree, a local dispensary doctor who lived at Moorefield Lodge, Newbridge, recalled that armed men called to his house that night to attend to a wounded escapee. He said there was no need for the revolvers, as he never needed persuasion or enticement to make his professional services available to the sick and needy. The presence of armed men at the scene established that there was a certain amount of outside help with the escape.[16]

O'Connor and his group continued on their freedom flight. He said, 'There were Free State posts at Naas and Blessington. It was important that we went between them. Our star carried us right through.' The seven escapees were treated to a breadcake at a friendly house and then went on to Brittas, Co. Wicklow, where they had a bottle of stout each. They then continued on to Rathfarnham, where they arrived on Tuesday morning. O'Connor and four others later made their way back home to the south, travelling across country through Wicklow, Carlow and Tipperary.[17]

The breakout from Newbridge Barracks was the largest escape of prisoners in Irish penal history. All told, 112 men escaped successfully; a further thirty-seven were captured in the tunnel. In total, thirty-five men from Co. Kildare escaped from Newbridge Barracks on the first night of the escape, including T.J. Williams, who had received the plans of the sewer from Nellie Kearns. It was the largest group by county. Carlow was next with twelve escapees from the county, followed by Dublin with ten and Wicklow with nine. Three of the Kildare escapees – James Dempsey (Celbridge), Jimmy Whyte (Naas) and Paddy Bagnall (Kildare town), had been released from Dundalk Jail in August, when Frank Aiken's men had captured the town from the National Army. They had been subsequently recaptured and interned in Newbridge Barracks. After escaping from Newbridge, Patrick Bagnall joined the Rathbride column, and on 12 December he was recaptured in a dugout at Mooresbridge, outside Kildare Town. Tragically, if he had not escaped, Paddy Bagnall would have cheated the firing squad on 19 December 1922.[18]

Neil Plunkett O'Boyle, the engineer of the successful tunnel, led a group of escapees in the Wicklow mountains; they became a thorn in the side of the National forces for five months. They were responsible for several fatal attacks on National troops and for the burning of Senator Bryan Mahon's mansion at Mullaboden, near Ballymore Eustace. On 8 May 1923 the column was finally cornered at a cottage at Knocknadruce, Valleymount, where O'Boyle was shot dead after surrendering. It was alleged that Col. Roger McCorley shot O'Boyle twice in the face as he held his hands up in surrender. Neil Plunkett O'Boyle is remembered as the last man to die violently in the Civil War.[19]

CHAPTER 12

A TUNNEL TO FREEDOM

During the Civil War, the Provisional and Free State governments imprisoned thousands of anti-Treaty republicans without trial in prisons and internment camps throughout the country. The Curragh Camp was home to two internment camps: Hare Park Camp and Tintown Camp. M.J. Burke, Chief Architect at the Board of Works, designed the Tintown Internment Camp at the Curragh, converting former British Army horse stables into quarters for republican prisoners.

Construction on the camp began on 23 November 1922, and No. 1 Section was completed by 15 January 1923. No. 2 Section was completed by 24 January 1923. The construction was carried out in part by Dublin building contractors. Their work consisted of lining the inside of the huts with felt and timber sheeting, and, at a later date, the fitting of felt to the roofs. The sheeting of the huts left a space of about four inches between the outside galvanised iron and the inside sheeting. Continuation of the concrete floors was intended to render tunnelling an impossibility, although the floors were serrated rather than flat. The converted stables made very large huts – roughly 180 feet by 29 feet – each accommodating more than 100 prisoners. Three huts were assigned as a camp hospital. Control of electric lighting was completely in the hands of the camp authorities, with a power switch being placed outside the compound.

Comdt Billy Byrne was appointed the Military Governor of Tintown No.1 Camp on 28 January 1923. He was given little or no instruction on how to run the camp and only received index cards for each internee on 18 April 1923. Orderly officers were present at the morning count and were to monitor that prisoners appointed by their own line officers carried out their fatigues. The orderly officers were also to oversee the general running of the camp during the day and then were present at the evening count at 7 p.m. before prisoners were locked in for the night.[1]

The republican prisoners' commanding officer was Peadar O'Donnell, the prominent Donegal republican. O'Donnell became involved in Irish republicanism through his initial participation in socialism as an organiser for the ITGWU. When he was unsuccessful in establishing a branch of the Irish Citizen Army in Derry, he joined the IRA and led guerrilla activities in Donegal and Derry during the War of Independence. He was a member of the executive of the anti-Treaty IRA and was in the Four Courts when it was attacked by National troops in June 1922. He was arrested shortly after the fall of the Four Courts.[2]

He was at first held in Mountjoy Prison, but was transferred to Tintown, the Curragh, in April 1923. O'Donnell had no sooner set foot in Tintown than he was planning his escape. He was approached by Tómas Ó Maoláin and Paddy Cannon (Mayo), who suggested they dig an escape tunnel. Ó Maoláin had successfully escaped from the Rath Camp in September 1921, and he brought his tunnelling skills to this new escape bid. O'Donnell quickly identified one of the three huts assigned to the 'hospital wing' as the ideal location to begin digging a tunnel to freedom. The huts were then almost empty, so one, according to O'Donnell, could accommodate an escape tunnel. He approached the camp medic,

Dr Francis P. Ferran, a Derry native active in Co. Mayo. O'Donnell's plan involved some of the men pretending to be sick to facilitate their transfer into the hospital hut, from where they would start their tunnel. Dr Ferran listened attentively and then replied simply, 'That can't be. I won't have any part of the hospital used for that.' O'Donnell pressed his case but was to discover that the Derryman's principles would not be so easily compromised. Ferran even offered to resign as medical doctor if O'Donnell pressed ahead.

'No good,' O'Donnell wrote in his memoir *The Gates Flew Open*, 'Dr. Ferran would not have any part of his hospital improperly used. He had accepted the huts from the enemy M.O. as a hospital, and as a hospital he would use them. I had never met Dr. Ferran before we came together in Tintown,' recalled O'Donnell, '... but there was no mistaking the mettle of the man.'[3] O'Donnell was housed in Hut 1, and it was from there the Tintown tunnel began and not the hospital huts as originally planned. One night O'Donnell gathered everyone in the hut around him. The men were all sworn to secrecy and swore not to speak of the tunnel outside the hut.[4]

Time was of the essence, as even if the tunnellers succeeded in escaping from Tintown No.1 Camp, their exit would lead them into a similar camp under construction. This camp was surrounded by a further series of entanglements and obstacles, for which wire cutters would be needed. Newbridge Cumann na mBan activist Nellie Wallace, whose brother Edward 'Dixie' Wallace was in Hut 1, with the help of friendly guard smuggled in double action wire cutters.[5]

The duties of the hut occupants were divided out among them. Not everyone could work in a tunnel – only a select few did – but other men in the hut were assigned jobs as lookouts, carpenters, etc. Some men were given the task of arranging for the safe hiding of soil. Jimmy Kilroy (Mayo), one of the tunnellers, maintained there was a seven- or eight-inch space between the outer and inner walls all around the hut. This was where the clay from the tunnel would be hidden. Carpenters were assigned the job of taking down the wooden wall sheeting to enable the clay to be deposited and then putting the boards back up again. The first job of the tunnellers was to break an entrance through the concrete before beginning the actual tunnel. This was a very laborious job because the concrete was nine inches thick. They soon completed a 'trapdoor' in front of a large stove that stood in the centre of the hut and faced the main entrance. This position safeguarded the trapdoor from footfall as there were always numerous squatters sitting around such a stove in winter or early spring.[6]

Concealment of the trapdoor's uneven edges became an urgent problem – the solution lay in plastering soap along the crevices. Thereupon the tunnellers commandeered the hut's weekly soap ration, and beards became the fashion. Next, the tunnellers scooped out a ten-foot-deep shaft, which would lead into the tunnel. Soon, it was time to prepare the real task of digging the tunnel. By chance, the tunnellers had been able to procure the most efficient of all tunnelling tools, a bayonet acquired from a sympathetic soldier. This sped its way through the wall of clay. One by one, they removed and replaced the wooden panels in the hut wall for receipt of the clay.[7]

Speed was essential, and the tunnel became a twenty-four-hour job. This was in shifts of two hours underground at first, but these were shortened considerably as conditions worsened. When the air became so bad, Jimmy Kilroy created a fan system for ventilation. At night, there were always at least two workers underground. Candles provided light. The tunnel was dug without supports, so was kept low and arched. Occasionally, there was a frightening cave-in, but the main thing was not to panic when this happened. To deceive the nocturnal military police, who made frequent counts at every unlikely hour, they placed 'dummies' that were veritable works of art in the absentees' beds – usually situated in the gloomiest corner of the hut.

Acting on information supplied by a military chaplain, military engineers conducted raids looking for the tunnel. The raids were on surrounding huts, but Hut 1 only received a brief visit. The chaplain had allegedly reported that there was a tunnel in Hut 1, so Comdt Billy Byrne decided to make a 'casual' visit. As Byrne walked through the hut, he could not help but notice that the hut was a model for cleanliness with beds in order and the floor gleaming. Unknown to him a tunneller, Paddy Cannon, was crouched in the mouth of the shaft. Finding nothing untoward, Byrne and his escort left.[8]

Byrne's suspicions were not allayed, and in the early hours of 18 March 1923, Peadar O'Donnell was transferred to Mountjoy Prison. The tunnellers suspended all activities for two days as a precaution. They then returned to tunnelling, and inevitably, more problems arose – direction, lighting and fresh air. Jimmy Kilroy solved all three simultaneously. He suggested that the tunnel could be lit by electric light. His fellow inmates shook their heads in despair. At the time electric bulbs were rare, and electricians were even scarcer. A few days later Kilroy appeared with a stolen cache of electric wire, bulbs, fuses and other electrical implements, and – to his comrades' surprise – began hooking up the wire to the tunnel. Kilroy laid the wire inside the wall and under the roof, where he made his electric connection. He then ran the wire with bulbs attached along the ceiling of the tunnel. When the bulbs, viewed from the shaft, ran in a straight line, then the tunnellers also knew the tunnel was straight.

Meanwhile, the new internment camp alongside was nearing completion. The switching on of lights over the new barbed-wire entanglements meant the camp would soon be occupied by prisoners and more guards. Spurred on by this progress, the tunnellers forced a spike to the surface that revealed a spot beside the last entanglement. Another day's work would take them clear of the wire, but too close to the new glaring lights. They had no choice but to go the following night. Zero hour was fixed at 10 p.m., Saturday, 21 April.[9]

The prisoners were last checked at 7 p.m., and the orderly officer reported that there were 479 internees in No. 1 Camp and a further 37 prisoners in the hospital huts.[10] Those who were to leave through the tunnel said their goodbyes to the ones who were to remain due to illness, wounds or duty. Dr Ferran opted to stay with his patients. Unfortunately, Ferran should have gone, because he died of pneumonia on 10 June 1923.[11]

Among the seventy or so who escaped were: Tommy Reidy, known as the 'Prince of the Tunnellers'; Tómas Ó Maoláin; Jimmy Kilroy; Willie Malone; Jim Rushe; 'Gas' Hughes; Paddy Kelly, the two Paddy Cannons and Paddy Hegarty (all from Mayo); Maurice Liston (Limerick); Ed 'Dixie' Wallace, Patrick Brennan and – Byrne (Kildare); S. Scanlon (Sligo); Nicky Reid (Howth, Dublin); Mick O'Hanlon and John McCoy (Armagh); and J. O'Connor (Kerry).[12]

Tómas Ó Maoláin and Tommy Reidy were first out. Ó Maoláin had escaped through a tunnel from the Rath Camp, the Curragh, in September 1921. A national schoolteacher, Ó Maoláin had been active since 1917 and had been held as a prisoner in Athlone Barracks before being transferred to Tintown with Tommy Reidy. He crawled behind Reidy, his face and hands blackened, and his boots tied around his neck. Reidy pulled back the last layer of earth from the exit shaft and slowly stuck his head up, only to withdraw it immediately and whisper, 'It's as bright as day and there's a sentry not five yards from us!'[13]

The tunnel leading from Hut 1 into the new camp was about fifty yards long. An exit hole – fourteen to eighteen inches wide

– was about three yards inside the wire of the new camp, at a point where there was complete darkness at night. The night of the escape was quite misty and stormy, with some occasional very heavy showers. The two waited patiently, and then the sentry moved away on his rounds, presumably to keep warm. Reidy exited the tunnel, followed quickly by Ó Maoláin. He said:

> So ever on the alert, we forged ahead to the entanglements on the far side of the new Camp ... By the time we had cut our way through the entanglements, there was a bloodstained trail in our wake, but that was a minor detail just then. Now that we were technically free, it was a case of each Group for itself ... Once again our luck held, even in one extremely tight corner. Soon the whinny of horses was music in our ears, as we hastened past a famous Horse Stable. But, it was only when we crossed a main road and headed for the open country, that we really began to breathe freely.[14]

Each group went their separate way towards their respective home areas. Some escapees did not even get out of the new camp compound. A military-police patrol accidently came across six escapees in the riding school. Several more military police arrived, and they rounded up four more prisoners who were hiding behind cement blocks in the new camp. None of the prisoners had their boots on.

With the alarm now raised, troops and military police rushed into Tintown No.1 compound. On opening No. 1 Hut, they discovered that the entrance to the tunnel was fully exposed. A count was taken of No. 1 Hut that revealed 71 men missing from the previous roll call of 114. Two men, Patrick Brennan and John McCoy, were also found to be missing from the hospital, bringing the total to 73.[15]

The camp authorities met with considerable opposition from the prisoners in ascertaining the names of the men who had escaped. This opposition was the result of orders issued by the prisoners' leaders contained in a document with instructions to hinder any attempt at discipline by the camp regime, found on one of the prisoners. Subsequently, two other tunnels were discovered. To effectively prevent any other escape by tunnel, the camp authorities issued orders that steps should be taken to make the prisoners in Tintown dig trenches around each compound. The prisoners' leaders were removed from the camps before the prisoners were made to commence this work, and a number of those leaders were transferred to the nearby Military Detention Barracks. The leaders later claimed they were handcuffed day and night. In response the camp authorities claimed that because the prisoners were dangerous, they were handcuffed only during the night.[16]

Among the escapees recaptured was Ed 'Dixie' Wallace of Newbridge. After being returned to the Curragh Camp, Wallace spent fourteen days in handcuffs, in the military prison. It was Dixie Wallace's sister, Nellie who had smuggled in the wire cutters. However, she was unaware of the escape, as she and her sister Lily were arrested at their Newbridge home on 6 April 1923 and imprisoned in Kilmainham Gaol. It was then that Nellie's name appeared on captured documents.[17]

Peadar O'Donnell, the originator of the tunnel, was elected to the Dáil in 1923 while in prison. Following the end of the Civil War, he participated in the mass hunger strike of October–November that was launched in protest at the continued imprisonment of anti-Treaty IRA men. He remained on hunger strike for forty-one days. O'Donnell was returned to the Curragh Camp, but in March 1924 he walked out of the front gate dressed in a National Army officer's overcoat provided by a sympathetic guard. The gates were also left open, and the searchlight pointed in a different direction. O'Donnell never revealed who his sympathetic guard was.[18] He hid out for several days before approaching a cottage where he said to the owner, 'I'm Peadar O'Donnell, IRA Executive. I want to get in touch with the organisation here.' The owner of the cottage put him in contact with the right people.[19] Following his escape, O'Donnell became editor of *An Phoblacht*, but later moved away from the republican movement, which he felt was too conservative. O'Donnell was involved in organising an Irish Brigade on the anti-fascist side in the Spanish Civil War. He was later editor of *The Bell*, the most significant literary magazine in Ireland from 1946 to 1954.[20]

'The Catalpa Six': Martin Hogan, James Wilson, Thomas Hassett, Michael Harrington, Thomas Darragh and Robert Cranston. These six men were rescued from Fremantle Prison, Australia, in April 1876. (Author's collection)

The *Catalpa* sailed from New Bedford, Massachusetts, on 29 April 1875, and half a world away picked up the six Fenian escapees from Fremantle Prison on 15 April 1876. (Author's collection)

James Stephens escaped from Richmond Prison on 11 November 1865, eleven days after he had been arrested. (Courtesy of Kilmainham Gaol Museum, 2023.0460)

John Boyle O'Reilly was the first prisoner ever to successfully escape from Fremantle Prison, in February 1869. He was picked up on a deserted beach by the whaling ship *Gazelle* and brought to the USA. (Courtesy of County Kildare Archives and Local Studies)

Nellie Kearns, a member of Cumann na mBan, smuggled in a plan of the sewer system to Newbridge Barracks, which internees used to escape on 14/15 October 1922. (Courtesy of County Kildare Archives and Local Studies)

Jimmy Whyte, Naas Company, IRA, was rescued from Dundalk Jail on 14 August 1922. Recaptured, he was interned in Newbridge Barracks, from where he escaped on 14 October 1922. (Courtesy of County Kildare Archives and Local Studies)

Mountjoy Prison escapees: Mae Burke, Eithne Coyle and Linda Kearns at an IRA training camp at Duckett's Grove, Co. Carlow, November 1921. Along with Eileen Keogh, the three had escaped from Mountjoy on 31 October 1921. (Courtesy of John Sweeney Collection)

Fr Patrick H. Delahunty, the only member of the clergy to escape from British custody, pictured in Chicago with a friend. Fr Delahunty escaped through a tunnel from Kilkenny Jail on 22 November 1921. (Courtesy of Jim Maher)

Royal Ulster Constabulary 'Wanted Poster' for Hugh McAteer, Jimmy Steele, Ned Maguire and Patrick Donnelly, who had escaped from Crumlin Road Gaol on 15 January 1943. (Author's collection)

An Phoblacht

REPUBLICAN NEWS

8-PAGE
PULL-OUT
SPECIAL
SUPPLEMENT

THE
DIARY
OF
BOBBY SANDS

Armed IRA jail break

● Crumlin Road jail, Belfast, after eight republicans shot their way to freedom on Wednesday afternoon

republican prisoners on remand in Belfast's Crumlin jail shot their way to freedom out of the heaviest guarded in Europe last Wednesday, in one of the most daring escapes of the last ten years.

escapees are: brothers Tony rry Sloan, Gerard McKee, erty, Angelo Fusco, Patrick and Tony Campbell, all Belfast and charged in on either with M60 machine ucks in 1980 on an RUC n Andersonstown in which 2 man was killed and three d, or with the siege on the Road in May 1980, when a in the SAS was killed; te Ryan from Ardboe, in Tyrone, who was charged ling an RUC Reservist and man

eight were also charged A membership, men came out the way they t last year through the

from gate: The elaborate, spectacular escape began around 4pm. when legal visits which they had all arranged for the same time had just ended and the prisoners were put in two cells.

When warders came to bring back one set of prisoners to their wing, one of the Volunteers produced a short-arm, forced the warders to release the other prisoners and then locked about ten warders in the cell.

They then made their way to 'B' wing's visiting area and arrested all the warders, visitors and solicitors who were there, before locking about thirty up in a room. One warder, named as Killen,

continued on page 2)

4 pages-25 pence

PENCE is the price of this week's special expanded 24-page issue of 'An Phoblacht/Republican News', which includes an eight-page supplement "The diary of Bobby Sands: the seventeen days of Bobby's H-Block hunger strike to the death"

HUNGER STRIKE
MARCH & RALLY
Sunday 14th June
BELFAST
Assemble 2 p.m.
Dunville Park

● British soldiers, a prison officer and RUC men, in despair, at the insecure gates of Crumlin Road jail

An exclusive report on the escape from Crumlin Road Gaol in
An Phoblacht/Republican News, 13 June 1981. (Author's collection)

THE GREAT ESCAPE

25th ANNIVERSARY

THE UNTOLD STORY BEHIND THE ESCAPE

THURSDAY 25TH SEPTEMBER '08
CARRICKDALE HOTEL, LOUTH.
STARTS 8.00PM   TAILLE 10.00

Twenty-fifth anniversary poster commemorating the 1983
Long Kesh escape. (Author's collection)

Frank Driver (Ballymore-
Eustace), who was
instrumental in the
Curragh escape on 2
December 1958 in which
fourteen men escaped.
He was first jailed in 1922
aged sixteen.(Courtesy of
Mick Healy)

Kevin Mallon, an IRA activist since the 1950s, escaped by helicopter from Mountjoy Prison on 31 October 1973, and again escaped from Portlaoise Prison on 18 August 1974. (Author's collection)

South Derry comrades Ian Milne and Francis Hughes. Hughes died on hunger strike in the H-Blocks on 12 May 1981. Milne escaped from Portlaoise Prison on 18 August 1974. (Author's collection)

From left: Long Kesh escapee Jim Clarke (Donegal), Thomas Kelly, and escapees Tony Kelly and Kieran Fleming (Derry) taken in November 1984. Kieran Fleming died after a confrontation with British troops on 2 December 1984. (Courtesy of Tony Kelly)

Former Dublin Brigade officer, Simon Donnelly, pictured at the cell door in Kilmainham Gaol in 1966, from where he had escaped on 10 February 1921. (Courtesy of Kilmainham Gaol Museum, 21PC-3K11-01)

Frank Teeling, arrested for his part in the Bloody Sunday assassinations of British agents, escaped from Kilmainham Gaol on 14 February 1921, along with Simon Donnelly and Ernie O'Malley. (Courtesy of Kilmainham Gaol Museum, 19PC-1K44-25)

CHAPTER 13

NINETEEN MEN ARE MISSING

On a gloomy November evening in 1925 nineteen IRA volunteers, either under sentence or awaiting trial, were in custody in two wings of Mountjoy Prison. The Civil War had petered out nearly two years earlier, but various incidents had followed involving clashes between republicans and the authorities. Despite the ceasefire in May 1923, the IRA was still determined to overthrow the Free State. Éamon de Valera still effectively controlled the IRA. The result was that its activities were directed to political rather than military matters. De Valera believed the Sinn Féin abstentionist policy of not taking its seats in Dáil Éireann was unproductive. The IRA, however, was disturbed at the downgrading of military operations and was suspicious of the political approach. At the General Army Convention held in Bullock Castle, Dalkey, on 14 November 1925, the IRA withdrew its allegiance from the 'Republican Government' controlled by de Valera and elected a new twelve-man executive. Andy Cooney was appointed Chief of Staff of the IRA, replacing Frank Aiken who was seen as a de Valera supporter.[1]

When Andy Cooney was appointed Chief of Staff, one of his first actions was to deal with British propaganda films being shown in Dublin theatres. Cinema managers had already been warned that if they persisted in showing such films, they would be drastically dealt with. On Armistice Day, 11 November 1925, armed IRA volunteers seized several reels of the film of 'Ypres' at Dublin's Masterpiece Theatre, Talbot Street. Two men, James Lee and Maurice Fenelon, were arrested at the scene. Two weeks later, on the morning of 25 November, four IRA volunteers – Charles Ashmore, William Merrigan, William Kinsella and John Doyle – arrived in a car and placed a bomb in the vestibule of the cinema. The resulting explosion blew away the box office and the entire front of the building. Luckily, no one was on the premises, so there were no injuries. As the raiders were leaving the cinema, two Civic Guards intercepted them. The volunteers abandoned their vehicle and began firing at the police, wounding both. One guard was shot in the abdomen, the other in the arm. William Kinsella and John Doyle, both of O'Toole's Arch, off Newfoundland Street, Dublin, were later arrested and detained on suspicion of being involved. Charles Ashmore and William Merrigan were also arrested and charged with the explosion and the shooting of the guards. All four were lodged in Dublin's Mountjoy Prison.[2]

One of the first actions of the remilitarised IRA was a prison break. Several important IRA men had been recently arrested and incarcerated in Mountjoy. These included Seán Russell, who was picked up just before the IRA General Army Convention, his pockets stuffed with documents and resolutions; Michael Carolan, Director of Intelligence, lifted in the midst of planning the jailbreak of the four Mountjoy prisoners at Adelaide Road, Dublin; and Jim Killeen, arrested at a farmhouse used as an IRA headquarters at Dunboden, Co. Westmeath, on 27 July 1925. Michael Seery and Patrick Norton were also charged, along with Killeen, with 'assisting in the formation of an illegal organisation'. They, too, were sent to Mountjoy Prison. IRA GHQ had a line in to Killeen through a sympathetic prison warder. A rescue plan was put in place, with Mick Price, Officer Commanding Dublin Brigade, in charge.[3]

At 8 p.m. on 29 November, a Ford Model T car drove up to the main gates of the prison. Six IRA volunteers were in the car, three of them in Civic Guard uniforms. George Gilmore, a veteran of the War of Independence and the Civil War, was the leader of the group. Gerald O'Reilly (Bohermeen, Co. Meath) and Patrick J. Farrell (Dublin) are the only other members known to have been in the party.[4] It was misty and murky when George Gilmore, wearing a Civic Guard sergeant's uniform, got out of the car and knocked on the door. He announced that he was in charge of an escort with three prisoners to be lodged and that his detainees would be serving three months' sentences in lieu of fines for poaching. He handed in a properly executed committal order and demanded entrance to the jail to hand over his prisoners. The unsuspecting warder opened the massive doors without hesitation, and the party drove through the inner gate without any hindrance. Inside, they quickly dismounted from the car.

The gate warder was suddenly surrounded by men waving revolvers, and George Gilmore, sticking a revolver in his back, said menacingly, 'Hands up.' The men took his bunch of keys and forced him into his own guardroom, where another warder on duty was held up, and the two were bound and gagged. Gilmore then unlocked the inner gate and, accompanied by his three 'prisoners', proceeded towards the general office in the main building about twenty yards away. The two volunteers in uniform took charge of the warders and the gate.

A military sentry was standing at the entrance to the office block. Since the beginning of the Civil War, it had been usual for a military guard to be mounted at Mountjoy Prison when political prisoners were in custody. In daylight, the soldier had a good view of the front gate from his position, but, in the darkness and in poor lighting, he had noticed nothing unusual. In his sergeant's uniform and with his three 'prisoners', Gilmore, suddenly sprang and disarmed the surprised soldier of his rifle and quietly marched him to the front gate to join the captured.

The raiders then entered the general office and held up the clerk on duty. He, too, joined the soldier and warders at the gate, while the IRA volunteers cut the telephone wires. Gilmore then led his three 'prisoners' to the gate of the circle, the central hall of the prison from which the four wings radiated. The warder in charge of the gate heard a voice call, 'Three on.' This announcement was familiar, signifying that three newly committed prisoners were to be admitted. He unlocked the gate, suspecting nothing out of the ordinary.

Gilmore strode through holding a revolver. He held the gate warder and the principal officer, Robert Grace, at gunpoint, as his accomplices entered the circle. They rounded up two other warders and locked all four warders in an empty cell. The republican prisoners were dispersed through various parts of the jail, but, with inside information provided by the sympathetic warder, the rescue party proceeded confidently to designated cells, and with their confiscated keys they methodically unlocked the cells in which the nineteen IRA prisoners had been housed.

The rescue party only made one mistake in the identification of the cells. A man named William Perry in D Wing gazed in puzzlement as his cell was unlocked, was handed a revolver and told 'Come on!' Perry, on remand on a charge of burglary, said, 'I'm not going anywhere!' Gilmore said to him, 'Are you not so-and-so?' Perry replied, 'Indeed, I'm not.'

'Do you know his cell number?' Gilmore asked.

He gave him the details and the prisoner was promptly freed. All the heavy iron gates that guarded the labyrinthine passages of the prison were opened, and the rescue party hurried through with their band of released men. Gilmore indicated the way to the main gate, and the prisoners trooped behind their rescuers. The soldier and the guards who had been held at the gate were put inside the inner gates and locked in. The group of IRA men left, taking the soldier's rifle and the gate keys but leaving behind the keys taken from Principal Officer Grace. Rescuers and rescued made their way out of the prison, abandoning their car. Unfortunately for the rescuers and escapees, only Tom Finlay turned up with his taxi car. Six men got into the car, while the rest escaped the scene on foot.

The whole operation only took minutes, because the rescue party had arrived with an almost complete list of the cell numbers and their location. It was clear that someone on the prison staff had cooperated with them, and also that some of the rescuers must have been prisoners in the jail at one time or another due to their familiarity with the surroundings. In fact, George Gilmore had served time in Mountjoy and knew the surroundings well. He had escaped from Mountjoy Prison in August 1923 – the aftermath of which resulted in riots, because the remaining prisoners were placed in solitary confinement and subjected to a stricter prison regime.[5]

Amongst the prisoners rescued was Michael Carolan, from Belfast, who described himself at his trial, on 27 October, as 'Commandant-General and Director of Intelligence' of the IRA. He was convicted at Green Street Courthouse of 'taking part in and assisting in the formation or organisation of a body purporting to be a military force not established or maintained as such by law'. At the time of his rescue, Carolan was serving a sentence of twelve months. He had joined the Irish Volunteers in 1914 and had served terms of imprisonment in Frongoch Internment Camp, Wales (1916), and in Mountjoy Prison, where he took part in a hunger strike (1920). During the Civil War he was director of intelligence for the anti-Treaty IRA.

Seán McGuinness was another of the rescued prisoners. He had been sentenced to eighteen months for assault and resisting arrest, and obstruction of gardaí. After his incarceration, he was disqualified as TD for Laois-Offaly. During the War of Independence, McGuinness was OC Offaly Brigade and took the anti-Treaty side in the Civil War. Several prisoners charged with the raid on Dublin's Masterpiece cinema the previous week were also among those who escaped.

In addition to Carolan and McGuinness, the others who escaped were: Seán Russell, James Donnelly, Maurice Fenelon and James Lee (Dublin), Frank O'Beirne and Michael J. O'Hara (Sligo), William Bolton (Carlow), James Nugent (Clonmel), Pat Norton, Michael Seery, Jim Killeen (OC Midlands Division) and Joseph Stephen Murphy (Westmeath), Patrick McCabe (senior) and P. McCabe (junior) (Meath), and Pat Ryan and David Reck (Wexford). Seán Russell was soon to become Chief of Staff of the IRA, while Jim Killeen was a member of the IRA general staff and was using the alias James Grace.[6]

In an attempt to recapture the prisoners and to combat what Irish Army Military Intelligence described as a 'marked revival in irregular activities', extensive raids were carried out in Dublin and its suburbs. The homes of those from Dublin who had escaped were kept under surveillance. Eight men, thought to have helped in the rescue or being among the rescuers, were arrested and brought to the Bridewell for questioning, but were later released. Among them were George and Jack Plunkett, sons of Count Plunkett, TD, and brothers of the executed 1916 leader Joseph Mary Plunkett.[7] Some of the escapees were subsequently recaptured and brought back to Mountjoy. George Gilmore, the engineer of the daring venture, was arrested and charged with riotous behaviour on Armistice Night, 11 November 1926. His run of bad luck continued in that while in the prison exercise yard, Gilmore was recognised by Principal Officer Robert Grace as the bogus police sergeant who had locked him up on the mass-escape night. Instead of a short sentence,

Gilmore had to serve eighteen months. He endured several violent beatings from prison staff. This resulted in his comrades carrying out an attack in which Grace was shot and wounded going home from work on the North Circular Road. Gilmore had held Grace responsible for his arrest and mistreatment and had warned him to 'make your peace with God'. Grace survived the attack.[8]

One of the Mountjoy escapees, Seán McGuinness, later fled to the United States, where he remained for five years before returning to Ireland and resuming his membership of the IRA in 1930. Over the years, McGuinness repeatedly clashed with the leadership of the IRA over the direction they should take in the post-Civil War era He was amongst those who believed the organisation needed to be tied to social issues in order to receive public support. He was a founder of the Saor Éire Party, and he died in 1978.[9]

George Gilmore was to serve three more terms in Mountjoy Prison, make another failed escape attempt, go on hunger strike, refuse to wear a prison uniform and remain naked in his cell for five months. In 1928 he finished his eighteen-months' sentence and was freed, only to be arrested again for challenging the right of people to fly the Union Jack. A large arms dump was discovered near the Gilmore home on 10 June 1931. George and his brother Charles were arrested and remanded in custody to Mountjoy Prison. On 10 October, with the use of two 'pistols' whittled out of wood and covered with silver paper, the Gilmore brothers bundled the warder in charge of their exercise into a nearby toilet. They then ran for the boundary wall, where they waited impatiently for some means of escape to appear over the wall. Shouts were exchanged with IRA volunteers on the other side, as the brothers held back several warders with their 'pistols'. The Gilmores waited twenty minutes for the expected ladder to appear, but, when it was clear the escape plan had miscarried, they surrendered and allowed themselves to be 'disarmed' and brought back to their cells. Four sections of a home-made ladder were found later on the other side of the wall. Evidently, the home-made ladder was not firm enough for its purpose.[10]

A military tribunal sentenced the two brothers on 8 December 1931; George was given five years' imprisonment, while Charles received three years. George Gilmore refused to recognise the court and stated, 'I do not want anybody to think I excuse myself for such a charge as having arms, I am admittedly hostile to British imperialism and international capitalism.'[11] When Fianna Fáil came to power, Frank Aiken, the new Minister of Defence, visited Arbour Hill military prison where those sentenced by military tribunal were held. There he conversed with his old comrade George Gilmore. Next day, 10 March 1932, twenty prisoners, including the Gilmores and Frank Ryan were released from custody. By 18 March the Fianna Fáil government had dissolved the military tribunals; special powers and detention were also suspended.

In August 1932 Gilmore and T.J. Ryan, of Kilrush, Co. Clare, were both shot and wounded by Criminal Investigation Department (CID) detectives in Kilrush, after a large crowd gathered at a house connected to local labour troubles. At a special court held in Kilrush Hospital, the two wounded republicans were charged with attempted murder of police. The state later dropped charges, when it became obvious at the trial that the two were unarmed and had been shot by a detective during an argument.[12]

Gilmore left the IRA in 1934 along with Frank Ryan and formed a new organisation Republican Congress, which led to their expulsion from the IRA. The following year Republican Congress split and gradually lost momentum over the central issue of whether it should devolve itself into a new revolutionary socialist party or remain as a united front of all progressive forces against fascism. Many supporters and members of Republican Congress, including Frank Ryan, later went to Spain to fight on the republican side in the Spanish Civil War.[13]

CHAPTER 14

I WISH I WAS(N'T) BACK HOME IN DERRY

On 12 January 1939 the IRA sent an ultimatum to Lord Halifax, British Foreign Secretary, demanding the withdrawal of all British armed forces and civilian representatives from every part of Ireland. When there was no reply to the ultimatum, IRA bombs began exploding across England. British security was immediately tightened, and thirty-three Irishmen were arrested in police raids. The bombing campaign was appallingly ill-conceived and resulted in the deaths of six civilians and the wounding of dozens. Britain introduced the Prevention of Violence (Temporary Provisions) Bill, while the Irish government passed the Offences Against the State Act on 14 June 1939. In the North, the Royal Ulster Constabulary (RUC) was always on alert, and an immediate crackdown on republicans followed. Arrests and jailings of republicans increased on both sides of the border.[1]

In the early morning of 2 November 1942 six IRA men escaped from Mountjoy Prison. They prised loose one of the cell windows in the exercise room and scaled down to the yard on a rope made of bedsheets. They then climbed onto a sentry post on top of the high boundary wall, slid across and dropped down to the outside. The six men were: Jackie Griffith and Pete Martin (Dublin); Jim Smyth (Oldcastle, Co. Meath); and Frank Kerrigan, Mick and Mort Lucey (Cork city). Jackie Griffith was shot dead by Special Branch detectives near Merrion Square, Dublin on 4 July 1943.[2]

Hugh McAteer was Chief of Staff of the IRA when he was arrested on 12 October 1942. A serving policeman from his old street in Derry had claimed he could supply the IRA with certain useful information, but when McAteer and his director of intelligence, Gerald O'Reilly, arrived at the man's house they were arrested. McAteer and O'Reilly were lodged in Belfast's Crumlin Road Gaol. While on remand, McAteer began sawing through his cell bars. However, before he had cut one half, his court case came up and he was sentenced to fifteen years for treason and moved to another wing with the convicted republican prisoners. McAteer was desperate to escape and redeem himself after his naive capture. Looking for another way out, he found a trapdoor in the ceiling of a toilet that led to an attic under the slates of the jail roof. He suggested to Paddy Donnelly, OC of the republican prisoners on A Wing, that an escape was possible using this route and that Belfast man Jimmy Steele, Adjutant IRA Northern Command, should go with them. They brought Edward 'Ned' Maguire into the conspiracy because he was a roof slater by trade.

On the morning of 15 January 1943, as the warders breakfasted, the four received permission to go to the toilet. They used a table, later removed by other inmates, to get into the attic, replacing the trapdoor beneath them. Once in the attic, Ned Maguire removed the roof slates, and the four made their way out onto the roof. They slid down from the roof on a rope made of knotted sheets and dashed to the twenty-foot perimeter wall. It was a cold frosty morning, and there were no prison staff around. At the wall, the escapees affixed a hook to a long pole made from brush shafts and strips of leather from the prison shoe shop. They wrapped the pole with cloth to prevent noise, and, after some trouble, hooked the barbed wire. McAteer was last to go over, but as he reached the top, he fell back into the prison yard and twisted his ankle. He struggled back up the pole, dragged himself over the barbed wire, where he ripped open his hand and fell again, this time on the right side of the wall. Even though they were wearing prison clothes, nobody noticed the four escapees, as Belfast's wartime shabbiness enabled them to blend into the crowd. A £3,000 reward was immediately posted for the capture of any or all of the four escapees. The four men returned to active service. In less than nine months, Jimmy Steele was to figure in another daring escape.[3]

Derry Jail, on Bishop Street in the loyalist Fountain area, had a long history of republican resistance. It was the scene of a daring escape of top Sligo republican Frank Carty on 15 February 1921. On Christmas Day 1939, republican prisoners took over the jail protesting against their continued incarceration without charges or trial. In October 1942, republican prisoners began digging an escape tunnel in Harry O'Rawe and Jimmy O'Hagan's ground-floor cell. The ground-floor cells were floored with wood, beneath which was nothing but clay. Working for over five months, a group of prisoners managed to sink a shaft extending fifteen feet straight down and turning sharply to extend eighty feet in a tunnel burrowed out towards a house in Harding Street. The tunnel's line of sight was on a chimney on Harding Street, its exit was the coal shed in the Logue family's backyard in No. 15 Harding Street. Over a period of five months, the prisoners removed fifteen tons of clay from the tunnel in pillowcases. They sifted and disposed of the clay around the prison yard or flushed it down the jail toilets. As a result, the sewers were clogged twice, but the authorities apparently never connected the sewer blockages with an escape tunnel. The sound of digging had often been masked by music practice held in other cells each evening. Nearby residents had heard noises at night, but never guessed it was prisoners digging an escape tunnel.[4]

Two men did the digging at night while another kept watch. Tunnellers were half-naked, because tunnelling is dirty work and their clothes had to be kept reasonably clean. The tools used for tunnelling were those which had been used to make a rockery in the prison grounds. Bits of wood salvaged from around the prison and sandbags made from pillowcases were used to prop up the tunnel. Large rocks, which the tunnellers encountered, were hidden under the floorboards of other ground-floor cells. The tunnel also suffered from waterlogging, and at one stage the tunnellers even had to dig under a coffin – at least five men had been hanged in the prison for murder. The last execution took place in 1908. Tunnelling was dangerous work, and a collapse buried Liam Graham but the others dug him out before he suffocated.[5]

Twenty men were picked to escape; the selection was based on those who would commit to reporting back for duty, north of the border. Among them were Albert Price, Liam Graham, Harry O'Rawe, Jimmy O'Hagan, Séamus 'Rocky' Burns and Paddy Adams. Anyone else who wanted to escape was to be given the opportunity to do so after the official escapees had left. Finally, when the tunnel was estimated to be nearly under the jail wall, GHQ in Belfast was notified. The escape, set for 21 March 1943, was to be supported by waiting IRA units in Derry and across the border in Donegal. The OC Tyrone, Jim Toner, and his adjutant, Joe Carant, were put in charge of moving the men out of Northern Ireland. GHQ would get them away from the vicinity of Derry Jail.[6]

A day before the escape, the Crumlin Road escapee Jimmy Steele and another Belfast IRA volunteer, Liam Burke, hired a large furniture lorry and driver and drove from Belfast to

Derry. On the way, the not so talkative driver suddenly stopped at Castledawson RUC station and went inside. Nervously, Steele fingered his revolver wondering had the driver recognised him – Steele's niece worked for the same firm. To make matters worse, Steele was sitting at the same level as a poster in the station window announcing a £3,000 reward for his capture and that of his fellow escapees from Crumlin Road, Hugh McAteer, Paddy Donnelly and Ned Maguire. The driver, however, unfamiliar with the route, had only popped in to ask for directions.

When they reached Derry, Steele produced his revolver and told the driver that his lorry was being commandeered by the IRA. The shocked driver looked at the revolver and then told Steele that he was a republican. When Steele explained why the furniture truck was being commandeered, the driver said that he could drive the lorry better than anyone else and agreed to remain with them and help out with the escape. A safe house had been provided for the Belfast men, while the lorry was left at the corner of Abercorn Place, so that the escapees, who were expected to emerge in Harding Street the next morning, could run down and jump into the back. There were three flights of steps at the top of Abercorn Place where it met Harding Street. That prevented the lorry being moved to outside No. 15, and also meant that the lorry was not close enough to arouse suspicion.

The escape was timed for 8.30 on Saturday morning, 21 March. Liam Burke positioned himself at the top of the steps at Abercorn Place to guide the escapees to the lorry. Outside the door of the cell a prisoner played the bagpipes to cover the noise of the escapees' departure. There was a brief panic when the escapees realised that the mouth of the tunnel was blocked. But it only turned out to be two bags of coal, which were then dragged back through the tunnel and into the prison, clearing the way for the escape.[7] The escapees, bare-headed and their clothes covered with clay and coal dust, crowded into the house of Joseph Logue, a shipping official, who was about to have breakfast. Startled, Logue said, 'What's this all about?'

One of the men made for the telephone, saying they must cut the wires. However, Mr Logue's daughter, Millie, who had come downstairs with her coat over her nightclothes, grabbed the telephone and prevented them. One escapee smiled and said, 'Watch out or you will catch a cold.' Millie later told press reporters, 'They were very polite. They told us nothing would happen if we kept quiet.' Before the Logues could figure out what it was all about, the escapees hurried down the hall, out the front door and quietly out to the street.[8]

Seán Hamill remained in the Logues' house to prevent them raising the alarm. By the time he left the house, the lorry had already driven off. He stayed in Derry, but subsequently crossed the border into Donegal. Jimmy Steele and Liam Burke gave up their places in the lorry to the fifteen escapees, and the vehicle drove off towards the border. A girl who was passing, and noticed a group of dirt-covered men getting into the back of a lorry, ran the quarter of a mile to the prison gate and told a policeman she thought an escape was in progress. He arrived as the furniture lorry drove away. The lorry drove toward the border and turned the escapees over to the next unit. However, the alarm had been raised, and submachine-gun-toting policemen were on the streets of Derry, holding up pedestrians and vehicles.

The journey to Donegal where the escapees were to link up with an IRA unit was uneventful, but the apprehension and tension among the escapees exploded in shouts of triumph when they crossed over the border at Carrigans. Customs officials at the border tried to stop the vehicle, which they believed was a 'border jumper' on a smuggling expedition, but it kept going. The customs officials reported it as such, unaware that the truck contained the

Derry Jail escapees. An Irish Army patrol accompanied by gardaí from several East Donegal stations were near St Johnston when the truck approached. The escapees abandoned the vehicle and fled to the hills, followed by the Irish security forces who rounded up eleven men on a hill at Glentown Slate Quarries. No shots were fired, and the eleven men surrendered quietly. It had been only six hours since they had escaped from Derry Jail. Unknown to the army patrol that loaded them on to an Irish military truck, a woman with a camera was standing behind a hedge and took a photograph of the men sitting in the truck. They were brought to Rockhill Military Barracks, Letterkenny. The remaining four men – Séamus Trainor, Rocky Burns, Alphonsus White and Séamus McCreevey – evaded capture.[9]

When told they were going to the internment camp at the Curragh, the eleven escapees said they would rather go back to Derry Jail where conditions were better than those in Co. Kildare. The Curragh internment camp was under military control, and it had harsher discipline and a poorer diet. Irish public opinion was outraged that the men had escaped gallantly only to be jailed yet again. A meeting of Letterkenny Urban Council passed a resolution unanimously, requesting President de Valera to release the men who had escaped from Derry Prison 'and are now held in custody by our own Government'. The government eventually saw the point that the Derry jailbreak was a grand stunt, and the escapees were released from the Curragh gradually in small groups.

The twenty-one escapees, the majority of them from Belfast, were: Paddy Adams, Seán Hamill, Liam Graham, Albert Price, Séamus P. Traynor, Séamus 'Rocky' Burns, Alphonsus White, Brendan O'Boyle, Hubert McInerney, Harry O'Rawe, Jimmy O'Rawe, Cathal 'Chips' McCusker, Liam Perry, Thomas McArdle, Séamus O'Hagan, Seán McArdle, Frank McCann, Daniel

McAllister, Kevin Kelly, Hugh O'Neill and Séamus McCreevey. Only fifteen of them had boarded the furniture truck. Harry O'Rawe, Hubert McInerney, Brendan O'Boyle, Cathal McCusker and Liam Graham did not go on the truck but successfully made their way on foot to Letterkenny, Co. Donegal.

Brendan O'Boyle was the last of the designated internees to escape through the tunnel. He got clean away and remained at liberty in Dublin throughout the war, only to die tragically on 2 July 1952 when planting a mine at Stormont telephone exchange.[10] Jimmy O'Rawe was the only non-designated escapee to go through the tunnel. Unfortunately, he was unfamiliar with Derry and was picked up by an RUC patrol on a road near the city during the blackout on the following night.[11]

Jimmy Steele and Liam Burke returned to Belfast by train. Ten months after his escape from Crumlin Road, Hugh McAteer was recaptured on the Falls Road. Jimmy Steele was arrested in late 1943. He was subjected to twelve strokes of the birch and sentenced to twelve years in jail; he served seven years. Steele was one of the most ardent critics of the IRA leadership in the late 1960s. When the republican movement split in 1969, he took the 'Provisional' side and founded the Belfast Republican Press Centre in 1970. He died later that year, the day after his seventy-third birthday.

The driver of the furniture lorry drove back towards Belfast, but was detained by the RUC at Sion Mills, Co. Tyrone. He was later released without charge. Curran Brothers, who had hired the furniture lorry to Jimmy Steele, subsequently received a letter from 'I.R.A. Military Headquarters, Ministry of Finance', with a remittance of £9 for the hire of the vehicle. In the letter was an apology for any rough treatment suffered by the driver of the vehicle.[12]

The *Irish Independent* of 26 March 1943 announced that three men arrested in Dublin were three of the Derry escapees.

However, only one, Seán Hamill, was a Derry escapee; another was Frank Kerrigan (Cork), who had recently escaped from Mountjoy Prison. Seán Hamill was sentenced to seven years for possession of arms and ammunition. Frank Kerrigan got ten years on the same charge. The owner of the house where they were arrested claimed he knew nothing about them.[13]

Two men arrested at a house in Donegal on 5 April by detectives assisted by the military were reported as being escapees. Ned Maguire, who had escaped from Crumlin Road Gaol in January, was one of those arrested. The other was Rocky Burns. Both men were taken to the Curragh Internment Camp.[14] Rocky Burns was subsequently ordered to sign a declaration distancing himself from the IRA to get out of the Curragh Camp. He made his way back to Belfast and continued in active service but was mortally wounded in a shoot-out with RUC detectives at Queens Street. At the time of his death, Burns was OC Belfast Brigade.[15]

Alphonsus 'Shuffles' White, from Rockmore Road, Belfast, was arrested in a safe house in Glasgow, six weeks after the escape. He was brought back to Belfast, where Belfast City Commission sentenced him to twelve years' 'penal servitude' for the possession of weapons. Shuffles was released in 1956 and moved to Dublin, where he worked as a painter for Dublin Corporation.[16]

On 19 September Liam Graham, Seaforde, Co. Down, was arrested on the Dublin Road in Newry. He tried to escape when challenged, but after a short chase by police, who opened fire, Graham was rearrested.[17] Thomas McArdle, Cullingtree Road, Belfast, was arrested in the city on 30 September 1943.[18] Another escapee, Cathal 'Chips' McCusker, was arrested in Belfast on 27 December 1943. On 2 October 1944 Paddy Adams, Abercorn Street North, Belfast, was arrested on a Belfast-bound train at Coraghwood by police on customs duty, when one of the constables recognised him. At this stage, six escapees were still at large.[19]

Following a tribunal inquiry into the escape, one prison warder was dismissed from the service. After the January 1943 escape, a further six warders were dismissed from Crumlin Road Gaol for 'negligence'.[20] Derry Jail was closed on 31 March 1953, and much of it was later demolished to make way for the redevelopment of the Fountain Estate. Its last remaining tower now houses a heritage centre.[21]

CHAPTER 15

HAVING IT AWAY

As early as 1948, the IRA Army Council had drawn up a plan of action for liberating the six northern counties. Its implementation, however, depended on the availability of arms. In the mid-1950s the IRA raided British Army bases in the north of Ireland and in England.[1] Some of the arms from a British Army territorial base were found in the lock-up of IRA volunteer James 'Séamus' Murphy. He became the only man to succeed in escaping from Wakefield Jail – a Category A prison in England – in 1959. When he escaped, twenty-four year old Murphy was serving a life sentence, but he remained free in Ireland for another fifty-six years and died at the age of eighty. Admittedly his sentence was harsh – a life term for stealing a quantity of arms and ammunition from a British Army base.

In an IRA raid on an arms depot at Arborfield, in Berkshire, on 13 August 1955, sixty-six weapons and 82,000 rounds of ammunition were taken. The raid was intended to obtain arms for Operation Harvest – a guerrilla-warfare campaign against targets in Northern Ireland. The IRA party consisted of seven volunteers and was led by Ruairí Ó Brádaigh. The others were: Donal Murphy, Jack Hicks, Tom Fitzgerald, Joe Doyle, Liam Walshe, Paddy Considine and an inside man – serving British soldier Frank Skuse from Cork. James 'Séamus' Murphy (Castledermot, Co. Kildare) was detailed to provide two Austin vans and a Vanguard car, and to set up a safe dump for the arms.

The operation went astray when one of the getaway vans, travelling at speed, was pulled over in a routine police check. A stack of crated ammunition was found inside. Joe Doyle (Bray, Co. Wicklow) and Donal Murphy (Dublin) were arrested. While Doyle and Murphy were being interrogated in Ascot Police Station, they heard the other van with the arms go by. The haul was brought to 237 Caledonian Road, a derelict and war-damaged shop in London, where it would stay until the heat died down. Meanwhile, in Ascot Police Station the police meticulously went through the contents of the confiscated van. Sixty-three cases of War Office ammunition were on board, along with two loaded revolvers, a hacksaw, fake documents, maps and a receipt made out to one James Murphy.

The police were soon on their way to London. Murphy, in charge of the arms dump, had hired the vehicles in his own name and the police easily traced him. He was captured while lying in bed in his digs. The arms and ammunition were recovered while police set up a round-the-clock watch to catch more IRA men, which proved futile: nobody turned up. The rest of the raiders, including Frank Skuse, returned safely to Ireland. Subsequently, Skuse, a native of Cork, was arrested in Dublin using the name Paul Murphy and was interned at the Curragh Camp.

At Berkshire Assizes in Reading, the two Murphys and Joe Doyle refused to plead. On their way to Arborfield, some of the raiders had stopped at a restaurant where the proprietor remembered that one of the Irishmen had spoken to him in German. The proprietor clearly remembered the strange group driving away in a Vanguard car, but he wrongly identified James Murphy as the German speaker when it was actually Jack Hicks.

James Murphy was not on the raid itself. Found guilty on two counts of robbery with aggravation, the two Murphys and Doyle were sentenced to life imprisonment. Before sentence was passed, Justice Cassels asked had they anything to say? Joe Doyle, acting as spokesmen for the trio, said, 'We're soldiers of the IRA. Those arms and ammunition were to be used against the British army of occupation in Ireland. We have no regrets and do not apologise for our part in this operation. Our only regret is that it wasn't a success.'

Sentencing them to life imprisonment, Justice Cassels said, 'This was an act of war upon your part and it was carried far enough to indicate your determination to go through and to stick at nothing in order to achieve your aims.' Even some of the arresting policemen were surprised at the severity of the verdicts – life sentences were quite uncommon. The sentences created as much of a stir in Ireland as the treason felony charges for the IRA raiders who had been captured after a similar foray on the British Army barracks at Omagh, Co. Tyrone, in 1954. However, they had only drawn ten and twelve-year sentences, while this looked like an act of malicious revenge against three young men who had made fools of the British Army.[2]

After a short period in Wormwood Scrubs, Séamus Murphy and Joe Doyle were moved to Wakefield, a Category A men's prison in West Yorkshire. Already in Wakefield was Cathal Goulding, IRA Chief of Staff, along with a future chief of staff, Seán MacStiofáin. An earlier attempt to free Cathal Goulding had failed, and he was eventually transferred to Dartmoor Prison. The Irish republican prisoners in Wakefield quickly made common cause with Greek Cypriot EOKA members, the two groups seeing in each other fellow freedom fighters. Ethnikí Orgánosis Kypríon Agonistón (EOKA) (National Organisation of Cypriot Fighters) was a Greek Cypriot nationalist guerilla organisation that fought a campaign for the end of British rule in Cyprus and for eventual union with Greece.

The regime at Wakefield was tough, because many of the inmates were 'lifers' serving mandatory life sentences for murder. Séamus Murphy quickly resolved to escape his bleak surroundings:

> This was almost an obsession with me by now. Hardly a waking hour passed but my mind was turning over thoughts of escaping this hell hole. I had been sneaking glances at the wall, eyeing keyrings, mentally measuring distances, seeking some weakness in this stone fortress that could be fruitfully exploited, but so far had found nothing that invited concentrated examination.[3]

Séamus Murphy had joined the IRA when he was a student boarding at Terenure College, Dublin. He was interested in politics and social injustice from his teenage years. Murphy was only twenty when he was sentenced, and so had to wait until he was twenty-one when he was transferred to the adult wing of the prison. While on A Wing, Murphy played chess with Klaus Fuchs, a German scientist serving a fourteen-year sentence for passing atomic secrets to the Russians. Murphy said, 'When Uncle Joe [Stalin] exploded his first nuclear device it was largely thanks to Fuchs.'[4] However, it was with the Greek Cypriot prisoners that Murphy expressed great solidarity. His fellow IRA prisoner, Manus Canning, learned Greek from the Cypriots, while George Ioannau, a Cypriot prisoner, translated the writings of James Connolly into Greek.[5]

A joint Irish/Cypriot escape committee was formed among the IRA and EOKA members. The Cypriots agreed that Ireland would be the natural place for them to head to – if they successfully broke out of Wakefield. Murphy said:

Both the IRA and EOKA had already something of a network among our respective exiles here in Britain. On the outside there were many practical advantages to be gained by this collusion, and in the prison we would not be working at cross purposes running around the place plotting and scheming independently of one another. All of us had the same end in view anyway, getting across that wall for a start.[6]

George Ioannau's younger brother, Nicolas, based in London, travelled to Dublin to discuss the breakout arrangements with IRA General Headquarters (GHQ). Unfortunately, he was killed in a hit-and-run accident in England while returning from meeting the IRA leadership. On 17 July 1958, he was riding a motorbike and was hit by a car, which left the scene. Many saw the hidden hand of British Military Intelligence in Nicolas Ioannau's death. According to J. Bowyer Bell, historian and terrorism expert, papers on his body relating to Irish–Cypriot connections disappeared, presumably into police or intelligence hands. His body was taken back for burial to Nicosia in Cyprus.[7]

The Cypriots smuggled cash into the prison; this was used to pay for six hacksaw blades that were secreted by a young Dublin criminal named Feeney. The blades were used to cut the bars on the window of one of the dining halls, which were fortified only by a single line of three bars spaced generously. This meant that only one bar would need to be cut.[8] With nothing forthcoming from IRA GHQ, outside contact was made through another prisoner, Pat O'Donovan, with Joe Christle, leader of a republican group who had split from the IRA over the northern border campaign. Christle, a noted racing cyclist, qualified as a solicitor after graduating in law at University College Dublin (UCD) in the 1950s. He lectured in law at the then College of Commerce in Rathmines, Dublin. He was considered one of the protagonists of the 1956–62 border campaign. In 1953 Christle was involved in the planning of a raid for arms on the officers' training camp in Felstead, Essex. Two years later, he was part of an IRA arms raid on the Royal Irish Fusiliers Barracks in Omagh, Co. Tyrone. Members of the 'Christle Group' also linked up with Saor Uladh on cross-border operations.[9]

Pat O'Donovan was a former IRA volunteer who had joined Saor Uladh. He was serving a seven-year sentence for armed robbery and through his work placement in the prison mailbag shop became the conduit for information from Christle.[10] The prison authorities were unaware, of course, that O'Donovan was anything but an ordinary criminal. Christle made contact with EOKA members in London, who were particularly anxious to get Nicos Sampson, another Cypriot prisoner, out. Klaus Fuchs was asked to go on the escape, but he declined. An ardent anti-Nazi who considered himself a revolutionary, Fuchs told Murphy, 'I wish you luck, but my war is over.' Five men were picked to escape – Séamus Murphy, Joe Doyle, Nicos Sampson, George Skotinos and Tony Martin, a British soldier who had defected to EOKA. Fuchs drew a map of the proposed escape route – from the dining hall to the prison wall where a rope could be thrown over – and had it sent out to Christle, who confirmed that it represented a reasonable chance of success.[11]

Several more trusted prisoners were brought in on the escape plan and they took turns cutting through the bar in the dining hall at different times. It took four days to make the first cut through the bar; the second cut took just as long. It was left with a minimum piece to hold the bar in place until the night of the escape. At the designated time of 6.30 p.m. on the evening of 12 February 1959, midway through the time when the prisoners were drawing their tobacco rations and the prison warders would be distracted, a rope was thrown over the prison wall. Séamus Murphy and Tony Martin were the first to go out. With great difficulty, Martin broke the iron bar on the dining hall window, and the two slipped out into the darkness. A ball of twine had been thrown over to lead them to the place where the rope was.

Murphy said, 'The rope was very thin and despite the knots hard to grip … All of my weight was on my arms and despite the knots my sweating hands were finding it hard to grasp … but slowly the top of the wall was coming nearer to me …' Martin pushed Murphy up from below until he was standing on the big man's shoulders. 'Then suddenly I was lying on top of the wall heaving great mouthfuls of air into my lungs. A tremendous feeling of elation came over me, intoxicated me. The top of this wall had been a tantalizing goal for years, years of frustrated plots and intrigues. I had finally made it. I was out!'

After dropping down from the twenty-foot prison wall, Murphy waited with his rescuers, two men he did not know, Hughie Farrell and Pat Farrelly. They waited for several minutes, but the rope remained slack. Neither Nicos Sampson nor Martin could grasp the rope and were left standing there helplessly. They returned to their cells before they were missed. It was obvious to those on the other side of the wall that something had gone wrong, so reluctantly Murphy and his rescuers left.[12] They made their way to two parked cars. In one car were republicans Áine Grealy and her brother Séamus, acting as decoys by pretending to be a courting couple.[13]

Murphy and his two rescuers got into the second car. He stripped off his blue prison uniform; his shoes had been left behind in his struggle to climb the wall. The two cars drove to Manchester, which was further than the nearest city, Leeds, where the police would search first. Pat Farrelly dropped off Murphy and Hughie Farrell at a house in a Manchester suburb. The getaway cars were driven on to Liverpool and Bradford respectively, where they were abandoned.[14]

The alarm was raised in Wakefield, when Murphy was missed at the 6.30 a.m. roll call. A thorough search of the prison grounds and outbuildings was made without success, but marks were discovered on the inside of the boundary wall of the prison that had been caused by Murphy climbing up the masonry. A police cordon thrown around the city brought no trace of the escapee. One of the getaway cars was discovered at Gladstone Road, in Liverpool, with Murphy's prison clothes on the back seat. It had been hired the previous day from a garage in Liverpool by a man giving his name as Brian McDowell, and an address at Haddington Road, Dublin. He had produced an Irish driving licence, paid £5.10s. for the car hire and £5 deposit. This led the police to believe that Murphy had sailed that night from Liverpool to Dublin.[15]

It was all part of an elaborate deception plan. Murphy had disappeared into a maze of carefully laid false scents, errant clues and even a spurious interview given by his family in Castledermot, Co. Kildare. When an *Irish Press* newspaper report on 17 February proclaimed Murphy's return to Ireland, his sister, Carrie, went along with the ruse and said Séamus was home and had talked to their mother, who was postmistress in Castledermot. Carrie said that neither she nor her mother had been questioned by the Irish police about his whereabouts. 'In fact,' she added, 'we have not seen the police at all since James escaped ...' Asked how he was, Carrie said, 'He is as good as you can expect. The treatment he got in the prison was not what it should be. He was pale and the strain has told on him. But he is safe and content in this country now.'[16]

The financial cost of the rescue operation, which involved the rent of flats and the hire of two cars, was generously paid for by a Cypriot woman, Katerina Pilina, with her £500 wedding dowry. Murphy, meanwhile, hid in the Manchester flat for three weeks, while Hughie Farrell made all the arrangements for his return to Ireland. Farrell booked a taxi to a Manchester train station, from where he and Séamus Murphy took a train to Glasgow Airport and an Aer Lingus flight to Dublin. Joe Christle was waiting to meet them at Dublin Airport. 'He looked very pleased,' Murphy wrote, '"Welcome home, lads," he said.'[17]

When Vivas Lividas launched the Greek-language edition of his book *Cypriot and Irish prisoners in British Jails 1956–59* in 2007, Séamus Murphy and his wife Betty went to Cyprus. While there, he was reunited with some of the Cypriot prisoners from Wakefield Jail, including Nicos Sampson, who had been freed in an amnesty in 1959. He also met Katerina Pilina, who had funded his escape with her wedding dowry, and he was finally able to personally thank her for this great sacrifice.[18]

Séamus Murphy died aged eighty on 2 November 2015. His memoir *Having it Away: A Story of Freedom, Friendship and IRA Jailbreak* was launched by historian and broadcaster Tim Pat Coogan at Wynn's Hotel, in Dublin, on 31 March 2018.[19]

CHAPTER 16

LITTLE ROCK

Operation Harvest, the plan to liberate the six northern counties, began on 12 December 1956 with a series of border attacks. IRA columns of around twenty men crossed the border and attacked specific targets. Under pressure from Britain, the Irish government deployed hundreds of troops and gardaí along the border.[1] On 8 July 1957 the Irish government announced that Part II of the Offences Against the State Act was in force, and internment without trial was invoked. The Curragh Internment Camp, sometimes referred to as Tintown, was reopened. Barbed wire was hastily erected around the old Second World War-era German naval internment camp, adjacent to the Military Detention Barracks. On 8 July 1957 a contingent of military police from the Curragh Camp brought thirty republican prisoners held in Dublin's Bridewell remand centre to the new camp. A further thirty-three men arrested in countrywide sweeps that weekend were also taken to the Curragh. In one go, most of the IRA leadership had been rounded up and jailed – sixty-three men. It was broadly anticipated that this figure would increase as raids for known republicans continued.[2]

The camp consisted of six wooden huts capable of accommo-dating 200 men. The camp was protected by five sets of fences.

Two fences lay between the camp and a six-foot-deep and eight-foot-wide trench, which was booby-trapped with flares and trip-wires. Three more fences had to be surmounted when, and if, this obstacle was negotiated. A raised sentry post guarded each corner of the camp, each manned by armed soldiers around the clock. In addition, guards armed with revolvers and ammonia grenades patrolled the fence perimeter.

Conditions in the camp were better than in the regimes of the 1920s and 1940s. Food was plentiful and could be supplemented by foodstuffs from outside or by meals cooked in the huts on electric rings. Tea could be made constantly using an immersion boiler. Guards opened the huts at 7 a.m., and breakfast was served in the dining hall an hour later. Until they recovered or were sent to the hospital, sick prisoners were given their breakfast in the huts, served by a member of the Legion of Mary. Showers were compulsory, and orderly duty was divided among the internees. Prisoners spent most of their time reading and making wooden Celtic crosses and leather wallets for sale outside the camp to raise funds. A nearby field was made available for Gaelic games.

Each hut had its Officer Commanding, and there was a camp council of prisoners. OC of the prisoners was Thomas (Tomás Óg) MacCurtain, the son of Cork Lord Mayor Thomas MacCurtain shot dead by the RIC in his home in 1920. Four of the huts in the camp were occupied, each housing about thirty internees. At the peak of internment, in June 1958 152 men were interned in the camp.[3]

Escape, of course, preoccupied the minds of many of the prisoners, and on Whit Monday night, 25 May 1958, three internees sawed through the bars on the windows of the bathroom in the camp hospital. They were Vincent Conlon, Drumsollen, Killylea, Co. Armagh; Terry O'Toole, Portarlington, Co. Laois; and John A. Kelly, Ballybough Flats, Dublin. The three men were patients in the special detention ward in the Curragh Military Hospital. They escaped at around 9.30 p.m. by cutting through an iron grating covering a narrow window. There were two military policemen on duty at the time, one outside the ward and one inside with the patients. One of the internees asked to use the bathroom at the end of the ward. He was followed shortly after by the second internee, and then by the third man. Soon after, the military policeman became suspicious, and, when he opened the bathroom door, he found all three had escaped through the window. The water taps had been left running to disguise the sound of sawing through the iron grating, which was forced outwards when sawn through.

The site of the hospital helped in the escape, as once out of the ward the men had only to cross the road to find cover among the trees. After clearing the trees, the escapees were out on the open plains of the Curragh, away from the camp's defences. They headed towards the village of Kilcullen and decided to knock on the door of the first house they came to. Amazingly, this happened to be a republican family, the Conways, living at Yellow Bog, six miles from the camp. They stayed there for the night, too nervous to sleep, and left early the next morning as a huge army and police search party combed the area. Around 6.30 a.m., Conlon and O'Toole were found hiding in a double ditch covered by sacks.[4] Kelly narrowly evaded detection and was captured ten days later, on 6 June, sleeping at a farmhouse at Gormanston, Co. Meath. He was subsequently taken back to the Curragh.[5]

Back in the camp, Terry O'Toole joined a group of four of the most militant prisoners who were planning a mass breakout for two dozen prisoners. The four consisted of Charlie Murphy (Dublin), Joseph 'J.B.' O'Hagen (Lurgan, Co. Armagh), Willie Gleeson (Limerick) and Frank Driver (Ballymore-Eustace, Co. Kildare). Charlie Murphy was Adjutant General of the IRA and one of the chief organisers of the 1956 border campaign. Frank

Driver had been an activist since his early teens, and in 1922 aged sixteen was the Curragh Camp's youngest internee. He had also been interned at the Curragh for several years in the 1940s when the government had jailed around 400 republicans. The camp was divided between militants led by Murphy, who believed it was their duty to escape, and the camp council who frowned on escape attempts, believing it was best to avoid anything that might get someone killed. The camp council had not sanctioned the earlier escape – so the breakout caused dissension between the two groups. Most of the escape group lived in a hut that was known as 'Little Rock' after the organised-crime safe town in Arkansas run by Irish-American gangster Owney Madden.[6]

The escape group was working on a tunnel, but this was discovered by an alert guard who spotted some clay from the tunnel that had been carelessly dumped on a pathway. However, the next escape venture paid off. This escape had the sanction of Tomás Óg MacCurtain and the camp council, which had been pressed into sponsoring the breakout. As a result, they were able to suggest who was to go out. They nominated Daithí Ó Conaill (Cork) and Ruairí Ó Brádaigh (Longford), both veterans of the Brookeborough raid, in which Seán South and Fergal O'Hanlon were killed. Ó Brádaigh had won a seat for Sinn Féin in Longford-Westmeath in the 1957 general election.[7]

When the grass from the playing field was cut, it was put in piles around the edge. Each time the internees were out, they brought in bunches of grass and glued it to a ground sheet. On 24 September, the men went out to play football as usual, bringing the grass-camouflaged ground sheet with them. Under cover of the football match, Noel Kavanagh cut open the bottom of the inner fence for easy access for the planned escape. They put the ground sheet in the corner of the playing field and covered it with more cut grass. Ó Conaill and Ó Brádaigh slipped under the ground sheet, while a group of men stood around to conceal them from the sentries. When it was dark, the two men simply slid under the cut wire and made their way under the outer wire, while back in their hut two dummy beds were made up to throw off a head count. Both escapees made for a rearranged pick-up.[8]

Earlier, Christy Kelly, from Rathangan, Co. Kildare, had been released from his internment on compassionate parole. While at home, he contacted Paddy O'Neill, from Kilbelin, Newbridge, and told him of the impending escape. Paddy O'Neill agreed to meet the escapees in his car at Brownstown Cross, near the Curragh Camp. He was waiting at the rendezvous point when Ó Conaill and Ó Brádaigh rapped on the window. The two hopped into the car, and O'Neill drove them to Athlone, Co. Westmeath, where they were met and spirited away to safe houses. The escapees were not missed until roll call the next morning.[9]

The men in Little Rock were disappointed that none of them had been picked to go out, but the orders for the escape of Ó Conaill and Ó Brádaigh had come from GHQ. Ó Conaill and Ó Brádaigh would later play prominent parts when they resurfaced and formed a revitalised Army Council with Ó Brádaigh as chief of staff.[10] The 'militants' wanted Charlie Murphy and J.B. O'Hagen to escape, so they began planning another breakout, gaining two new recruits, Frank Armstrong and Jimmy Devereux (Limerick). Among those involved in the plot were Mick Kehoe, John Power and Paul Stephens, who were among twenty-two men who had tunnelled to twenty feet from the wall in Mountjoy Prison before their exploits were discovered and their escape attempt foiled. The tunnellers were subsequently transferred to the Curragh.

As a result of Ó Conaill and Ó Brádaigh's escape, the hacksaws used in the making of crafts had been withdrawn, and the only wire-cutting equipment the escape group had was a pair of pliers. Devereux, a fitter by trade, made three wire cutters from lengths of angle iron and a poker taken from the laundry. Despite the fact that there had been a few releases and rumours that the internment camp would close by Easter 1959, Murphy decided to go ahead with a mass breakout. The escape was planned for 1 December 1958, but had to be called off after the Minister for Justice, Oscar Traynor, arrived at the camp and a general stand-to had been ordered. The next day it went ahead as planned. Twenty-six men were to break out, and they were to make their way to Meath, where they would regroup and form an active service unit for action on the border. All the men went to confession the night before the escape.[11]

At about 3 p.m. roughly 100 men were playing football and hurling on the recreation field. Some minutes later, the men began to disperse in groups as if they were selecting teams for further games. Suddenly, some of the internees started a demonstration, shouting and waving their arms, while some others set off smoke bombs under the sentry boxes surrounding the camp. A group of about six seized and held the officer in charge of the guard; further smoke bombs were set off and soon the camp was enveloped in dense smoke. Then, around thirty men rushed the wire fence and four of them cut their way through the first fence before the guards realised what was happening. Sentries on duty tried to stop the rush, and a military policeman, who was watching the match, was pushed aside when he tried to block their path. He drew his revolver and fired two shots, missing the escapees. The guard fired again as the prisoners continued running, hitting one man, Brian Boylan, in the leg. An officer disarmed the policeman as he prepared to fire point blank at the escapees.

Charlie Murphy, who had stayed with Frank Driver at the gap in the wire helping the other men through, ran to Boylan's assistance. The rest of the escapees cleared the second and third fences and reached the trench without further casualties. Here, the guards threw ammonia grenades at them. Blinded by the ammonia, the escapees floundered among the coils of barbed wire as trip flares went off and more shots were fired. Terry O'Toole was shot in the right thigh but kept running. Jim Cullen was also hit and was recaptured. By the time the last fence was reached, the escape group had been halved and the wire cutters were abandoned. The escapees pulled the fence down with their hands and ran across the plain towards Lisieux Stud. Meanwhile, other groups of internees gave the impression that they had wire cutters and converged at different points of the fence, which helped divert attention away from the main escape.

The alarm bells went off at 3.15 p.m. and troops were rushed in lorries to cordon off the area around the camp. As the alarm sounded, a military policeman on a motorcycle sped towards the escapees but missed them and went on towards Brownstown. About 400 troops from the Curragh Camp and the nearby artillery barracks in Kildare Town began follow-up searches. Armoured cars and motorcycles assisted in the search, which was impeded by thick fog. At one stage, the troops thought they had the escapees cornered, and they burned a large section of furze to flush them out, but no one appeared. An Electricity Supply Board truck that failed to stop after being waved down by troops at a checkpoint at Ballymany, near Newbridge, was hit by several bullets, but the driver, who kept going until he reached Newbridge Police Station, was unhurt. As dusk fell the search was temporarily suspended for the regrouping of forces and the arrival of more troops from Dublin.

Meanwhile, the escapees carried out what first aid they could in the nearest cover, a field with a thick ditch that was about a mile away. All the men had cuts. Pat McGirl (Leitrim) was temporarily blinded from the ammonia grenades. Liam Fagan (Dundalk) had been wounded in the knees by shrapnel and could go no further.

First aid had to be abandoned as the pursuing soldiers neared, and McGirl and Fagan were both captured. The rest of the escapees split up – one group heading towards Moone in South Kildare, the others towards Portarlington. Joe Cunningham's group, which headed to Moone, called inadvertently to the house of a republican who was being waked. His widow paused in her grief to arrange safe houses for the men. Terry O'Toole's group – Willie Gleeson, Jimmy Devereux, Gerry Haughian and Dan Donaghy – circled Kildare Town and headed for Portarlington, following a route that took them thirty-five miles instead of the normal eighteen. They reached a friendly house on the outskirts of Portarlington the next morning. O'Toole stayed on to receive treatment for his leg wound, while the others, after a brief rest, were taken to safe houses.

Fourteen men escaped successfully: Vincent Conlon, J. Thompson and J. Ferris (Armagh), Joseph Cunningham (Enniscorthy), Robert Keogh (Galbally, Co. Wexford), Jimmy Devereux and Willie Gleeson (Limerick), Terry O'Toole (Portarlington), Donal O'Shea (Kilgarvan, Co. Kerry), John Joe McGirl (Ballinamore, Co. Leitrim), Dan Donaghy (Co. Down), James McQuaid (Monaghan), Gerry Haughian (Lurgan) and Norman Daly (Lifford, Co. Donegal).

Two of the would-be escapees were wounded by gunshots: Brian Boylan and Jim Cullen (Cavan). An emergency operation was performed on Brian Boylan at the Curragh Military Hospital to remove a bullet. Three others sustained minor injuries from tear gas: Patrick O'Sullivan (Whitehall, Dublin), James Columb (Loughgowna, Co. Cavan) and Pat McGirl (Cambar, Co. Leitrim).

Despite an extensive sweep through Co. Kildare, the failure to catch more of the escapees strengthened the belief that they had had outside help and were assisted once they got clear of the camp. As soon as the alarm was sounded, local republicans came to their aid in the escape. One local republican was known to have led a group of escapees to safety, assisting in carrying the wounded Terry O'Toole. Paddy O'Neill and Christy Kelly went driving around the area hoping to pick up escapees. As their car drew up to a checkpoint, a soldier on duty recognised Kelly as a former internee and called for police backup. O'Neill and Kelly were arrested and held overnight in Newbridge Garda Station, before being released without charge the following morning when there was no evidence to suggest they were involved in the escape.[12]

Most of the escapees remained free. However, in February 1959 escapee Gerard Haughian was arrested at a farmhouse near an arms cache discovered at Maghera, Co. Derry. He was wearing a uniform with a tricolour flash. Haughian was jailed in Northern Ireland.[13] On 7 June 1959 Robert Keogh was captured in a dugout at Omeath, Co. Louth, but, despite extensive questioning in Dundalk Garda Station, he was released the next day, as no weapons were found.[14]

While the escape was a spectacular success, the breakout deepened the split in the IRA, both in the internment camp and the movement throughout the country. For a time, the escapees were ostracised by the movement, but eventually, as the need for experienced and reliable men was a necessity, GHQ overlooked the 'unofficial escape' and reinstated the escapees.[15]

The Fianna Fáil government, however, had decided to end internment and to close the Curragh Camp. There were several reasons for this, but it was mainly the sputtering out of the campaign in the North after the summer operations. Internees began to be released unconditionally in batches. On 15 March 1959 the last twelve internees were released, and the Curragh Internment Camp was closed for good. Among those released were former British Army corporal Frank Skuse, J.B. O'Hagen, and Kildare man Frank Driver, who had held the wire back allowing his comrades to escape in December 1958.[16]

CHAPTER 17

THE CRUMLIN KANGAROOS

The civil-rights movement staged its first protest march, from Coalisland to Dungannon, in August 1968. However, it was the Royal Ulster Constabulary (RUC) attack on the demonstration in Derry on 5 October of that year that led to the descent into violence that left over 3,500 people dead. In August 1969 rioting between Catholics and Protestants at the Apprentice Boys' march escalated into the Battle of the Bogside. The RUC lost control of the city due to a full-scale uprising by the Catholic majority and had to call on the British Army to help to restore order. The violence spread to Belfast to divert attention from the Bogside, which in turn led to British soldiers appearing on the streets of Northern Ireland's capital. Belfast always had higher sectarian tensions than Derry, and Protestant mobs burned 1,800 Catholic families out of their homes. Catholics welcomed the arrival of British soldiers, which brought a temporary respite from the violence. However, relations soon broke down when it was seen that the army was taking the side of loyalists/Protestants. A revitalised IRA had appeared on the streets to protect Catholic communities during the loyalist attacks, and it began to clash with British soldiers. On 9 August 1971 the Northern Ireland (Stormont) government introduced internment to defeat the IRA. The first swoops led to

340 arrests, but almost immediately it was realised that little was going to plan. Resistance to the British Army/RUC increased and violence escalated to new levels. Northern Ireland's jails were soon overcrowded, and internment camps were built at Magilligan, outside Derry, and at Long Kesh, near Lisburn.[1]

No building has symbolised Belfast's dark history more than Crumlin Road Gaol. The brooding Victorian structure was built in 1846, designed by renowned architect Sir Charles Lanyon. It had a central area called the circle with four wings branching out in a radial cellular system. Modelled on London's Pentonville Prison, it was the first jail in Ireland to use the 'silence and separation' approach, where there was only one prisoner per cell. There was also a rule of silence, and prisoners were hooded when outside their cells. The idea was to keep prisoners isolated from each other, and so it was one of the most advanced prisons of its day. A more 'humane' regime was introduced later, when it was seen that this system did nothing to reform inmates. Its prison graveyard contains the remains of sixteen former inmates who were hanged, including IRA volunteer Tom Williams, executed for his part in the killing of an RUC constable at Easter 1942.

In addition to the jail, a courthouse, also designed by Charles Lanyon, was built on the other side of the road, and was completed in 1850. The jail and courthouse were linked by a tunnel, so the prisoners were led to the courthouse without having to go outside for their trial or to be sentenced.[2]

By 1971 the jail, known as 'the Crum', held 860 inmates, mostly due to the outbreak of the 'Troubles'. Political prisoners were held on C Wing, sometimes with two and three to what used to be a one-man cell. The prison conditions became so bad, republican Terence 'Cleaky' Clarke said darkly, 'The Crum is so bad it would put you off going to jail.' It was, by the 1970s, an old prison, overcrowded and unable to cope in any positive way with its increasing number of inmates. As part of a protracted campaign for segregation, republican and loyalist prisoners had agreed to exercise separately on alternate days. As only one hour's exercise was permitted, it meant prisoners were on almost total lock-up in their cells. Their only breaks were that brief exercise period and other short excursions into the wing for slopping out, washing, and collecting meals and food parcels sent in from outside.[3]

Republican prisoners in Crumlin Road Gaol were organised as 4th Battalion, Belfast Brigade, with a battalion staff, public-relations officer, education officer, training officer – and an escape committee. The last named met secretly once a week to develop escape techniques. By the 1970s the 'Crum'– despite it being one of the most secure and heavily guarded prisons in Europe – had witnessed some dramatic escapes. The first attempt was made in September 1970, when five republican prisoners, using ropes made of sheets to which were tied hooks from the metal struts of two tables, succeeded in getting on top of the outside wall, during a football match. The escape had been timed to coincide with an explosion outside the wall, but this backfired when the men heard a nail bomb go off on the Antrim Road. They mistook this for the signal and climbed to the top of the wall. However, the would-be escapees were confronted by several armed British soldiers, who had coincidentally been alerted by the explosion. The five men jumped back down and mingled with the prisoners, who were restraining the prison warders. An immediate investigation to determine the identity of the five would-be escapees was prevented, when all the men in C Wing threw their sheets out onto the landing in a pile so that the escapees could not be identified.[4]

It was over a year before republicans would successfully escape from the prison in what was the first major jailbreak of the period. Twenty-one-year-old Christy Keenan had been arrested in October 1971 and had only been in Crumlin Road Gaol for four weeks when he was asked by the republican prisoners' OC if he wanted to escape. 'I thought it was a joke, a set-up and said, "Of course". The escape was brought forward, as one IRA volunteer came in on Thursday and went back out on Tuesday. He was facing a murder charge.' The plan was for the eleven men to escape while the prisoners were playing football. Keenan said, 'OC, I can't play football. Never kicked a ball in my life ...', he laughed, 'I was [made] centre forward!'[5]

During the exercise period on the morning of 16 November 1971, two teams of republicans began playing a game of football on one of the recreation fields near the rear of the prison. The teams were in green jerseys and blue jerseys, while dozens of prisoners stood in civilian clothes around the pitch watching the game. At 11.10 a.m., two rope ladders were thrown over the wall near some sheds at the Clifton Park Avenue side. At the blow of a whistle, eleven men dressed in football jerseys and shorts ran to the wall. 'All anxiety lifted,' Keenan said. 'An automatic sense takes over. I ran across a ploughed field in a cold November. Your legs felt like lead. You overcome it. One of the team grabbed the screw and held him back. It wasn't haphazard, it was well organised. A remand prisoner from 1st Battalion set it all up.'

Most of the men began climbing one of the rope ladders, and Christy Keenan said there were so many men on the rope ladder they began to pull over those on the outside holding their end of the rope. 'Nobody had seen the other ladder,' he said. Fifteen men had been designated to hold back the prison warders. Although outnumbered, the warders managed to regain control of the situation. Nine men eventually climbed the two rope ladders, dropped over the wall and went out through a hole cut in the perimeter fence earlier by IRA volunteers posing as workmen. Two cars were seen to approach the prison wall from the Clifton Park Avenue side. When the nine escapees piled into the two vehicles, they found a change of clothes for each of them. Christy Keenan said, 'There was a full set of clothes for everyone … the driver was very calm, cool. "Take the football gear off and put the clothes on," he said. Not everyone got out. One didn't.' Two of those designated to escape were left behind. One of them was Seán Convery. He would soon get his chance.[6]

However, the prison authorities claimed that they had stopped a further sixteen men from escaping, and that two prison officers were slightly injured when they stepped in and blocked their way. 'Screws made only half-hearted attempts to stop us,' one unnamed escapee later said.[7] To cover the security failure, the authorities said that twenty-five men were meant to escape, but the fact that only two getaway cars were provided belies this claim.

Roadblocks were set up around the city within minutes of the escape. Meanwhile, after the breakout, the remaining prisoners were put back in their cells and prison staff held a roll call. All visitors were told to leave, and those arriving were turned away. The nine escapees were all from Belfast. They were: Séamus Storey (18), Annalee Street; Thomas Maguire (28), Norglen Road; Peter Hennessy (21), Quadrant Street; Bernard Elliman (26), Ballycastle Street; Thomas Fox (31), Ladybrook Drive; Thomas Kane (23), Whitehall Road; Terence 'Cleaky' Clarke (24), Etna Drive; Daniel Mullan (17), Oakfield Street; and Christopher Keenan (21), Anderson Street. One escapee was on remand for attempted murder, while the rest had been charged with firearms and explosive offences.[8]

Christy Keenan and three other escapees were brought to a safe house in north Belfast, where they stayed with a married couple and their young children. On the following day, Christy Keenan and Daniel Mullan were picked up at a nearby chapel and given clerical garb. 'We got priests' clothes, not monks' clothing, right down to the underwear,' Keenan said. Three cars drove towards the border on Thursday night, 18 November. 'There was a scout car ahead, and two cars with two escapees in each. I was in the front; Danny Mullan in the back.'

As the convoy headed towards the border, the cars stopped at a red light near Omagh, Co. Tyrone. Keenan said, 'As the light went green three RUC men stepped out in front of our car, as the two other cars drove through.'[9] A prison officer from Crumlin Road Gaol identified Keenan and Mullan as escapees and they were detained.

Two Cistercian monks, Father Thomas O'Neill and Brother Patrick Joseph Skehan, along with several local businessmen, were subsequently charged with aiding and abetting the escapees. The monks were from Our Lady of Bethlehem Cistercian Monastery at Portglenone, Co. Antrim, which was later raided and searched by troops and police. Nothing was found. Fr O'Neill and Br Skehan were later fined £250 and £500 respectively for the offence.

The other seven escapees successfully made it across the border and six of them appeared at a press conference at the Kevin Street headquarters of Sinn Féin, in Dublin. During the conference, an RTÉ film crew recorded in sound and film an interview in which veteran republican Daithi O'Connell was talking to escapee Bernard Elliman. However, the interview was later banned by the station under the Ministerial Order banning IRA publicity which had been made on 1 October 1971. RTÉ also turned down a BBC request for the film, although a film of the news conference was shown with the report on national television.[10]

The escape caught the imagination of the Irish public, and, shortly after the jailbreak, the Wolfhound folk group recorded the now-famous 'Crumlin Kangaroos' ballad, which became an instant hit in Ireland and among the Irish abroad. Another ballad, 'Over the Wall', by the Dublin City Ramblers was just as popular.

There was further embarrassment a month later, in November 1971, when Seán Hanna (Henrietta Street, Belfast) walked out the front gates of Crumlin Road Gaol. Hanna had just finished a two-month sentence and was to be brought to court to appear on an explosives charge, but by a complete stroke of luck it had been overlooked that Hanna was on remand for this charge. However, two of his accomplices, James Goodman and Arthur Maguire, were jailed for a total of eighteen years, while another, Anthony Lundy, who was acquitted of the charge, was rearrested under the Special Powers Act. Hanna disappeared completely and was believed to be in hiding in the Republic. As a result of these two escapes, the Stormont government announced that security was being tightened.[11]

Two weeks later, an even more embarrassing escape was made. Martin Meehan and Tony 'Dutch' Doherty, two of the most wanted local IRA volunteers, were picked up by British troops. Both were severely beaten up in Palace Military Barracks. They were moved to Crumlin Road Gaol in the last week of November. On 2 December the prison authorities got a phone call from the press about an escape. Reporters had asked some people in Ardoyne why bonfires had been lit and were told that it was because Meehan and Doherty and another republican, Hugh McCann, had escaped; could the prison authorities confirm this, the reporters asked. The authorities were stunned. It was the first they had heard of it. A check was made, and the claim confirmed. Meehan, Doherty and McCann were, indeed, missing from their cells. In fact, Meehan and McCann had crossed the border before the prison authorities even knew they had escaped. Doherty stayed behind to take care of some business and, unhurried, crossed over the next week. For five hours they had hidden, uncomfortably, in a manhole in the exercise yard, up to their knees in water, until the rest of the prisoners had gone in from exercise. Then, under the cover of darkness and a thick fog, they went over the prison wall, using a rope of knotted blankets and sheets. Their comrades on the inside wrecked the normal head count by staging an 'incident' – a pretend fight that kept the warders busy until 'all' prisoners were in their cells. The three prisoners made their escape when the prison fell silent after lock-up.

A furious prime minister, Brian Faulkner, ordered an inquiry into prison security. Crumlin Road Gaol was leaking like a sieve, and as Faulkner announced that Sir Charles Cunningham was being called in to conduct a review of the security arrangements at the prison, the escapees were conducting a news conference in Dublin. Faulkner's administration staggered on through the rest of 1971, but, in March 1972, was replaced by direct rule from London.[12]

CHAPTER 18

THE MAGNIFICENT SEVEN

Seán Convery was one of the would-be escapees left behind in the Crumlin Road jailbreak of 16 November 1971. Due to overcrowding, and maybe because he was wearing football gear on the morning of the Crumlin Road escape, Convery was transferred by helicopter to the British prison ship HMS *Maidstone*, which was moored on Belfast Lough. On the night of 17 January 1972 Convery was one of seven republican internees who escaped from the *Maidstone* and swam to freedom. The escapees achieved fame in news headlines across the world as 'The Magnificent Seven'.

After the introduction of internment on 9 August 1971 it was found that Crumlin Road Gaol and Long Kesh prison camp were unable to cope with the huge amount of internees. HMS *Maidstone*, a former British warship docked at the coal wharf in Belfast Docks, was hastily and crudely adapted as a prison ship. The prison itself was at the stern of the ship and consisted of two bunkhouses and two messrooms. At the time, 124 men were held there in cramped and inhumane conditions, where prospects for even the most basic of needs, like exercise, were virtually non-existent.[1]

None of the internees were happy with their new accommodation, and some began planning their escape immediately. A small group of them – Martin Taylor, Tommy 'Tucker' Kane, Tommy Gorman and Peter Rogers – had noticed a seal swimming through the ring of barbed wire that surrounded the ship, and they figured that the gap was also sufficient to allow a human through. They began throwing scraps of food to the seal, tempting him to come close to test the guards' alertness. The prisoners also tossed tin cans and plastic bottles overboard to monitor the movements of the current around the ship. Word came through from outside that top IRA men Jim Bryson and Tommy 'Todler' Tolan, from Ballymurphy, were to be given a chance to escape, and they were brought into the equation.[2]

Jim Bryson had moved to Ballymurphy with his wife and son after being burned out of their home at Excise Street. He had a reputation as a fearless activist, and, after having been arrested, he single-handedly fought free from a British Army Saracen armoured car, using only his fists.[3] Another Belfast man, Seán Convery, was also brought on to the escape team. A few months earlier, Convery had stayed behind fighting off the prison warders to ensure that his comrades – who had jumped over the wall at Crumlin Road Gaol – got away safely. For this honour, it was decided that he should also be given a chance to escape.

The plan was first to camouflage their bodies with boot polish and butter to insulate them from the cold water. They would then saw through a steel bar in the ship's porthole and climb down the ship's steel cable into the water. They had to avoid both the barbed wire surrounding the ship and the beam of the sentry's searchlight on deck. After that, they would swim to the other side of the harbour where cars would be waiting to pick them up. In preparation for the escape, the men acclimatised themselves for their gruelling swim by taking ice-cold showers. Hacksaws were smuggled into the prison and were used to saw most of the way through the bar on the porthole where the men would make their exit. They had timed exactly how long it would take to saw through the other half, so on the appointed night, it would be just a matter of finishing the job.

A new internment camp had also been opened at Magilligan, near Limavady, Co. Derry, and when fifty internees were transferred there on 15 January, the would-be escapees from the *Maidstone* had to urgently move their daring escape plan forward. The escape was planned for shortly after 5.30 p.m. on 17 January, but then things began to go wrong. A delay in the nightly head count of internees by guards caused the escape to go twenty-five minutes behind schedule. This was the time designated to swim to the other side of the docks, where the escapees were to rendezvous with the IRA getaway drivers waiting to take them to safe houses. The delay meant that the crucial meeting never took place. By 4.55 p.m., each of the seven had blackened his entire body with boot polish and butter, except for their hands and head. The rest of their bodies and their underpants were also blackened immediately after the head count.

Aware they were running late and that everything needed to be on time, the seven men made their way out through the porthole. Wearing only their underwear and with socks on their hands, the men slid down the ship's hawser one-by-one. This brought them just barely over the surrounding ring of barbed wire. They dropped into the freezing waters, cutting themselves on the barbed wire as they did so. However, because of the sub-zero temperature no one felt the barbed wire cuts until later. They waited in the water until all had emerged from the porthole, and they then set off on the 400-yard swim across the Musgrave Channel to the nearby power station. As they swam away from the ship, they could see the army sentry on the deck.[4]

Peter Rogers said:

I climbed out the porthole with help from my comrades. I grabbed and then climbed onto the hawser ... We wore socks over our hands to protect our skin from being cut by the hawser steel rope as we slid down it into the water. To my surprise it was the smoothest of steel ropes. I gently and effortlessly slid down the rope into the water. As I did so I found five pairs of discarded socks floating around. The mixture of boot polish and butter had very effectively waterproofed our skins. The polish irritated our skins, causing heat, which the butter then insulated within our bodies. I hardly felt the cold as I entered the water.[5]

As well as the cold, there was the fear of being nipped by the seals that frequented the area or being caught by the Royal Marines who patrolled the harbour in boats. The plan was for each man to swim the breaststroke so as not to splash and make noise, but Martin Taylor recalled, 'as most of us got across any form of swimming took over. You're exhausted. It was freezing, and I know that I was only too glad to do the front crawl when I got close.'

Several of the men got into difficulty and had to be helped by their comrades. Seán Convery was not a strong swimmer, but he made it, with the help of his friends. He said, 'About halfway, I too felt I wasn't going to make it. My strength seemed to give way and I thought I'd had it. I shouted for help and some of the others came and swam alongside me until we reached the other side.' Another prisoner, Peter Rogers, said he had nearly given up hope at one stage. 'I prayed so hard I even invented a few new saints,' he said afterwards.[6]

Peter Rogers also ran into difficulty. He said:

The current was too strong, my arms were tired and I was getting weaker. I turned over on my back and floated for a while and did the back paddle. Water then seeped into my right ear, which had been damaged by the RUC during interrogation in Holywood Barracks some weeks before. I then developed a sharp pain in my ear. So I'm shaking my head to get the water out of my ear to ease the pain while I am trying to swim. And then I thought I saw a ship coming towards me. I soon forgot the earache and resumed swimming. The phantom ship turned out to be a buoy, but the fright gave me the spur I needed. It took away that moment of doubt. Todler joined me as I approached the pier. We tried to climb up it but it was too dark and we cut ourselves to pieces on the barnacles. Fortunately, we found another opening. But there was no time to dally. We had to get to our pick up. We met up with the rest of the lads hiding in the dark shadows. Some of them had lost their underpants in the swim. They were naked.[7]

They found they had landed 500 yards down from the agreed rendezvous point and were twenty minutes late. Their getaway drivers, fearing the operation had been cancelled, had long since dispersed. The men hid near the power station for a few minutes, mainly to avoid being spotted by British patrols. They had seen three Saracens in the vicinity around 4.30 p.m. while they were still on the ship. Agreeing that they needed alternative transport, the seven men made their way to a nearby car park. Jim Bryson and Peter Rogers broke into a car and, after failing to 'hot-wire' it, took whatever they could find. Bryson found a bowler hat and an umbrella, while Rogers wrapped a rug around himself to keep warm.[8]

Bryson and Rogers met up with the other escapees, and the group made their way stealthily along the pier towards the Queens Road bus terminus, with the intention of commandeering a bus.

Tommy Gorman, wet, filthy and shivering, and clad only in his underpants, entered the busmen's hut. He told the driver of a bus, which was parked outside, that he had fallen into the Musgrave Channel and had to strip off his clothes as they were dragging him down. The busman put his overcoat around Gorman, who then ran out of the hut. Before disappearing, Gorman stopped briefly to throw money and other contents from the coat pockets back towards the busman.

Peter Rogers, formerly employed as a bus driver, knew the routes and time schedules. The escapees' original intention had been to commandeer the bus, but it was decided to wait for the next one because of the commotion caused by stealing the coat. They waited twenty minutes for the bus to return from doing its round. When it got back, the driver got out and headed towards the security hut to report the loss of his coat. The seven escapees darted out of hiding and boarded the bus. Peter Rogers took the wheel of the double-decker and revved up the engine to a high pitch to build up enough air in the brakes for the engine to engage. Alerted by the engine starting up, the bus driver and a security guard came running over. As they neared the bus, two of the men rushed out, and one of them, Tucker Kane, punched the security man, who fell into the arms of the bus driver. The bus took off at breakneck speed, desperately trying to make the dock gates before they would be closed following the inevitable alert. They made it just in time. A security man had run out to close the gates, and, as he saw the bus approaching, he desperately tried to wave it down but the bus careered past him.

The road was clear, so the men easily spotted a security Land Rover in pursuit. They decided to head for the Markets area of Belfast to dump the bus and seek help. The bus zigzagged across the road to prevent the Land Rover catching up with them, while the men were shouting at Rogers, letting him know which side the

Land Rover was trying to overtake them on. Rogers successfully manoeuvred the bus, which was automatic, despite the difficulty of having to use the accelerator and brake with bare, frozen and slippery feet.

Rogers drove into Cromac Square practically on two wheels and manoeuvred the bus into Verner Street beside a local bar. He said, 'It was a tight squeeze, like putting a cork into a bottleneck. Our pursuers left us, afraid to venture into the area.' The seven men piled into the bar. Punters were in shock, looking at seven-near naked strangers standing in front of them, one with a bowler hat on, another with a busman's coat and another with a rug. One escapee shouted, 'IRA, we need your help. We escaped off the *Maidstone*. We need clothes.'

Jackets and overcoats were quickly given to the escapees, and someone handed over the keys of their car. Within minutes they were off again, piled into the car – four in the back, three in the front – with Tommy Gorman driving. At one stage in the journey, Gorman said, 'I'll stop for some petrol.' They all burst out laughing. That was the mood. They travelled through loyalist areas to safe houses in Andersonstown, where they were split up into different houses. They watched the nine o'clock news with great delight, and laughed as Colonel Budd, of the Royal Horse Artillery, told the media that he was confident the escapees were still in the Markets area and that he would have them back on the *Maidstone* by midday the following day. The next day the men were moved from their safe houses across the border to freedom.[9]

On 24 January the seven escapees appeared at a press conference organised by Sinn Féin at Power's Hotel, Kildare Street, Dublin, to announce details of the escape to the world. The men were quickly dubbed 'The Magnificent Seven'.[10]

The following September escapee Jim Bryson was arrested again and charged with possession of a handgun. He was held in

Long Kesh and then taken to Crumlin Road Gaol. On the morning of his trial, 22 February 1973, Bryson staged a spectacular escape. While being escorted to Crumlin Road Courthouse through the underground tunnel that connects the jail with the courthouse, Bryson produced a small .25 pistol, and he and another prisoner stripped the prison guards of their uniforms. They then casually walked through the courthouse towards freedom, but Bryson's accomplice was apprehended. Bryson made it outside, discarded his uniform, headed for the Shankill Road, and hitched a lift from two unsuspecting off-duty Ulster Defence Regiment (UDR) soldiers who thought they were running a mercy mission to the Royal Victoria Hospital. From then on Bryson was a seriously wanted man. On 31 August 1973 he was mortally wounded and a fellow volunteer, Paddy Mulvenna, shot dead by a British Army sniper hidden in the roof space of a building in Ballymurphy's Bullring. Bryson died three weeks later, on 22 September.[11]

Tucker Kane died in a horrific car accident on the Glen Road, West Belfast, in July 1976 while on IRA active service.[12] Todler Tolan was captured a second time and sent to the Cages in Long Kesh. Released in 1975, he remained an active volunteer until he was shot dead during a feud between the Provisional IRA and the Official IRA, on 27 July 1977. He had just returned from his honeymoon with his wife of two weeks, when he was ambushed outside his home.[13]

Peter Rogers later settled in Knocktown, Duncormick, Co. Wexford. He remained in the IRA, and on 13 October 1980 was transporting explosives in his van when gardaí, investigating a bank robbery in neighbouring Co. Kilkenny, appeared. Detective Gardaí Seamus Quaid and Donal Lyttleton recognised the vehicle. In an ensuing shoot-out, Rogers was shot in the foot, while Detective Garda Quaid was shot dead. Rogers was captured the following morning at a nearby house. He was sentenced to life imprisonment in Portlaoise Prison, but was released in 1998 under the terms of the Good Friday Agreement after serving eighteen years. Rogers later left the IRA, apologised to Seamus Quaid's family, and refused to return to his homeplace in Wexford, opting to move back to Northern Ireland.[14]

CHAPTER 19

UNDER AND OVER, UP AND OVER

Dublin's Mountjoy Prison was always the main prison in the Republic, and in 1972 accommodated nearly 400 prisoners. Of these, thirty-five men were republicans who were located on B2 landing in the prison's B wing. The republican prisoners – Provisional and Official IRA – had been agitating for some time for better conditions, in particular for a move to a prison separate from what they termed 'common criminals'. On 18 May 1972, when most of the prisoners in three wings of Mountjoy Prison were being locked up, the republican prisoners in the remand wing overpowered three prison officers and took possession of their keys. The prisoners wrenched a cell door from its hinges, and in an attempt to escape rammed the door through a large window at the end of their landing. They could not proceed further, as more prison officers arrived on the scene. However, the disturbance spread to the entire prison, resulting in systematic destruction of cell doors, cell furniture and bedding, toilet bowls and wash-hand basins. A newly fitted dental surgery and much of a new kitchen were wrecked. The prison roof was also extensively damaged. The riot was encouraged by about 1,000 republican supporters outside the prison. It took 200 soldiers and several hundred gardaí to bring the riots under control.[1]

As a direct consequence, the republican prisoners were moved the next day to the Curragh Camp, where the government had recently spent £200,000 on security and infrastructure upgrades to the Military Detention Barracks. The Curragh was chosen in the likely expectation that its remoteness would preclude riots such as that outside Mountjoy. However, within weeks a major clash took place on the Curragh Plains. Again, it was prisoner grievance – the denial of parole to a Belfast prisoner who was due to be married – which led to the disturbances. On 9 July 1972 a peaceful demonstration of 2,000 people, organised by Provisional Sinn Féin and People's Democracy, degenerated into a full-scale riot, involving around 200 breakaway demonstrators, gardaí and riot-gear-clad soldiers. This was the first time such troops had been deployed in the Republic. The crowd set fire to a building at the Curragh complex and attacked the troops and gardaí with petrol bombs, fireworks and stones. An army baton charge eventually dispersed the crowd.[2]

Things were about to get worse for the government. On 29 October 1972 seven IRA men escaped from the Military Detention Barracks at the Curragh Camp through a tunnel. Some prisoners who had been recently discharged from the detention barracks were instrumental in laying the groundwork, and they later coordinated well-timed transport arrangements. One of the prisoners was Eddie Gallagher, who had been arrested in Pettigo, Donegal, by gardaí after his unit bombed UDR man Mervyn Johnston's garage across the border in Tullyhommon, Co. Fermanagh. He was an experienced tunneller, having worked on some projects in England. Fellow republicans in the Curragh Military Prison asked Gallagher to put his tunnelling skills to use. Eddie had three others with him on his team: Joe O'Connell, who would later become part of the

Balcombe Street Unit in England; Joe Coughlan, Tullamore; and Thomas Dignam, Clara, Co. Offaly. Together, they started sinking a shaft in the cell of an Official IRA member.[3]

The cell from which the tunnel led to the compound had a wooden floor. This helped the tunnellers escape the attention of the prison guards. The flooring in the cell was well above ground level, and the tunnellers stowed the excavated material from the tunnel out of sight under the floor. On 29 October 1972 the tunnel was ready. The escape, which was carried out with precision timing, saw the seven men emerge from the tunnel entrance at 6.45 p.m. With makeshift ropes made from sheets and blankets, they scaled two high walls that were topped with barbed-wire entanglements. During this dash, they overpowered an unarmed military policeman who spotted the escape. They tied and gagged him, before running clear of the heavily guarded military camp to waiting cars which whisked them away to safe houses. The duty officer prevented four other unnamed prisoners from escaping.

Four of the seven escapees were from Northern Ireland. They were Thomas McGrath and Patrick Carty (Coalisland, Co. Tyrone), James Hazlett (Dungiven, Co. Derry) and Colm Murphy (Belleek, Co. Fermanagh). The rest were from the Republic: Michael McVerry (Dundalk, Co. Louth), Chris Murphy (Rathbane, Limerick) and James McCabe (Rathfarnham, Dublin). Five of the escapees were Provisional IRA men.[4] Within a year Michael McVerry and Patrick Carty were killed in attacks on British forces. Michael McVerry was mortally wounded in an attack on an RUC barracks at Keady, Co. Armagh, on 15 November 1973. Patrick Carty and two other volunteers, Dermot Crowley and Seán Loughran, were killed when a bomb they were transporting in a car near Omagh exploded prematurely on 25 June 1973.[5]

After the successful escape, the army claimed in its defence that the Military Detention Barracks was under Department of

Justice Regulations, and this was why the military policeman was unarmed and easily overpowered. The Department of Justice retorted that the Military Detention Barracks was completely under the control of the defence forces. Meanwhile, a massive nationwide search took place with troops, gardaí, detectives and tracker dogs. Uniformed police and detectives called to people of known republican sympathies in Kildare and west Wicklow, but none of the men were found.[6]

Eddie Gallagher served three months of his four-month sentence and was then released. He went back to England to a tunnelling job in Tunbridge Wells, Kent. Later that year, Gallagher met heiress Rose Dugdale in London.[7]

At noon on 31 October 1973 an IRA volunteer using the name 'Mr Leonard', and wearing a white suit and imitating an American accent, arrived at the Westpoint Hangar at Dublin Airport to take a flight in a five-seater Alouette II helicopter. The 'American film director' had earlier phoned Irish Helicopters Ltd and said he needed a helicopter and pilot to fly over Co. Laois to take some landscape shots. Captain Thompson Boyes, who had only been a month with the company, was detailed to take Mr Leonard to Stradbally, Co. Laois, at 1.30 p.m. to photograph ancient monuments. The helicopter had seen service in the French Air Force, after which President Charles de Gaulle had presented it to the wife of the South Vietnamese leader, President Thieu. The South Vietnamese later sold the helicopter to Irish Helicopters Ltd.

As requested by Mr Leonard, Capt. Boyes landed the helicopter in a field beside a farmhouse at Dunamase, near Stradbally, to pick up some photographic equipment. On landing, the unsuspecting pilot saw two masked men coming out of the trees in front of him, one armed with a revolver and the other carrying an Armalite rifle. Mr Leonard exited the helicopter as the two armed men, one of them later identified as Brendan Hughes (Tyrone), climbed on board. One said, 'We're the IRA. We are going to Mountjoy Jail to pick up three prisoners.' The IRA volunteers produced a Dublin street map and ordered the pilot to fly to the city, directing him to follow the path of the Royal Canal and railway lines, and not to register his flight path with air-traffic control.[8]

Capt. Boyes later said to reporters, 'They told me that if I fouled up they would put a bullet through me.'

Nothing more was said during the flight. As Boyes entered the Dublin area, he dropped his helicopter height to 700 feet and approached the prison from the rear. The helicopter made an initial pass over the prison before it touched down in the centre of the compound outside D Wing just after 3.30 p.m.[9] At the time there were 372 prisoners in Mountjoy, of which 88 were Provisional IRA and 10 were Official IRA volunteers. As the helicopter approached, there were twenty-three Provisionals in the exercise yard being supervised by thirteen prison officers. At this stage, because of the arrival of the helicopter, alarms had been activated in the prison, but the containment plans had simply not considered an aerial escape.[10]

Kevin Mallon, an IRA activist since the 1950s' campaign, had been arrested a few months earlier after a spate of armed robberies in the south of Ireland and was incarcerated in Portlaoise Prison. He devised the daring plan, which was undertaken by another top activist, Brendan Hughes, from Ardboe, Co. Tyrone. Informed of the plot in advance, several IRA prisoners worked to restrain nearby warders, while others hustled Kevin Mallon; Séamus Twomey, Chief of Staff of the IRA; and J.B. O'Hagen, his adjutant, on board the aircraft. The occupants prevented a fourth prisoner, Gerry O'Hare (Belfast), from getting on board, as he had not been designated to escape. It took two minutes for the entire operation, which had been clearly minutely planned.[11]

One prison officer on duty initially took no action, as he believed the helicopter contained the Minister for Defence, Paddy Donegan. The other warders realised what was happening too late, and fights broke out as they realised an escape attempt was in progress. A legendary story emerged of a warder shouting to close the gates as the helicopter flew away.

Capt. Boyes felt slight panic as the helicopter took off with its extra passengers, as he recalled that he also had no extra fuel on board. He said that at one stage he told the hijackers that the overloaded helicopter would not make it, but he was ordered to proceed. The aircraft, luckily, managed to clear the prison walls. It was supposed to land at a pitch-and-putt course owned by a republican sympathiser in south Dublin. However, the owner was sick, and the helicopter subsequently landed at the disused Baldoyle Racecourse in north Co. Dublin. Here a gruff Kevin Mallon turned to his rescuer Brendan Hughes and said, 'Well done as usual, but you were fuckin' late!'[12]

A getaway car, a taxi that had been hijacked in Dublin city centre by members of the IRA's Dublin Brigade, was waiting. Capt. Boyes was ordered to remain where he was for five minutes while the escapees were spirited away. The getaway car was abandoned at nearby Portmarnock. After five minutes, Capt. Boyes flew back to his base, a mere three minutes away, where he raised the alarm.[13]

Back in Mountjoy, the republican prisoners continued to run around the exercise yard to confuse the prison officers, who were attempting to carry out a head count to discover the identities of the escapees. Éamonn Mac Thomáis, Officer Commanding the republican prisoners, eventually held a parade in the yard and addressed the men. He said he had been informed by the prison authorities that a helicopter had landed in the yard and that a number of prisoners had escaped. 'I didn't see a helicopter, and this being Halloween, the prisoners that escaped must have gone out on witches' broomsticks.' Mac Thomáis continued, 'I don't see who is missing but the prison authorities want to do a head count, which necessitates all men going to their cells.' A count was carried out as the men filed inside, and it was discovered that three prisoners were missing. Their identities were only confirmed after a cell check.

A classically downbeat IRA statement referred to the Mountjoy escape at the end of a list of operations against the British forces: 'Three republican prisoners were rescued by a special unit from Mountjoy Prison on Wednesday. The operation was a complete success and the men are now safe, despite a massive hunt by Free State forces.' The defence forces and gardaí launched a massive manhunt for the escapees. In Dublin over 300 gardaí searched hundreds of homes in a vain attempt to track down the escapees. Within two days of his release, Twomey was back as Director of Operations for the North. Twomey gave an exclusive interview with Germany's *Der Spiegel* magazine shortly after his escape. Throughout Europe the exploit was termed, 'the escape of the century'.[14]

The helicopter escape was a massive publicity boost for the IRA and was a huge embarrassment to the Irish coalition government, led at the time by Fine Gael's Liam Cosgrave. It had been planned meticulously, and the three escapees had been selected because of their high profile within the media rather than men who were serving longer sentences. The primary purpose was to embarrass the Fine Gael/Labour coalition, which had boasted the previous year that their government was having greater success than the British in crushing the republican movement. An emergency debate on security was held in the Dáil on 1 November. Jack Lynch, leader of the opposition, stated:

> It is poetic justice that a helicopter is now at the heart of the government's embarrassment and in the centre of

their dilemma. Indeed, it was hard to blame the prison officer who observed that he thought it was the Minister for Defence paying an informal visit to Mountjoy Prison because, of course, we all know the Minister for Defence is [wont] to use helicopters, as somebody observed already, as other Ministers are [wont] to use State cars.[15]

Quick to celebrate the escape, Seán McGinley wrote 'Up and away' (The Helicopter Song), which became a No. 1 hit for the Wolfe Tones rebel band. RTÉ immediately banned the song from being played by its stations However, the song sold 12,000 copies in the first week it was released, only being knocked off the top spot by Slade's 'Merry Christmas Everybody'.[16]

On 13 November 1973 Brendan Hughes was arrested at a flat in Rathmines, Dublin, and jailed for three years for his part in the escape. Kevin Mallon was subsequently recaptured following an appearance at a GAA dance near Portlaoise on 10 December 1973.[17] J.B. O'Hagen was also quickly recaptured, but Séamus Twomey remained free, only being arrested in Dublin four years later on 2 December 1977.

The helicopter escape resulted in all IRA prisoners held at Mountjoy Prison and the Curragh Camp being transferred to the maximum security Portlaoise Prison on 9 November 1973. However, the change of location only brought a temporary respite. More trouble, and prison escapes, lay ahead.[18]

CHAPTER 20

REDUX: NINETEEN MEN ARE MISSING

In 1973 the Irish government decided to transfer 120 republican prisoners to the newly converted top-security Portlaoise Prison, where armed soldiers from the defence forces, gardaí and prison officers guarded them around the clock. This decision came in the wake of two significant events – the 1972 summer riots at the Curragh and the helicopter escape of Mallon, Twomey and O'Hagen from Mountjoy Prison in October 1973. Minister for Justice Paddy Cooney had previously insisted that there was no internment-by-remand system in the Republic, and the Curragh Camp would be used for detaining only a handful of prisoners while those sentenced would need to be jailed elsewhere. In March 1973 the prisoners' OC, Dan Hoban (Mayo), and Adjutant Martin McGuinness (Derry) signed a statement condemning the prison facilities at the Curragh. Two months later, 1,000 relatives and supporters of the prisoners demonstrated at the camp.[1]

Republican prisoners were housed in E Block, a four-floor structure over a basement at Portlaoise Prison. Inmates were allowed to wear their own clothes, to associate at given times and to do prison work that suited them, like kitchen and orderly duties.

The prison authorities gave implicit recognition to the command structure of the various republican groups. In May 1974, gardaí discovered an elaborate eighty-foot tunnel being dug from outside Portlaoise Prison. It started in the shrubbery in the grounds of the psychiatric hospital opposite the prison and stretched under a road and a row of cottages, and was to emerge in the prison yard through a manhole. Inside the tunnel were found hacksaws, axes, crowbars, spades, buckets, ropes and a trolley. The prisoners were undeterred, and almost immediately began plans for a more daring escape operation. Nineteen men serving long prison sentences were selected to escape in mid-August.[2]

A member of the IRA escape committee spotted a weakness in the jail security in the area of the prison where the laundry house was situated. The laundry led to an outside stairway and down into the courtyard, where the governor's house and warders' mess were located. Prisoners discovered that they could gain access to the laundry area quite easily. It was a doorway at the top of the courtyard that led out onto the streets of Portlaoise Town itself that gave the prisoners hope that their plan would work.

The escape committee decided that they needed explosives to get through this gate, and they sent word outside to this effect. On the outside, the IRA agreed that the plan was viable, and smuggled in the explosives needed: gelignite hidden in 'Lucky Numbers' sweet wrappers. Tunneller Eddie Gallagher, recently released from the Curragh Military Detention Barracks, arrived in Portlaoise to lead a team ready to help republicans escape from the prison. The prisoners were waiting for a signal to say that they were about to escape. Gallagher and his team had a line of getaway cars waiting, and had designated safe houses for the escapees, but the signal did not come.[3]

On the night of 15 August 1974 Gallagher met Kilkenny republican Richard Behal and an unnamed female activist in

Tracey's Bar in the town. Later, as they drove home the worse for wear, their Mini car was stopped by the Garda Special Branch. Gallagher jumped out of the car and made a run for it, but was rugby tackled by a detective, who stuck a gun in his face. He thought it wise to surrender. Gallagher and Behal were placed on remand on the republican wing in Portlaoise. As soon as he could, Gallagher asked why nothing had happened with the escape attempt. He was told the prisoners were waiting for the right time. Gallagher offered to take over, and the plans were set in motion.[4]

The date set for the escape was Sunday, 18 August 1974. The escape group had new additions, including Gallagher. Twenty-five men, many of them senior IRA activists, were earmarked to break out. Planning went ahead inside the prison. The prisoners detailed to escape set themselves to work making prison officers' uniforms. The idea was that when the escapees were running through the courtyard, the troops on the roof of the jail would not be able to distinguish between them and the real prison officers, and so would not open fire.

On the morning of 18 August nervous tension prevailed. At 12.30 p.m., one of the prisoners, Liam Brown, approached the prison officer at the gate of the lower landing and asked to be let in. This was the signal for the first team of escapees to rush forward and get the key to the laundry. The prison officer was quickly overpowered, and he gave up the key without too much resistance. With this first stage of the plan successfully completed, the escapees opened the door to the stairwell and rushed through to the courtyard. They used their keys to get onto an adjoining flat roof before climbing down to ground level and running to the walls of the governor's house. By now, some of the prisoners were wearing the home-made prison officers' uniforms. A warder sounded the alarm; soldiers on the turrets were about to shoot when they spotted the uniforms and held fire, fearing the prisoners had taken hostages. This gave those escaping vital seconds to clear the courtyard and continue their escape. The escapees ran the seven yards to the governor's walled residence where they placed their first explosive charge at a gate leading to the prison walls. After this had exploded, a second charge was planted in an iron doorway in a perimeter wall. The door and a part of the wall were blown in, and nineteen men made their dash for freedom through the hole created by the explosion.

One of escapees, who was from Armagh, explained how a bomb blew a hole in an inner courtyard wall. He said, 'That took us into the small courtyard where the Governor's residence was and we'd blown the glass out of the windows. This was just before midday on a Sunday and I can remember him standing, looking out, completely mesmerised, wearing a pair of pyjamas and a jacket.'[5]

As the prisoners made the final dash for freedom, the soldiers fired warning shots over their heads. One or two of the prisoners dropped to the ground fearing the worst, but as the prison officers raced from their mess, they called on the soldiers to stop firing. The six would-be escapees who were captured were escorted back into the prison again. After a 100-yard dash through fields and bushes outside the prison, the men who had successfully escaped reached the Borris Road, where they commandeered five cars and sped away.

Back at Portlaoise, the governor demanded a head count. However, the prisoners refused to comply with his order, adding to the confusion and preventing the prison authorities' attempts to identify the escapees. They held out for several hours, until the governor threatened to send in the riot squad. After the head count it was confirmed that nineteen men were missing.[6]

When the prisoners realised that nineteen of the twenty-five men had escaped, they were overjoyed. Those who escaped were: Liam Brown, Paddy Devenny and Micky Nolan (Belfast), Tom

McFeely and Ian Milne (Co. Derry) Thomas McGinty and Eddie Gallagher (Donegal), Patrick Thornberry, and brothers Kevin and Martin McAllister (Armagh), Brendan Hughes and Kevin Mallon (Tyrone), Oliver McKiernan (Fermanagh), Bernard Hegarty and Sam O'Hare (Louth) brothers Michael and Seán Kinsella (Monaghan) Seán Morris (Meath) and Tony Weldon (Dublin).[7]

Among the escapees were Kevin Mallon and his Mountjoy rescuer, Brendan Hughes, and two brothers, Michael and Seán Kinsella, who had been convicted of murdering Senator Billy Fox. Mallon spent the first few days of his freedom in a wood near the town of Emo with seven other escapees and two female volunteers, Margaret McKearney and Marion Coyle, who were trying to arrange transportation. Local republicans aided their journey to Gorey, Co. Wexford, via Wicklow. Paddy O'Neill, from Newbridge, Co. Kildare, and a friend drove their cars to Emo and picked up the group. As they headed to Gorey, they drove through a garda checkpoint. McKearney and Coyle were in the front seat with Paddy O'Neill, while Mallon and two escapees were in the back seat. O'Neill managed to drop the group off, but he was followed by a patrol car and stopped at Arklow. The next day, he was brought to the Special Criminal Court, in Green Street, Dublin, and sentenced to a year for aiding the escapees. O'Neill served his term in Portlaoise Prison with some of the men he had been trying to help escape.[8]

In an attempt to recapture the escapees, the government launched a statewide search operation. Helicopters, tracker dogs, and thousands of troops and police – many called back from holiday – were part of a massive manhunt for the escapees. Roadblocks were thrown up throughout the country, and the town of Portlaoise was sealed off. The Irish Navy was even called in and put on the alert. British troops and police sealed escape routes into the North. Searches went on for over a week but to no avail.[9]

The singer and songwriter Dermot Hegarty wrote 'Nineteen men' while travelling from his native Longford to Kilkee, Co. Clare. Driving with his friend, Brendan Kearney, they were regularly stopped by police and military checkpoints until they were told in Monasterevin, that 'the boys' had blown a hole in the wall in Portlaoise Jail and escaped. They performed the song in Kilkee that night, and the place erupted. 'Nineteen men' was recorded the next day and was released during that week. Larry Gogan played it on *New Releases* on the Friday, but halfway through the song, the producer pulled the plug and took it off the air. The *Evening Herald* ran a headline saying, 'RTÉ bans Hegarty's new single', and 'Nineteen men' became a huge success, staying at number 1 in the charts for four weeks.[10]

Many of the escapees returned to active service in the North. In September escapee Martin McAllister was wounded in a shoot-out with British troops at Crossmaglen, Co. Armagh. Samuel O'Hare, a native of Newry with an address in Dundalk, was arrested after he was recognised by gardaí, in the town, on 15 November. Paddy Devenney was picked up in Belfast in the first week of December, while Thomas McGinty was recaptured at a house at Carrigart, Co. Donegal, on Christmas Eve. Kevin Mallon was arrested again. He was charged with possession of a weapon, and with escaping from Mountjoy and Portlaoise Prisons, which drew him a ten-year sentence. Despite extensive follow-up searches, by the end of 1974 fifteen of the escapees were still at large.[11]

The breakout was a serious embarrassment for the Fine Gael–Labour coalition government. A judicial inquiry into the episode was set up by Justice Minister Paddy Cooney, which led to a much tighter security regime with an increased garda and military presence being deployed in the prison. Parcels were routinely confiscated, and random cell searches took place – 'Lucky Numbers' sweets were put on the banned list. Additionally, strip searches became the norm along with restrictions on free association among the prisoners. By December 1974 conditions within the prison had deteriorated to the point that the republican leadership within felt compelled to riot or go on hunger strike to draw attention to their grievances.[12]

Paddy O'Neill was in Portlaoise Prison on St Patrick's Night, 17 March 1975, when, during an attempted breakout, Volunteer Tom Smith, Dublin Brigade, was shot dead by soldiers on guard duty. After his sentencing for assisting escapees, O'Neill had spent much of his time in the workshop, but on that night he was told to stay in the recreation hall. He was there when the lights went out. The auxiliary generator cut in within minutes. O'Neill heard an explosion as a bomb blew open a door gate to the exercise yard. This was followed by shots. The IRA had tried to break into the prison at the farm gate, which was to be breached by a purpose-built armour-plated dumper truck that could accommodate twenty men. The co-driver had only recently been released from the prison. He took the wrong turn, but the truck broke down as it reversed and did not make the last gate. The twenty designated escapees got as far as the final wall around the jail, but armed troops patrolling the prison perimeter held them back with a hail of bullets. Tom Smith was shot through the head as he ran back into the prison. Top IRA strategist Brian Keenan was among several wounded would-be escapees, sustaining gunshot wounds in the hand and leg. There was a sombre atmosphere in the prison that night as twenty-six year old Tom Smith lay dead in the infirmary. Paddy O'Neill was released two months later, after serving a total of nine months.[13]

Eddie Gallagher became leader of a maverick republican group responsible for the aerial bombing of Strabane RUC Station, the theft of the Beit art collection from Russborough House and the kidnapping of Dutch industrialist Dr Tiede Herrema. One of

Gallagher's accomplices in the Beit art robbery was Rose Dugdale, an English-born heiress who joined the IRA in 1972, while a co-conspirator in the Herrema kidnapping was Marion Coyle, who had helped transport escapees from Portlaoise in August. Gallagher demanded the release of Dugdale, Kevin Mallon and Laois republican James Hyland. After the release of Dr Herrema, on 7 November 1975 without any of the demands having been met, Gallagher returned to Portlaoise Prison to serve a thirty-year sentence for kidnapping.[14]

CHAPTER 21

LONDON CALLING

Brian Keenan was Britain's most wanted man and one of the IRA's most capable military operatives. When he was arrested in Banbridge, Co. Down, in March 1979, and brought to London, the IRA launched a rescue attempt almost immediately. He had been appointed IRA Quartermaster General (QMG) in 1973, also assuming responsibility for the IRA's activities in Britain. Beginning in 1972 the IRA's twenty-five-year campaign in Britain involved nearly 500 recorded incidents and caused the deaths of 115 people and the wounding of 2,134. Keenan played a significant role in establishing contacts between the IRA and sympathetic regimes in the Eastern bloc and the Middle East. He had contacts with the Libyan regime of Muammar Gaddafi, when he visited Libya to arrange an arms shipment in 1972. Keenan was arrested in the Irish Republic in July 1974, and he spent a year in prison after being convicted of IRA membership. On St Patrick's night, 17 March 1975, he was one of the leaders of the attempted breakout from Portlaoise Prison, in which Volunteer Tom Smith was shot dead by soldiers on guard duty. Keenan was among several would-be escapees who were wounded, when he sustained gunshot wounds in the hand and leg.

Believing that extending the IRA campaign to Britain 'was a necessary appendage to the armed struggle in the Six Counties',

Keenan maintained, 'It sent a powerful message to the British Establishment, political and military.' After his release in July 1975, Keenan went to London to organise logistics for an IRA bombing team. That team later became known as the Balcombe Street Gang, when they were captured at that address after a six-day siege. Keenan's fingerprints were discovered on bomb parts in one of the unit's arms depots, and he became one of the most wanted men in Britain. He spent some time in the United States, where he organised an arms pipeline from the American side to Britain and then to Ireland via the QE2. He was arrested in 1979, and in June 1980 Keenan was charged in connection with explosives offenses and was held on remand in London's Brixton Jail.[1]

It was the successful Mountjoy helicopter escape that gave GHQ the idea of repeating it in London to rescue Keenan, who was their top man. The Keenan rescue team included Bobby Campbell, Bobby Storey, Dickie Glenholmes and Gerard Tuite, all prominent members of the IRA. However, the rescue attempt never happened after Storey, Glenholmes and Tuite were arrested on 14 December 1979 at Holland Park, London. The RUC had tipped off British police that the IRA was planning a Christmas bombing campaign in England. After a two-month intelligence operation code-named Otis, Scotland Yard detectives raided a luxury flat in Holland Park, west London, where Tuite and Glenholmes were staying.[2]

After his arrest, Gerry Tuite was held on remand in Brixton, awaiting trial in connection with IRA bombings in London and Essex in December 1978, and for plotting the jailbreak of Brian Keenan, ironically out of the same jail: Brixton. In the summer of 1978 Tuite, posing as David Coyne, a young businessman of German–Irish extraction, had met a young nurse, Helen Griffiths, at a party in London. Within a short time, he had moved into her flat at 144 Trafalgar Road, Greenwich. Griffith's shift work as a nurse facilitated Tuite having many hours in the flat on his own, and his purported business enabled him to travel throughout the country. During his ten-day trial, over sixty witnesses, including his former girlfriend Helen Griffiths, gave evidence. Her flat was searched by police in February 1979, and traces of explosives were found on a bag and a briefcase. Gelignite, Semtex, detonators and safety fuses were also found. A sawn-off shotgun found in the flat was linked to pieces of wood from a shotgun found at the scene of a car-bomb explosion in London in December 1978. Mini-cassette tapes found hidden under the floorboards contained a recording in which a voice recited a number of names and addresses of a 'hit list'. Two male voices were heard on a tape, detailing information about British politicians and military installations. This included names, addresses and movements of people such as Home Secretary William Whitelaw, former Foreign Secretary Lord Carrington, former MP Enoch Powell, Sir Keith Joseph and Northern Ireland Shadow Secretary Airey Neave, killed by an Irish National Liberation Army (INLA) bomb in March 1979. Gerry Tuite was found guilty of possession of explosives with intent to endanger life.[3]

Gerry Tuite was from a traditional republican family but was never suspected of being an IRA operative. One of a family of eleven children, his parents' wedding party had been the scene of a shoot-out between gardaí and Tuite's uncle, Patrick Dermody, who was on the run after an IRA bank robbery. Dermody, from Hilltown, Castlepollard, Co. Westmeath, was OC Eastern Command, IRA. On 30 September 1942, armed gardaí surrounded a house at Lismacanigan, Mountnugent, Co. Cavan. They had been tipped off that two wanted men, Patrick Dermody and Harry White, were among the guests seen arriving at the wedding of Dermody's sister, Jane, to Michael Tuite, a local farmer. With the house cordoned off, gardaí burst in the door and rushed the kitchen. Both sides opened fire simultaneously as wedding guests dived to the floor.

Dermody and White ran to the back of the house. Detective Garda Michael J. Walsh, following the two, was mortally wounded and died from his injuries later in Cavan Hospital. The police claimed the IRA men shot him, while wedding guests said he was shot by gardaí firing blindly from outside through a window. Dermody was shot in the back and killed instantly, as he was trying to escape through a rear window. Harry White successfully got through a window, firing as he ran. Despite being wounded twice in the leg, he made good his escape. White made it to a nearby field where a sympathetic soldier involved in the follow-up searches found him two days later lying in a ditch. The soldier brought White to a barn, dressed his wounds, and contacted the local IRA who got him safely out of the area. Gerry Tuite was born in that house thirteen years later.[4]

During his late teens, Gerry Tuite went to sea as a merchant seaman. It was during this period, when he was away from home for many months at a time, that he became an IRA volunteer. He entered Britain in August 1977 and operated at a high level within the IRA. Tuite's skilful elusiveness merited him a grudging tribute, 'master of disguise', following his arrest. As late as May 1983, searches of several London flats used by Tuite turned up expertly concealed caches of firearms and bomb-making equipment.

At one time the Sinn Féin organ *An Phoblacht/Republican News* carried a story that Gerry Tuite had been assaulted while in prison, with the headline 'Tuite beaten in Brixton'. After a follow-up cautionary letter from Tuite to the paper, it carried another headline 'Tuite bruised but not beaten in Brixton', emphasising that the republican prisoner could be battered and bruised but never 'beaten'. It was while on remand in Brixton Jail, awaiting trial on the London bomb charges, that Tuite made his daring escape. Although Tuite was a Category A prisoner – in Britain, 'those that would pose the most threat to the public, the police or national security should they escape' – he was not held in a high-security cell.[5]

At that time Brixton Jail was Europe's biggest remand centre. Built in 1820, overcrowding was an early problem, and its small cells and poor living conditions contributed to its reputation as one of the worst prisons in London. In 1980 its capacity was 600, but there were 1,000 inmates held there, more than three-quarters of them on remand.[6] Gerry Tuite was originally remanded to A Wing, where he immediately began planning to escape. He began exploring ways of breaking out of his cell which, when discovered, led to him being moved to D Wing. This annexe held fifteen Category A men guarded by a senior officer and seven staff, one of whom was tasked with keeping vigil overnight when the area was locked down. Brian Keenan was also on D Wing, but he was moved to Wandsworth Jail when became involved in a dispute with prison staff. Tuite managed to get himself moved to an upper-floor cell, where he became friendly with bank robbers 'Big Jim' Moody and Stan Thompson.[7] Jim Moody, whose mother was Irish, was a former associate of south London's feared Richardson mob and was known as an extremely violent robber and gangland killer. Essex man Stan Thompson was one of the most successful escapees in Britain, having got out of three different prisons within five years.[8]

Both Moody and Thompson were on remand on armed-robbery charges. The three began planning an escape. Moody's brother Richard smuggled in hacksaw blades, masonry drill bits, screwdrivers and superglue in his socks. He handed them over at visiting time to his brother, when the supervising officer's attention was elsewhere. Richard Moody had noticed that the scanner used to detect such equipment was not passed over the lower part of visitors' legs. The prisoners also managed to get a tin of white paint as Tuite's cell was to be redecorated when he moved in.[9]

Tuite obtained a tubular bar, which, mounted on a broom handle, created a highly effective brace for the drill bit. The trio devised a routine in which one man worked on the wall separating Tuite's cell from Thompson's, while the others made themselves visible to staff and kept watch. Searches were not as frequent or thorough as was expected, so the work progressed at a remarkable rate. Wooden lockers were screwed into position to cover the compromised brickwork. They used the paint used along with cardboard and tape to disguise damage to the seventeen-inch-thick walls. When they ran out of glue, marmalade was used to stick the cardboard to the wall. Tuite then toiled steadily on a second wall breach that would give access to an exterior roof area. The final step entailed Moody cutting into Thompson's cell.

On the late evening of 14 December 1980 Moody and Thompson opened their shared cell, but Moody could not fit his large muscular body through the hole into Tuite's cell. Tuite had not broken out through the roof yet, so they had to wait until the following night to widen the hole so Moody could fit through. Thompson appeared in court later that day, and to his surprise found he was to be acquitted of the robbery charge. However, the escape went ahead as planned at 3.15 a.m. on 16 December. When the hole was complete the three escapees dropped into a yard; avoiding CCTV and dog patrols, they used builders' planks and scaffolding piled up for repairs to scale a twelve-foot mesh fence and the fifteen-foot perimeter wall. Later, prison staff found a scaffold plank with a hook on a nearby roof.

A getaway car which was intended to speed them away did not turn up, probably because of the last-minute change in dates. However, the three escapees flagged down a passing cab within minutes. The driver later told police he was looking for a pre-booked passenger and thought the three men were his fares. He dropped them off at Herne Hill outside the city, saying the men paid him £5.00 for a £1.50 journey. The escapees were not missed for seven hours. Tuite later attributed the successful escape to 'efficient lookouts and inefficient guards'.[10]

Gerry Tuite's escape came at the height of the Armagh/Long Kesh hunger strike for political status in December 1980, and was a tremendous morale boost to republicans. British police immediately issued 16,500 wanted posters of Tuite – whose escape angered Scotland Yard and embarrassed the prison department. Tuite's escape was the first jailbreak by a republican prisoner in England since the beginning of the IRA campaign in 1969.[11]

A national manhunt began in the Greater London area. Following raids on suspected republicans, police made four arrests, but Tuite was nowhere to be seen. Two days after the escape Stanley Thompson was cleared of armed-robbery charges in his absence, and, after a TV appeal by his girlfriend, he phoned her to say he was giving himself up. He walked into Brixton Police Station with a solicitor on 19 December. He later received a twelve-month sentence, suspended for two years, for breaking out of Brixton.[12]

Brian Keenan was subsequently convicted of explosives offences and was sentenced to eighteen years in prison. He was released after serving fourteen years. In March 1981 Dickie Glenholmes and Bobby Campbell were convicted of planning to spring Keenan from Brixton Jail using a hijacked helicopter. Bobby Storey was acquitted due to lack of evidence, while Gerry Tuite was no longer in Britain.[13]

Gerry Tuite and Jim Moody hid out in a succession of IRA and underworld safe houses in London, until Tuite found it safe to travel to Ireland. He lived at a flat in Drogheda, Co. Louth, for fourteen months, until routine garda enquiries ended his run of luck.

On 4 March 1982, members of the Special Detective Unit were searching a flat in Dwyer Street, Drogheda, when there was a knock on the door. 'I opened it,' said Detective Sergeant John Biggins, 'and Tuite was standing there. He just froze.' Tuite had got a lift from Dublin to Drogheda, and was unaware a search was ongoing at the address. Completely surprised by the turn of events, Tuite offered no resistance. He was taken to Drogheda Garda Station along with a man who lived in the flat above him. This man was later released without charge.

Tuite became the first person to face trial in Ireland for offences committed in Britain. He was later charged in the non-jury Special Criminal Court under a previously unused section of the Criminal Law Jurisdiction Act 1976, permitting trial in Ireland for offences said to have been committed abroad. It was at the request of the British government that the Irish authorities decided to invoke that Act. No attempt was made to extradite Tuite to Britain, because Irish law forbids the extradition of people wanted for politically motivated offences. Subsequently, in the following July, he was sentenced to ten years' imprisonment. Tuite raised his eyebrows and smiled when he heard the sentence. He was happy he could not be tried for escaping from Brixton Jail because only jailbreaks that had occurred on the island of Ireland were prosecutable.[14]

Richard Moody received eighteen months for smuggling escape equipment to his brother, James. Gangland hitman and armed robber James Moody was on the run for thirteen years. It was thought that he spent some of his time on the run in Ireland. Ultimately, on 1 June 1993, he was gunned down in a London bar in a gangland-style hit.[15]

Eleven years after Gerry Tuite's spectacular escape, two more IRA prisoners absconded from Brixton Jail before their sentencing. Nessan Quinlivan (Limerick) and Pearse McAuley (Strabane, Co. Tyrone) had been arrested at Stonehenge in November 1990 after a year-long search by police. They had both been charged with conspiring to murder British brewery executive Sir Charles Tidbury and conspiracy to cause explosions. On 7 July 1991 the two men were being escorted back to their cell after attending Sunday morning Mass when McAuley produced a gun from his shoe and pointed it at the prison guards. McAuley suddenly fired shots at the prison guards, and the pair managed to somehow get over the massive perimeter wall. Desperately searching around for a vehicle, they shot a prison officer in the leg, stole his car and drove off.

The two escapees later fled to the Republic. In 1993 Nessan Quinlivan was rearrested and jailed for possession of arms, but was released in 1996 as part of the Irish government early-release programme for republican prisoners. Later, in 1999 Pearse McAuley was convicted of manslaughter in Dublin's Special Criminal Court for his role in the killing of Detective Jerry McCabe after a robbery in Adare, Co. Limerick, on 7 June 1996. He was sentenced to fourteen years in prison, and was released in 2009, having served just ten-and-a-half years. In August 2009 the Crown Prosecution Service in Britain announced it was no longer seeking the extradition of Pearse McAuley and Nessan Quinlivan for their escape from Brixton Jail. Subsequently, in 2015 McAuley was sentenced to twelve years for assaulting and stabbing his then estranged wife, Pauline Tully, a Sinn Féin councillor on Cavan County Council. He was released in June 2022.[16]

CHAPTER 22

TAKING THE M60 TO THE CRUMLIN ROAD

The M60 Squad's dramatic escape from Crumlin Road Gaol in the midst of the 1981 H-Block hunger strikes in Long Kesh was a huge morale boost to the republican movement and the nationalist people. The Belfast IRA unit was known as the M60 Squad because of their use of the powerful American-made general-purpose M60 machine gun during ambushes of Crown forces. The M60 was a prestigious weapon for the IRA, and it was used by two active-service units operating in north and west Belfast. On 2 May 1980 – as a four-man active service unit was about to open fire from a house on the nearby, heavily fortified Antrim Road RUC barracks – it was surprised by undercover Special Air Service (SAS) troopers. As the SAS unit rushed into the house next door in the ensuing gun battle, Captain Herbert Westmacott was fatally wounded. Following a stand-off where a priest, Fr Hutton, negotiated their surrender, the M60 Squad gave themselves up. Angelo Fusco, Joe Doherty, Robert Campbell and Paul Magee were captured. Capt. Westmacott was posthumously awarded the Military Cross.

In early June seven Belfast IRA members were within days of

their trial on charges of M60 machine-gun attacks that had left two members of the Crown forces dead and three wounded. They were: Joe 'Doc' Doherty (28), Spamount Street; Paul 'Dingus' Magee (33), Glenalina Gardens; Robert 'Fat' Campbell (27), Ballymurphy Crescent; Michael 'Beaky' McKee (24), New Barnsley Crescent; brothers Tony (26) and Gerry Sloan (27), Summerhill Drive and Westview Pass; and Angelo Fusco (24), Slieveban Drive, Four of them had been captured after the shoot-out with the SAS. The other three members of the M60 Squad had been arrested on information supplied by James Kennedy, who acted as a driver for the M60 Squad.[1] The courthouse was situated just across the road from the jail, but the M60 Squad members had other plans regarding their attendance at their forthcoming trial.

Within three months of being incarcerated in Crumlin Road Gaol, Joe Doherty was appointed to the six-man escape committee. Doherty was an experienced IRA volunteer and had served short prison terms in the *Maidstone* and Long Kesh when, aged seventeen, he was arrested on charges of being a member of Fianna Éireann. He had also tried to escape from Crumlin Road in 1974, when convicted of possession of explosives. Doherty and a companion sawed through the bars of their cell and lowered themselves to the prison yard on a rope. As they made their way to the perimeter wall with ropes and a grappling hook, they were caught in a searchlight beam and apprehended. His escape attempt earned him another eighteen months. Back again in Crumlin Road in 1980, Doherty put his experiences into practice and once more planned to escape. He later said to author Martin Dillon:

> We were formulating about three or four escapes. We had a few ideas. Some were to go over the wall. There were another couple of ideas for digging tunnels. Security was so tight that the tunnels, and plans for going over the wall,

were out. A volunteer suggested to the committee that maybe we should go out the way we came in, and that was to go out the front gate.[2]

An escape plan was sent outside to Belfast Brigade, proposing that fourteen prisoners should be involved. Belfast Brigade conveyed its approval for the plan to the escape committee with the proviso that only eight named volunteers should participate, deeming that fourteen escapees was too ambitious. Joe Doherty was on the list along with his six M60 comrades and another veteran volunteer, Pete Ryan, from the republican heartland of Ardboe, Co. Tyrone. Ryan had been charged with the killing of an RUC constable in April 1980. The verdict on the M60 killings was due on 12 June and the breakout date was set for 10 June. Two weeks prior to the event, two small .25-calibre handguns broken down into separate parts were smuggled into the prison and assembled in the jail.

Meanwhile, the hand-picked group of eight volunteers was assigned to map out the security measures throughout the prison. Positions of remote-control cameras were noted, and the men designated to escape were to listen to codes or passwords used by prison officers when they were coming on or off duty and unlocking or locking doors. The time picked for the breakout was in the middle of the H-Block hunger strike, when four volunteers had died and, according to Doherty, 'it was important for the escape to come off as the morale in the country was very low'.[3]

Sixteen prisoners, including the eight selected for the escape, arranged simultaneous visits with their lawyers for 10 June. This was done so that they could be together in the visiting area set aside to provide a place for legal teams and accused to discuss their business in private. The escape group even went through a 'dummy run' two days earlier, and, according to Dingus Magee, 'it went sound, everyone we wanted was there'.

On the day itself, several men from A and C Wings were called for visits as normal. The operation began at about 4 p.m., when prison officers came to bring back one set of prisoners to the holding area. Two prison officers, Bell and Tweed, accompanied Doherty, Tony Sloan, Paul Magee and Robert Campbell into the passageway, one in front and one taking up the rear. Magee suddenly pulled a pistol and put it to Officer Bell's head. Bell made a move towards the holding room but Magee pushed the gun tight against his head and said, 'You better stay where you fucking are and do nothing.'

Doherty had also produced a pistol, and he ordered the other prison officer to stand alongside Bell and to remain silent and still. Doherty, Magee and Campbell rounded up other prison staff from the holding rooms and the visiting area, and gathered the three designated prisoners – McKee, Fusco and Sloan. The five visiting solicitors were also pushed into the holding room with the prison officers. Some of the officers were told to remove their uniforms, which were given to prisoners who in turn removed their civilian clothes and dressed as prison officers.

Everything was going according to plan, but the escapees needed to gain access to an area designated B Division, which led to the front gates. Their path was blocked by a door locked from the outside and secured by Officer Richard Kennedy, a big intimidating guard. His role was to search prisoners entering the visiting area. Kennedy opened the door as the escapees and a 'prison officer' approached. Fat Campbell, carrying one of the automatic pistols, and Angelo Fusco, carrying a confiscated baton, pushed through the door. Campbell cocked the pistol, pointed it at Kennedy and said, 'Kennedy, this is no fucking joke. We're taking you as a hostage.' The gun was pushed into his back, and Kennedy was marched along the passageway towards Holding Room 3. When he entered the room, Kennedy suddenly swung around and hit Campbell on the side of his head with his baton.

Dingus Magee said, 'Fat Campbell knocked a warder named Kennedy to the ground with his own baton after he had attempted to break it on Fat's head. He was lucky he was only hit by the baton and not shot.' Kennedy was beaten on the head with the butt of a pistol, and, as he fell to the ground, he was repeatedly punched and kicked and then dragged semi-conscious and locked in a holding room.

The escapees made their way towards the jail's front gate, with two of them, Doherty and Ryan, in prison guards' uniforms, marching six prisoners to where they normally would be taken for daily visits by relatives. They bluffed their way through the inner gate of the airlock-type exit, but a warder, David Batchelor, on the outer gate recognised Joe Doherty wearing a prison officer's jacket and brown trousers. As he fumbled to close the last gate to freedom, he was hit and fell to the ground. Suddenly, the eight escapees were above him, and, while he tripped one of the prisoners, the escapee quickly rose to his feet and rushed through the visitors' gate with the others.

Prison Officer Thomas Killen was standing near the gate when he saw Robert Campbell coming towards him holding a pistol. Campbell held the gun to the officer's neck and said, 'Touch that fucking alarm and you're dead.' The eight escapees then went out onto the Crumlin Road. Killen started to go after them, but when he heard three gunshots he wisely returned inside the gate.

As the escapees ran from the prison, an alarm was sounded, which attracted the attention of RUC men and British troops at the courthouse on the Crumlin Road. British troops were stationed at five guard towers, known as sangars, surrounding the prison. They were confused by the sight of prison officers and 'civilians' running out and did not open fire. IRA support units had parked three cars, their ignition keys hidden under floor mats, outside the prison, in the car park of the Crumlin Road Health Centre, which was adjacent to the courthouse. The prisoners ran across the road towards the health centre, where some of them availed themselves of the cars.[4] 'I thought the guards were chasing the men in civilian clothes [prisoners] but then they jumped into the cars with them,' said a witness. As RUC men opened fire on them, other escapees took cover and returned fire. An IRA active-service unit, touring the Crumlin Road area, provided covering fire for them, while RUC detectives in civilian clothes also joined in the fray. One detective recalled Pete Ryan firing two shots at him. In the midst of the gun battle, Joe Doherty stood up and shouted, 'Police, police, don't fire.'

The RUC men, thoroughly confused, temporarily lowered their weapons, giving three of the escapees time to jump into the getaway cars and drive away. Doherty and the other escapees made off on foot in two groups. Three of them broke into a house at California Close in the nearby loyalist Shankill Estate, discarded their prison-officers' uniforms, hijacked a car and made their getaway. Among them was Michael McKee, who had a gunshot wound to the head which was treated later that day by a sympathetic doctor. Doherty and another escapee made their way on foot to the safety of the republican stronghold of Lower Falls. Doherty discarded his prison-officer's tunic as he ran through the maze of tiny side streets linking the Crumlin Road and Shankill Road.[5]

As the men made their daring escape, clearly visible to republican prisoners in cells on the top landing of A Wing, loud cheers and chants went up, and makeshift flags were flown from the windows. All eight escapees reached safe houses in west Belfast within the hour.[6] Crown forces found one car abandoned in the Shankill Road. They said that a group of escapees had fled on foot across the nearby 'peace line' into republican west Belfast. A second getaway car was found near the city centre, where the RUC said more prisoners had commandeered a taxi and headed to the republican Falls Road district.[7] Despite huge follow-up searches, none of the men were recaptured. After lying low for a few days, they were spirited to south Armagh and crossed over the border to the Republic.

One week later, in Bodenstown, Co. Kildare, at the annual pilgrimage to the graveside of Theobald Wolfe Tone, the father of republicanism, the crowd was given an added morale booster when, at the closing ceremony, one of the Crumlin Road escapees, Dingus Magee, made a dramatic appearance on the platform. Sporting a close-cropped hairstyle under his cap and wearing dark glasses, Magee was introduced to the 5,000-strong crowd by Owen Carron, hunger striker Bobby Sands's election agent in the Fermanagh-South Tyrone by-election. Magee referred briefly to his 'release' before being whisked from sight. He did stop, however, to sign autographs, before disappearing from the cemetery.

In a bid to catch Magee and Michael McKee, who was also present, gardaí and troops set up roadblocks on all routes out of nearby Sallins village. Ugly incidents developed at the main checkpoint at the Naas end of the Dublin–Naas dual carriageway. Republican supporters exited their homeward-bound buses and blocked the dual carriageway as Magee and McKee yet again made their escape along the adjacent railway line. Bottles and stones were thrown at gardaí, who resorted to a baton charge to clear the road. Neither of the two escapees were found.[8]

Robert Campbell was the first of the escapees to be recaptured, three months later. He was arrested in September 1981 at a house in Dundalk and served a ten-year sentence in Portlaoise under extra-jurisdictional legislation for his escape from Crumlin Road Gaol. Michael McKee was arrested in a house at Dundalk on 3 December 1981, while Anthony Sloan was apprehended at a house in Holyhill, Cork, on 3 January 1982. Paul Magee's and Angelo Fusco's run of luck ended in January 1982 when they were arrested in Dundalk. In February 1982, after they opted for a trial in the Republic, Anthony Sloan, Angelo Fusco, Paul Magee and Michael McKee were each jailed for ten years by the Special Criminal Court in Dublin for their part in the escape from Crumlin Road Gaol.[9]

By the middle of January 1982 five of the eight escapees had been recaptured in the Republic and, due to the improbability of the others remaining free, Joe Doherty was smuggled out of Ireland to America. It was important for republican morale that the last remaining members of the M60 Squad not be recaptured. Doherty was given a false passport and a one-way plane ticket from Shannon to New York. Helped by the Irish-American community in New York, Doherty worked at several different jobs until 18 June 1983, when he was arrested at his workplace, Clancy's Bar, by the Federal Bureau of Investigation (FBI). He fought a lengthy extradition battle from the USA, but was eventually deported in 1992. He remained in Long Kesh Prison until 1998, when he was freed under the terms of the Good Friday Agreement.[10]

Gerard Sloan was arrested at Dublin Airport in November 1988 as he waited to board a flight to Toronto via Amsterdam. In April 1989, after he too opted for a trial in the Republic, Sloan was jailed for five years for escaping from Crumlin Road Gaol. His brother, Anthony, successfully challenged attempts to extradite him to the North. In December 2000 he and the six other members of the M60 Squad, were granted a Royal Prerogative which enabled them to return to Northern Ireland without fear of prosecution.

Shortly before his release from prison in 1989, Paul Magee was served with an extradition warrant. He started a legal battle to avoid being returned to Northern Ireland, but in October 1991 the Supreme Court in Dublin ordered his return to serve his sentence for the killing of Capt. Westmacott. Magee had jumped bail, and a warrant was issued for his arrest. He fled to England, where he became part of an IRA active service unit. On 7 June 1992, Magee and another IRA volunteer, Michael O'Brien, were travelling in a car near Tadcaster, when they were stopped by the police. The unarmed police officers questioned them, became suspicious and called for backup. Magee opened fire and Special Constable Glenn Goodman was mortally wounded; another officer, PC Kelly, was shot four times, but survived. Magee and O'Brien evaded capture for four days by hiding in a culvert before they were arrested in Pontefract.

Magee was sentenced to life imprisonment, but on 9 September 1994 along with five other prisoners, escaped from Whitemoor Prison. The prisoners, in possession of two guns that had been smuggled into the prison, scaled the prison walls using knotted sheets. A guard was shot and wounded during the escape, but the five prisoners were captured after being chased across fields by prison officers and police. On 5 May 1998 Magee was repatriated to the Republic to serve the remainder of his sentence in Portlaoise Prison. He was released in late 1999 under the terms of the Good Friday Agreement.[11]

Angelo Fusco tried to escape from Portlaoise Prison, which earned him another three-year sentence. Fusco was released in January 1992 and was immediately served with papers ordering his extradition to serve his sentence at the Maze Prison for the killing of Capt. Westmacott. He won a landmark victory three years later, when the High Court overturned the original Dublin District Court's order. Fusco settled in Tralee, Co. Kerry, but again went on the run in February 1998, just before the Supreme Court, the Republic's highest legal authority, ruled against him. He was arrested at a roadblock on New Year's Eve 2000, but as he was being rushed towards the border two days later, the High Court temporarily halted the extradition after a successful court application by his lawyers.[12]

Pete Ryan was the only escapee who was not recaptured. As a highly motivated volunteer with extensive operational experience, Ryan was among a unit that drove straight into the Derryard British Army checkpoint in an armoured Bedford dump truck in December 1989. They opened fire with two belt-fed machine guns, AK47s, hand-grenades, RPG-7s and a flame-thrower, killing two soldiers and wounding two more. On 3 June 1991 Ryan, along with two other volunteers, was killed in an SAS ambush in Coagh, Co. Tyrone.[13]

Within hours of the jailbreak the escape became known as 'The Great Escape' and the escapees as 'The A-Team'. There were many more attempts to break free from Crumlin Road Gaol before it finally closed its doors in April 1995, but the M60 Squad escape from the Crum was the most audacious jailbreak of the period. That was until 1983, when there was another Great Escape, this time from the H-Blocks of Long Kesh.

CHAPTER 23

OUT OF THE LONG KESH MAZE

L ong Kesh, or the Maze Prison, as the British preferred to call it, was considered Europe's most escape-proof jail. It consisted of eight blocks, in an H-shape, contained within three segments, each surrounded by concrete walls and connected by large hydraulic gates. The H-Blocks were designed to be jails within a jail. Each was a secure unit inside high steel fences and razor wire. The segments were themselves surrounded by an eighteen-foot-high perimeter wall with, at regular intervals, lookout posts manned by armed British soldiers. The sheer number of gates and segments was intimidating.

Republican prisoners had been fighting against Britain's criminalisation policy in the H-Blocks of Long Kesh since 1976. They had been protesting for years on the blanket and dirty protest for recognition as political prisoners. The republican prisoners had fought against the jail administration and loyalist prisoners to achieve segregation. They had seen ten of their comrades die on hunger strike to get what was, in name only, political status. In the aftermath of the hunger strike, republican prisoners had decided on a strategy of entering into the system in order to destroy it. They forced the loyalist prisoners into protest action after months of fistfights and attacks, which led to segregation. In November 1982 the republican prisoners presented themselves for prison work.[1]

The Northern Ireland Office was ecstatic when republicans began prison work, but they were duped. As buses and vans brought prisoners to and from visits to the kitchens, woodwork and stitching workshops, and vegetable gardens, republicans gained access to every corner of the prison. They gained a sense of the geography of the prison, which helped in developing plans to escape. In early 1983 an escape committee was set up to evaluate escape plans and to help organise any feasible ideas. In H-Block 3 (H3), Belfast man Larry Marley led a team of five, selected by the camp leadership, to organise a mass escape from the prison. Marley's team focused on a lorry which delivered meal trolleys from the prison kitchen to all over the prison. The food lorry travelled to every corner of the prison several times each day and also left the camp on occasions. It soon emerged that security around the food lorry was lax, and that it was used unofficially to transport consignments of alcohol to the prison officers' social club. Security policy directed that all vehicles had to be searched whenever they passed through any of the inter-segment gates, but the food lorry was never searched on its way around the prison.[2]

Three members of the escape committee – Brendan 'Bik' McFarlane, Brendan 'Brendy' Mead and Tony McAllister – were in H7, and they began working on a plan to seize an entire block, load the men onto the food lorry and drive out the main gate! Each of the H-Blocks was controlled by a 'circle' – the central wing that served as an entrance hall and administrative area. A circle contained a control room, several offices, stores, a medical room and a canteen for prison officers. If the circle could be seized, the prisoners would have control of the H-Block. To do this, there needed to be a relaxed atmosphere in the blocks so the prison officers would drop their guard. As the prisoners had agreed to do prison work, they were given jobs as orderlies, which gave them access to the circle. Bik McFarlane, Brendan Mead and Tony McAllister were designated by the escape committee as the circle orderlies, because they were serving life sentences with no prospect of release. They began working on gaining the prison officers' trust by making them tea and toast, cleaning the canteen and other areas used by the staff. Eventually, the prisoners nurtured a more trustworthy atmosphere, becoming friendly with prison officers who had only months before brutalised and beat them – something that was not easy for the republican prisoners. It became normal to see 'trusted' prisoners walking in and out of the control room.[3]

While the food lorry passed unchallenged through all internal gates, it underwent a security check at the main-gate tally lodge before it left through the gate in the perimeter wall and out through the external gate in the fence surrounding the camp. The escape committee came to the conclusion that weapons would be needed to subdue the prison officers on the block and to seize the main-gate tally lodge at the prison exit. In the summer of 1983 the escape plan was presented to the camp leadership, and the proposal was accepted. This was then submitted to the IRA Army Council, which cleared the operation and organised a backup force of IRA volunteers from Belfast Brigade and South Armagh Brigade to assist the escapees once they broke out. Subsequently, at least four small-calibre .25 automatics and two silencers were smuggled into the prison and passed on to H7. In the two months before the escape thirty-seven men in H7 received fifty-two special family visits, even though this was against regulations. There was no metal detector used on visitors and, because of the relaxing of security, none was used on the prisoners returning from such visits. It is thought the pistols and silencers were smuggled in on these visits.[4]

The camp leadership appointed Bobby Storey as OC of the escape, with Bik McFarlane as his adjutant. They designated men to various roles. Storey was a seasoned operator and had been on the team to take part in the rescue of Brian Keenan in Brixton Jail in 1980. He had only arrived in Long Kesh in 1981, convicted of possessing a rifle.[5] Storey found out that Seamus McElwaine had a smuggled pistol in his possession. He approached McElwaine and asked him for the pistol. McElwaine refused, saying he needed it for an escape he was planning. Storey took him into his confidence and outlined his plan. McElwaine was invited to go along, and Storey got his pistol. The advice from the camp leadership and the IRA Army Council was that only those serving more than four years should go out on the food lorry, but anyone that wanted to go was cleared to do so.[6]

However, while some men knew about the plan for weeks in advance of the escape, others only found out hours before the breakout. The first men to be briefed were those with essential and complicated roles. They would need to time to learn their tasks. Tony Kelly had already served six years when he was approached by Robert 'Rab' Kerr. 'Rab asked me would I like to escape. I said of course, looking around, thinking how would you get out of here? Months later Bik McFarlane said to me your answer was being recorded – not physically, but mentally in his head. Bik said, "If you had given the wrong answer you wouldn't have been on the escape",' Tony recalled. In the days ahead Bobby Storey and Bik McFarlane went over every detail of the plan with those assigned crucial tasks to make sure they knew precisely what to do.[7]

Sunday was chosen for the breakout because it was the quietest day on the blocks. There were no visits, no prison work and there were fewer prison officers on duty. On the two Sundays before the designated day, 25 September, the men assigned to take the block circle made dry runs. Small watches had been smuggled in for each of the men, as the takeover required precision timing. On each occasion everything went off smoothly. The dry runs even accustomed the prison staff to having more than the usual number of prisoners in the circle on a Sunday afternoon. The purpose of the republican orderlies' cooperation with the prison officers now became clear to men who had resented their fellow prisoners for doing this.[8]

On 25 September 1983 Long Kesh Governor John Baxter's journal for Sunday morning recorded, 'Carried out morning rounds accompanied by Senior Officer on duty. Visited H3, H4, H5, H6, H7, H8 and prison hospital. Assistant Governor visited H1, H2, Cells and kitchen, found all in order.' Baxter was right in many ways. Floors were swept and mopped. The prisoners went through their normal routine, taking showers and eating breakfast. Mass was said in C Wing. Most of the 125 republican prisoners were engaged in recreational activities, moving freely within each wing. Twenty-four prisoners employed as orderlies were cleaning up and performing other tasks around the block. At 12.30 p.m. all prisoners were locked in their cells.[9]

In a double cell built to accommodate four men, Eddie O'Connor and Seán McGlinchey spent their time making ties and ponchos, which, along with pillowcases, were intended for use when the warders were captured. These would be used to disguise the rearguard group and put over the heads of warders so they would not recognise their 'captors'. It was only then that they told Kevin Barry Artt, the last prisoner to be informed, that there was to be a mass escape in a little over an hour.

'Ha,' replied Artt doubtfully, 'such a yarn!' He had been sentenced to twenty years a few weeks earlier, and he thought his cellmates were pulling his leg. It took them some time to convince Artt that an escape was really about to happen. It had been decided to let Artt go on the escape, as he was innocent of the charge that had brought him to Long Kesh. Kevin Barry Artt was a twenty-four-year-old from north Belfast. On the word of informer Christopher Black, he had been convicted of the killing of Long Kesh Assistant Governor Albert Miles in 1978.[10]

As soon as the cell doors were opened at 2.05 p.m., the circle team of Bobby Storey, Bik McFarlane, Brendy Mead, Tony McAllister, Gerry Kelly, Rab Kerr and Seán McGlinchey moved into position. The men were armed with four pistols, two of which had silencers; two replica pistols; and a chisel. They blockaded the store with chairs and large bins, and flooded the governor's office and the welfare office with liquid polish – all to keep staff out. The different teams of prisoners, armed with hammers and chisels taken from the hobby rooms, then moved into their positions to seize the wings. Alarm buttons in the canteen and at the top and bottom of each wing were covered by teams of men talking or lounging around. Everyone was waiting for the signal to begin the takeover.

When the circle was empty, Bik McFarlane shouted out the signal to get into position: 'A and B is the bumper [floor polisher] there?' The teams in A and B Wings moved into position. 'It's not here, Bik,' Seán McGlinchey roared back. McFarlane moved across to the C and D side of the circle. 'Sammy,' he shouted to the prison officer on duty, 'is the bumper there?' Sammy shouted down the wings for the bumper and Bobby Storey replied, 'It's here. I'll bring it out.' On hearing the signal word 'bumper', the teams in C and D Wing moved into position.

Bobby Storey and Tony McAllister walked into the prison-officers' canteen in C Wing. They pulled out their pistols, pointed them at the prison officers and ordered them to lie on the floor. The officers looked up disbelievingly until Storey cocked his weapon, and then they hit the floor in seconds. McAllister left the canteen and nodded to Gerry Kelly, who moved to the control room. Kelly drew his pistol and, holding the small weapon in two hands, pointed it at Prison Officer John Adams's head said, 'Don't move an inch or I'll blow your head off.' He gave Adams instructions to act normally if the central control room contacted him. 'Make them believe you, or you're dead,' Kelly warned him.

Bik McFarlane shoved his silenced pistol into the ribs of the officer guarding the gate and ordered him to lie on the floor. They next apprehended the medical orderly along with a warder who sauntered out of the toilet beside the control room. They were ordered to lie on the floor, but, while Gerry Kelly was distracted keeping an eye on the warder and Adams in the control room, Adams got up from the floor and tried to close the door of the control room. He could not reach the alarm button unless he got the door closed, but Kelly had got his pistol through the door and fired two shots. Adams was hit above the eye and slumped against the door. The shots alarmed Supervising Officer Geordie Smiley, who was being held at gunpoint by Brendy Mead in the principal-officers' office. Smiley lunged at Mead, and the two traded blows, until Bobby Storey burst in and ordered Smiley to the floor. When Smiley refused, Storey ordered Mead to shoot him. Smiley slowly got down, realising that the man he had joked with over the last few months was now about to put a bullet in him. Mead, no doubt, was relieved he did not have to shoot the prison officer.

In the area between C and D Wings, Rab Kerr produced his pistol and held up the prison officer on duty. With a gun to his head, the warder was pushed to the floor and a pillowcase put over his head. This was the signal for the two wings to be seized. There was no resistance in C Wing, but one warder on D Wing received a slight stab wound from a chisel when he put up a fight. At the other side of the block, A and D Wings were quickly taken and again a warder was injured by a hammer blow when he resisted. The block was now under control of the prisoners and no alarms had been sounded.

Seán McGlinchey and Joe Corey stripped two warders of their uniforms. They put on the uniforms to pass themselves off as warders and not arouse suspicions when they approached the gate. The two escorted Bik McFarlane up to the front gate.

McFarlane had a brush and shovel slung over his shoulder and a silenced pistol in his pocket. It was customary for him to sweep the gate area. The prison officer at the gate, suspecting nothing, admitted McFarlane to the area between the two front gates. Once inside McFarlane stuck his pistol to the back of the warder's neck, relieved him of his keys and marched him away from the front gate with a warning not to try anything. McGlinchey and Corey in prison-officers' uniform took over duty at the gate. The entrance to H8 was opposite to H7, only thirty yards away, but it was unoccupied, and so no prison officers were on duty there.

All of H7 was now secure, and preparations had begun for the arrival of the food box-lorry. The captured warders were brought to the two classrooms and tied together in pairs. They were relieved of their uniforms and dressed in ponchos with pillowcases over their heads. Twenty-four warders in total were taken captive. Prisoners not going out, and operating as a rearguard, wore balaclavas made from pillow cases to disguise themselves and against later retaliation. Thirteen escapees put on prison-officers' uniforms, and some even shaved off moustaches to disguise themselves.[11] Bobby Storey received reports from all areas of the block and marked off each task on a clipboard. Tony Kelly was then given the job of locking up those prisoners on his wing who had no part of the escape or were not part of the rearguard. Locking up his fellow prisoners was not a job he relished, but it was for their own safety so they would not be liable to later retaliation from prison officers.[12]

At 3.30 p.m. a prison van delivering the Sunday papers arrived. Noticing nothing untoward, the driver threw the papers on the ground outside the gate. As the van drove off, the blue box food lorry arrived, twenty minutes late. McGlinchey and Corey opened the first gate, allowing the lorry into the area between the gates. In keeping with routine, they closed the gate behind the lorry before opening the inner gate to allow it into the front yard of the block. The driver was oblivious to anything out of the ordinary, but he was soon made all too aware of what was happening. Bobby Storey opened the driver's door, while Gerry Kelly pulled him out. Bik McFarlane took the orderly out from the passenger side. They were brought inside at gunpoint.

'This block is now in the hands of the IRA,' Storey said to the driver. 'All screws who obeyed our orders are safe. One who didn't was shot in the head.'

Storey explained what he needed the driver to do and what would happen to him if he didn't. Looking around at all the armed and masked prisoners, the driver assured his captors that he was willing to cooperate. He was tied into his cab, told there was a grenade primed under his seat – there wasn't – and that Gerry Kelly lying on the floor with a pistol pointed at him would shoot him before pulling the pin if the driver tried to alert anyone. The driver replied, 'It's only a job. I'll do exactly as I'm told.'

The meals were unloaded from the lorry, and thirty-seven men jumped into the back, those wearing uniforms at the rear. Two men of the rearguard took over at the front gate, while others wished their comrades good luck.[13] Dermot McNally said, 'I was told two days before the escape. I was glad it was only two days. I couldn't have coped with knowing earlier, I would've burst. Sitting in the back of the lorry was the worst. You could hear the grass grow, it was that silent. Everybody lost in their own thoughts, not a word said.' Tony Kelly said, 'It was complete silence. Boys mentally counting the gates they were going through.'[14] The lorry drove the short distance to the first obstacle – the 'airlock' – the space between the two gates, manned by a single prison officer. He opened and closed the first gate and said hello to the driver as he walked around to open the next gate. The lorry drove into the administration area. In the cab Kelly told the orderly to lie on the floor, as he would not be allowed past the administration gate. Once again, the lorry drove safely through. It drove towards the Tally Lodge and the main gate, and parked near the van pool.

Nine prisoners dressed in prison-officer uniforms and armed with pistols and chisels exited the lorry and entered the Tally Lodge, arresting several warders there and in the vicinity. However, they were behind schedule, and their efforts to overpower the warders and take it over were hampered by the arrival of large numbers of staff coming on duty. Within five minutes the escapees had thirty warders under guard. A warder coming on duty was told to lie on the floor, and when he drew his baton, he was immediately stabbed with a chisel. Two more warders drew their batons and were also stabbed, although not seriously injured. The other warders under guard became emboldened by their weight of numbers. One warder managed to push an alarm button, but when the emergency control room responded, he was forced to say it had been an accident, thereby averting the launch of a full escape alert. At this point, Officer Jimmy Ferris got up and made towards an alarm button, but he was stabbed in the chest and fell to the floor.

More and more warders came on duty and were arrested, until the position in the Tally Lodge became impossible to hold. It was decided to board the lorry and get to the external gate, but three men had to be left behind as a rearguard to hold the Tally Lodge. As they were boarding the lorry, two vigilant warders arriving for duty realised what was happening and drove their cars across the gateway, blocking it. With that, a warder burst out of the Tally Lodge. The alarm was raised. It was 4.12 p.m., nearly two hours after the escape had started. Bobby Storey opened the back door of the lorry. He shouted, 'Everybody out. The bubble's burst! Go! Everybody go!'[15]

Prisoners streamed out of the back of the lorry, as a large body of prison officers surged forward. Twenty-nine of them ran to the barbed wire; only two were caught, as the rest made it over the top of the hill, down a thirty-foot gully and up the other side where they could see farmhouses. Jim Clarke said, 'One lad threw his coat down on the fence and stamped on the fence and we all got over.'

'I remember looking over and seeing the gate and everybody heading towards the fence,' Tony Kelly said, 'so I ran over to the fence. Once we got over the fence into the field and ran up the field zig zagging and ran as fast as we could into this farmyard. At this farmyard there was a van and two cars. Eight of us got into each car and two got into the van. I don't know why only two got into the van. But we were lucky; they were captured.'[16]

Jim Clarke said, 'We got into a car and there was about eight of us and Bik we said we'd head to Belfast, but Seamus [McElwaine] said no at this stage Belfast will be cordoned off.' At a safe distance from the prison, they abandoned the car, and the eight escapees headed off on foot to safety, hiding out at a farmhouse near Dromore, Co. Down. Setting out from the farmhouse the group walked at night through the countryside towards Newry where they found a nationalist house. 'They were not republican, but sympathetic to our plight,' Clarke said.[17]

There were also eight escapees in the other car. Tony Kelly said, 'There were too many in our car, legs and arms sticking out everywhere, so we decided we needed another car. We pulled into a layby and seen two women sitting at the side. We said, "Look, we're taking your car," and the younger woman said, "My mother needs that car." I said, "We need it more," so we took the car and drove off.' The two cars went in separate directions with four escapees in each vehicle. Tony Kelly said, 'We didn't know at the time but we were outside the three-mile cordon around the jail. We saw a sign for Leitrim. Paddy McIntyre was a football fan and he read all the GAA books in jail, he said there is a GAA club there, so we knew we were on the right road.' They drove on to Castlewellan, Co. Down, which they knew was a nationalist town. Tony Kelly, Jim Smith, Joe Corey and Paddy McIntyre found refuge in a republican safe house in Castlewellan. Kelly and Smith were taken away separately to another safe house, and were later brought safely across the border, the first escapees to reach the Republic. McIntyre and Corey were later arrested when a large force of RUC surrounded the safe house. They only surrendered when a local priest was brought to mediate, as the escapees did not trust that they would not be shot 'while trying to escape'.[18]

Some prisoners tried to escape in prison officers' cars. Brendy Mead ran out the gate into the car park. He opened a car door and pulled the driver out, but the driver took the keys out of the ignition and threw them away. Mead struggled with the warder, retrieved the keys and drove off with four others along the prison wall towards the external gate leading to the public road outside. They were followed by another warder in his car, flashing his lights and sounding the horn. He swerved into Mead's path, forcing the car to crash. The escapees scrambled out of the car. Two were caught, but three of them – Mead, Kevin Barry Artt and Paul Kane – managed to get out on the main road, where they hijacked a passing car.

Harry Murray shot a pursuing warder in the leg. The warder had one of the escapees' pistols and was pointing it at him when Murray fired first. As Murray ran away, a soldier in a watchtower shot him in the leg. Warders gave him a severe beating and dragged him back to the prison. Pursuing soldiers and prison officers found four escapees hiding in reeds at the side of the River Lagan, about half a mile from the prison. All were taken back into custody. The main gate was closed again and the prison secured. Troops from the adjoining military complex joined in the search. Within an hour, checkpoints had been set up at strategic points.

Gary Roberts was picked up by troops as he crossed a field, and he was handed over to the RUC at a checkpoint where he received a beating. When he got back to Long Kesh, Roberts got another beating.[19]

Nineteen of the original thirty-eight escapees successfully evaded recapture and were brought across the border to relative safety. They were: Kevin Barry Artt, Paul Brennan, Seamus Clarke, Gerard Fryers, Dermot Finucane, Gerry Kelly, Anthony McAllister, Gerry McDonnell, Brendan McFarlane, Robert Russell, Terence Kirby, Jim Smyth (Belfast), Jim Clarke (Donegal), Tony Kelly, Kieran Fleming (Derry), Seamus McElwaine (Monaghan), Seamus Campbell, Padraig McKearney (Tyrone) and Dermot McNally (Armagh). Most of them were returned to jails north and south over the ensuing years. Gerard Fryers and Seamus Campell were never heard of again. Three of the escapees were later killed on active service – Kieran Fleming (1984), Seamus McElwaine (1986) and Padraig McKearney (1987).

Four of the escapees were recaptured after a short spell of freedom: Paul Kane and Brendan Mead (Belfast) were spotted and arrested on a deserted road near Castlwellan, Co. Down, the day after the escape. Hugh Corey (south Derry) and Paddy McIntyre (Donegal) surrendered after their safe house was surrounded by RUC the following day. Fifteen of the escapees were unlucky to be recaptured very close to Long Kesh almost immediately after the breakout. They were: James Burns, Denis Cummings, James Donnelly, William Gorman, Peter Hamilton, Rab Kerr, Jim McCann, Seán McGlinchey, Martin McManus, Harry Murray, Marcus Murray, Edward O'Connor, Gary Roberts, Joseph Simpson and Bobby Storey.[20]

Many of the thirteen prisoners initially recaptured were stripped, beaten and dragged along the ground near H7 by prison officers. The prison orderly who was on the kitchen lorry, and was not involved in the escape, lost two teeth from a baton blow to the mouth. The remaining eighty-eight prisoners in H7 were relocated to the unoccupied H8 to allow the block to be searched and thoroughly examined by crime-scene police officers. These prisoners, many barefoot and naked from the waist up, were made to run a gauntlet between two lines of prison officers and dog handlers, where they were beaten, kicked and bitten by the German Shepherd dogs. Twenty-two prisoners were later given compensation for their injuries sustained at the hands of prison officers.[21]

In April 1988, after a thirty-five-day trial, sixteen prisoners were acquitted of the murder of Prison Officer James Ferris, after the judge said he could not be satisfied that the heart attack that caused Ferris's death had been the result of his stabbing. James Ferris was posthumously awarded the Queen's Commendation for brave conduct. Prison Officer John Adams took years to recover from his gunshot wound.[22]

The mass escape from Long Kesh remains a landmark in Irish and British penal history. It was the biggest jailbreak in Europe since the Second World War, and to republicans is forever known as 'The Great Escape'. In more than a century of republican jailbreaks, the methods of escape had evolved from ropes and wax keys to helicopters, explosives and guns. Each escape in each phase of the republican struggle had inspired others to break out, so that the continuity of republican escapes continued as long as Irish republicans were incarcerated. There were as many failures as there were successful jailbreaks, but each attempt gave hope and encouraged other prisoners to try, as well as raising morale both inside and outside the prisons and camps. While many escapes have been billed as 'Great Escapes', in truth every successful breakout was a great escape.

ENDNOTES

INTRODUCTION

1   Béaslaí, Piaras, *Michael Collins and the Making of a New Ireland* (Dublin, 2008), p. 361.

CHAPTER 1

1   www.dib.ie/biography/stephens-james-a8277 (accessed 8 May 2024).
2   Golway, Terry, *Irish Rebel: John Devoy and America's Fight for Ireland's Freedom* (Dublin, 2015), p. 29.
3   Ramón, Marta, *A Provisional Dictator. James Stephens and the Fenian Movement* (Dublin, 2007), pp. 177–8.
4   *Waterford News and Star*, 17 November 1865.
5   Ibid.
6   See Ramón, *A Provisional Dictator*, pp. 184–5.
7   *Carlow Morning Post*, 2 December 1865.
8   See Ramón, *A Provisional Dictator*, p. 188.
9   Ibid.
10 Devoy, John, *Recollections of an Irish Rebel* (Shannon, 1969), p. 85. John Breslin and John Devoy must have had their doubts about Stephens's leadership as they both came to the conclusion during his escape that he was half-hearted.
11 *Westmeath Independent*, 23 December 1865.
12 *Carlow Morning Post*, 2 December 1865.
13 See Ramón, *A Provisional Dictator*, p. 189.
14 www.dib.ie/biography/stephens-james-a8277 (accessed 8 May 2024).
15 See Golway, *Irish Rebel*, p. 65.

CHAPTER 2

1   Ó Lúing, Seán, *The Catalpa Rescue* (Tralee, 1965), p. 50.
2   Ibid., p. 12. In 1865, according to James Stephens, Fenian strength in Ireland and Britain stood at 80,000, which did not include the 15,000 Fenians in the British Army.

3   Ibid., p. 50.
4   Ibid., pp. 52–3.
5   Golway, Terry, *Irish Rebel: John Devoy and America's Fight for Ireland's Freedom* (Dublin, 2015), p. 62.
6   Ó Lúing, *The Catalpa Rescue*, p. 57.
7   Ibid.
8   Ibid., p. 61.
9   Ibid., p. 66.
10 Ibid., pp. 75, 82.
11 Ibid., pp. 92–3.
12 Ibid., pp. 96–8.
13 *The Rescue of the Military Fenians from Australia. With a Memoir of John Devoy who planned the rescue and the names and careers of the Rescued and their Rescuers* (Dublin, 1929). See https://kildare.ie/ehistory/index.php/the-rescue-of-the-military-fenians-from-australia/.
14 See Golway, *Irish Rebel*, p. 69.
15 See Ó Lúing, *The Catalpa Rescue*, pp. 115–19.
16 Ibid., p. 120.
17 Ibid., pp 123–37.
18 Ibid., pp. 161–3.
19 *Connaught Telegraph*, 16 September 1876; *The Nation*, 16 September 1876.
20 See Golway, *Irish Rebel*, p. 70.

CHAPTER 3

1   Durney, James, *The War of Independence in Kildare* (Cork, 2013), pp. 64–8.
2   Fanning, Ronan. *Éamon de Valera. A Will to Power* (Dublin, 2015), pp. 66–7.
3   O'Donoghue, Florence, *Sworn to be Free: The Complete Book of IRA Jailbreaks 1918–1921* (Tralee, 1971), p. 38.
4   See Fanning, *Éamon de Valera*, p. 68.
5   Ibid.
6   McCullagh, David, *De Valera. Vol. I: Rise 1882–1932.* (Dublin, 2017), p. 152.
7   See O'Donoghue, *Sworn to Be Free*, p. 34; *Irish Independent*, 24 January 1919.
8   *Evening Herald*, 23 January 1919.
9   See McCullagh, *De Valera*, p. 153.
10 Coogan, Tim Pat, *De Valera. Long Fellow, Long Shadow* (London, 1995), p. 125.
11 Béaslaí, *Michael Collins and the Making of a New Ireland* (Dublin, 2008), p. 174; see also Coogan, *De Valera*, pp. 125–6.
12 *Irish Independent*, 7 February 1919.
13 *Evening Herald*, 6 February 1919; *Irish Independent*, 7 February 1919; see also Coogan, *De Valera*, pp. 125–6.
14 See McCullagh, *De Valera*, p. 154.

15   Durney, James, *Stand You Now for Ireland's Cause. A Biographical Index of Co. Kildare Republican Activists 1913–1923* (Naas, 2023), p. 147.
16   *Nenagh Guardian*, 8 March 1919.
17   See O'Donoghue, *Sworn to be Free*, pp. 45, 47.
18   Hannigan, David, *De Valera in America. The Rebel President and the Making of Irish Independence* (New York, 2010), pp. 2–3.
19   Ibid., p. 69. The Rhode Island chapter of Clan na Gael had sold Wilson his house for $1.

CHAPTER 4

1   Durney, James, *On the One Road. Political Unrest in Kildare 1913–1994* (Naas, 2001), p. 46.
2   O'Donoghue, Florence, *Sworn to be Free: The Complete Book of IRA Jailbreaks 1918–1921* (Tralee, 1971), p. 49.
3   Béaslaí, Piaras, *Michael Collins and the Making of a New Ireland* (Dublin, 2008), pp. 184–7.
4   www.dib.ie/biography/beaslai-piaras-a0515; www.dib.ie/biography/duggan-ea monn-john-edmund-a2820 (both accessed 9 May 2024).
5   McLoughlin, Pat, 'Clara and Ballycumber men among twenty that went over the wall at Mountjoy in 1919', Offaly History Blog, 21 January 2023.
6   See Béaslaí, *Michael Collins*, pp. 187–90.
7   *Westmeath Independent*, 5 April 1919.
8   McLoughlin, 'Clara and Ballycumber men'.
9   *Westmeath Independent*, 5 April 1919; *Roscommon Herald*, 5 April 1919.
10   Borgonovo, John, Crowley, John, Ó Drisceoil, Donal & Murphy, Mike (eds), *Atlas of the Irish Revolution* (Cork, 2017), p. 443.
11   See Béaslaí, *Michael Collins*, pp. 233, 238–40.
12   *The Freeman's Journal*, 28 October 1919.
13   *Irish Independent*, 16 December 1919.
14   See O'Donoghue, *Sworn to be Free*, p. 108.

CHAPTER 5

1   Durney, James, *The War of Independence in Kildare* (Cork, 2013), pp. 92–3, 108.
2   Dwyer, T. Ryle, *The Squad and the Operations of Michael Collins* (Cork, 2005), pp. 180–1.
3   O'Malley, Ernie. *On Another Man's Wound* (Dublin, 1979), p. 257.
4   Simon Donnelly, Bureau of Military History Witness Statement (hereafter BMH WS) 481, Military Archives, Dublin.
5   Gillis, Liz, 'The Great Escape', Kilmainham Tales – remembering for the future, Kilmainhamtales.ie.
6   *Irish Press*, 2 January 1936.

7   O'Donoghue, Florence, *Sworn to be Free: The Complete Book of IRA Jailbreaks 1918–1921* (Tralee, 1971), p. 117.

8   O'Malley, Ernie, *On Another Man's Wound*, pp. 278–9; Martin, Harry F. and O'Malley, Cormac K.H., *Ernie O'Malley: A Life* (Dublin, 2021), p. 49.

9   See Gillis, 'The Great Escape'.

10 *Anglo-Celt*, 19 February 1921; see also Béaslaí, *Michael Collins and the Making of a New Ireland* (Dublin, 2008), p. 124.

11 See O'Malley, *On Another Man's Wound*, p. 274.

12 Ibid., pp. 274–5.

13 See O'Donoghue, *Sworn to be Free*, p. 121; O'Malley, *On Another Man's Wound*, p. 281; Martin & O'Malley, *Ernie O'Malley*, pp. 50–1.

14 *The Irish Times* 17 February 1921.

15 *Irish Press*, 2 January 1936; *Irish Press*, 28 November 1949.

16 The Anglo-Irish Treaty signed in London on 6 December 1921 by representatives of the Irish Republic and the British government effectively ended the War of Independence.

17 *The Cork Examiner*, 27 January 1976; *Irish Press* 27 January 1976; *Evening Herald* 7 February 1976.

18 www.dib.ie/biography/omalley-ernest-bernard-ernie-a6885 (accessed 9 May 2024); Dorney, John, *The Civil War in Dublin. The Fight for the Irish Capital 1922–1924* (Dublin, 2017), pp. 175–6.

CHAPTER 6

1   Durney, James. *Interned: The Curragh Internment Camps in the War of Independence* (Cork, 2019), p. 7.

2   Ibid., p. 50.

3   Ibid., pp. 20, 25.

4   Joseph Lawless, BMH WS 1043.

5   Daniel R. Ryan, BMH WS 1673.

6   See ibid.

7   Ibid.

8   See Durney, *Interned*, pp. 83–4.

9   See Ryan, WS 1673.

10 See ibid.

11 See Durney, *Interned*, pp. 86–7.

12 See Lawless BMH WS 1043.

13 See ibid. The Anglo-Irish Truce came into effect on 11 July 1921, ending hostilities between the IRA and Crown forces.

CHAPTER 7

1   *The Freeman's Journal*, 23 June 1921.

2 Durney, James. *Interned: The Curragh Internment Camps in the War of Independence* (Cork, 2019), pp. 113–4.
3 Ibid., pp. 126–8.
4 *Anglo-Celt*, 4 January 1936.
5 Ó Maoláin, Tomás, 'The inside story of famous I.R.A. escape from the Curragh Camp', *Mayo News*, 17 May 1959.
6 O'Donoghue, Florence, *Sworn to be Free: The Complete Book of IRA Jailbreaks 1918-1921* (Tralee, 1971), p. 243.
7 Conroy, John F., 'Escapes from the Rath Internment Camp, Curragh, 1921', *Western People*, 6 June 1964.
8 Byrne, Thomas, 'A tunnel to freedom. Escape from Kildare Camp', undated newspaper article, copy in author's possession.
9 See O'Donoghue, *Sworn to be Free*', p. 246.
10 Byrne, 'A tunnel to freedom'.
11 Andrews, C.S., *Dublin Made Me* (Dublin, 2001), p. 187
12 Ibid., pp. 187–8.
13 O'Callaghan, Micheál. *For Ireland and Freedom: Roscommon's Contribution to the Fight for Independence* (Cork, 2012), pp. 126–7.
14 *Roscommon Herald*, 17 December 1921.
15 See Durney, *Interned*, p. 162.
16 *Fermanagh Herald*, 17 September 1921.
17 Ibid.

CHAPTER 8

1 Borgonovo, John, Crowley, John, Ó Drisceoil, Donal & Murphy, Mike (eds), *Atlas of the Irish Revolution* (Cork, 2017), pp. 442–3.
2 Linda Kearns, BMH WS 404.
3 Ibid.
4 Ibid.
5 *Irish Independent*, 1 April 1921; *The Freeman's Journal*, 31 October 1921.
6 See Kearns, BMH WS 404.
7 See O'Donoghue, Florence, *Sworn to be Free: The Complete Book of IRA Jailbreaks 1918-1921* (Tralee, 1971), pp. 172–3.
8 www.dib.ie/biography/coyle-eithne-anne-a2132 (accessed 9 May 2024).
9 See Kearns, BMH WS 404.
10 *The Freeman's Journal*, 31 October 1921; *The Skibbereen Eagle*, 5 November 1921.
11 According to Kearns, Miss O'Rourke was an aunt of Dr Gogarty.
12 See O'Donoghue, *Sworn to be Free*, p. 177.
13 Ibid.

CHAPTER 9

1 Borgonovo, John, Crowley, John, Ó Drisceoil, Donal & Murphy, Mike (eds), *Atlas of the Irish Revolution* (Cork, 2017), p. 443

2 Durney, James, *Stand You Now for Ireland's Cause. A Biographical Index of Co. Kildare Republican Activists 1913–1923* (Naas, 2023), p. 173.

3 Durney, James. *Interned: The Curragh Internment Camps in the War of Independence* (Cork, 2019), p. 185. The names of the two other escapees are not mentioned.

4 Ibid.

5 www.kilkennylibrary.ie/eng/our_services/decade-of-centenaries-resources/the-kilkenny-jail-escape-1921/brochure-619x350mm-jail.pdf.

6 Martin Kealy, BMH WS 1003.

7 Swithin Walsh, Eoin, *Kilkenny: In Times of Revolution 1900–1923* (Dublin, 2018), p. 136.

8 See Kealy, BMH WS 1003.

9 Maher, Jim, *The Flying Column – West Kilkenny 1916–21* (Dublin, 1987), p. 158.

10 See Swithin Walsh, *Kilkenny: In Times of Revolution*, p. 137. Boland had been Governor of Mountjoy Prison when Thomas Ashe died in 1917 after forced-feeding while on hunger strike. He had become a hate figure to republicans and a scapegoat for the prison authorities. By the time he was Governor of Kilkenny, his attitude had changed. www.kilkennylibrary.ie.

11 See Swithin Walsh, *Kilkenny: In Times of Revolution*, p. 137.

12 See Maher, *The Flying Column*, pp. 159–60.

13 Ibid., p. 160.

14 See Swithin Walsh, *Kilkenny: In Times of Revolution*, pp. 138–9; see also Maher, *The Flying Column*, p. 159.

15 See Maher, *The Flying Column*, p. 161.

16 See Kealy, BMH WS 1003.

17 See Maher, *The Flying Column*, p. 161.

18 Donoghue, Fergal, *Kilkenny Jail, 22 November 1921*, Kilkenny Co. Library, 2021.

19 See Maher, *The Flying Column*, p. 163.

20 See Swithin Walsh, *Kilkenny: In Times of Revolution*, pp. 139–40.

21 See Kealy, BMH WS 1003.

22 See Swithin Walsh, *Kilkenny: In Times of Revolution*, p. 141.

23 See Kealy, BMH WS 1003.

24 Laurence Condon, Pension Application MSP34REF4098, Military Services Pension Collection, Dublin.

25 *Connacht Tribune*, 18 November 1922.

CHAPTER 10

1   Duggan, John P., *A History of the Irish Army* (Dublin, 1991), p. 98.

2   Younger, Calton, *Ireland's Civil War* (London, 1968), p. 374.

3   Dorney, John, 'Today in Irish History, August 14, 1922, The anti-Treaty IRA attack on Dundalk', www.theirishstory.com/2013/08/14/today-in-irish-history-august-14-1922-the-anti-treaty-ira-attack-on-dundalk/.

4   Hopkinson, Michael, *Green against Green: The Irish Civil War* (Dublin, 1988), p. 170.

5   See ibid.; see also Younger, *Ireland's Civil War*, pp. 374–5.

6   Howard, Marcus, 'Dundalk Gaol 1922. The Great Escape', www.youtube.com/watch?v=OXm7-LdO6W4 (accessed 11 May 2024).

7   *Evening Herald*, 28 July 1922.

8   Ó Ríordáin, Aodhán, 'The story of my grandfather's escape from Dundalk Jail 100 years ago today', 27 July 2022, https://m.facebook.com/AodhanORiordain

9   McCann, Lorraine, 'Dundalk Jail during the Civil War', Louth County Archives. www.youtube.com/watch?v=9gc9qKsCcSk.

10   *The Freeman's Journal*, 29 July 1922; see also McCann, 'Dundalk Jail during the Civil War.'

11   McCann, 'Dundalk Jail during the Civil War'; *Donegal Democrat*, 29 July 1922.

12   Andrews, C.S., *Dublin Made Me* (Cork, 1979), p. 243.

13   See Dorney, 'Today in Irish History'.

14   Neeson, Eoin, *The Civil War, 1922–23* (Dublin, 1989), pp. 197–8.

15   Jim Dunne, BMH WS 1571.

16   See Durney, James, *Stand You Now for Ireland's Cause. A Biographical Index of Co. Kildare Republican Activists 1913–1923* (Naas, 2023), pp. 265–6.

17   Ibid., pp. 332–3.

18   See Younger, *Ireland's Civil War*, p. 376.

19   www.dib.ie/biography/aiken-francis-thomas-frank-a0070 (accessed 11 May 2024).

CHAPTER 11

1   *Kildare Observer*, 12 August 1922.

2   Durney, James, *The Civil War in Kildare* (Cork, 2011), pp. 109–10.

3   O'Keefe, Patrick, 'My reminiscences of 1914–1923', *Oughterany. Journal of the Donadea Local History Group* (1993), p. 49.

4   Nellie Kearns, Military Pension application MSP34REF17238, www.militaryarchives.ie (accessed 19 May 2024).

5   'The escape from Newbridge Barracks', *Leinster Leader*, 31 December 1927; Mick Sheehan interview with Ann Donohue, 1989. Copy in Kildare County Archives & Local Studies, Naas.

6   O'Connor, Seamus, *Tomorrow was Another Day* (Tralee, 1970), pp. 67–8.

7   See ibid., p. 68.

8   'The escape from Newbridge Barracks,' *Leinster Leader,* 31 December 1927.

9   O'Connor, *Tomorrow was Another Day*, p. 68.

10   Ibid., p. 69.

11   Ibid., p. 68

12   Ibid., pp. 68–71.

13   See Durney, *The Civil War in Kildare*, p. 116.

14   See O'Connor, *Tomorrow was Another Day*, pp. 68–73.

15   See Durney, *The Civil War in Kildare*, p. 116.

16   *Leinster Leader*, 29 October 1960.

17   See O'Connor, *Tomorrow was Another Day*, pp. 68–73.

18   Durney, James. 'The Greatest Escape. Newbridge Barracks 14/15 October 1922', https://kildare.ie/ehistory/index.php/the-greatest-escape-newbridge-barracks-14-15-october-1922/.

19   *Kildare Observer*, 19 May 1923.

CHAPTER 12

1   File AW/889. Court of Inquiry re Escape of Internees from Tintown Internment Camp, 1 May 1923. Military Archives, Cathal Brugha Barracks, Dublin.

2   www.dib.ie/biography/odonnell-peadar-a6700 (accessed 19 May 2024).

3   O'Donnell, Peadar, *The Gates Flew Open* (London, 1932), pp. 103.

4   See ibid., pp. 103–5.

5   Durney, James, *Stand You Now for Ireland's Cause. A Biographical Index of Co. Kildare Republican Activists 1913–1923* (Naas, 2023), p. 368.

6   'Mayo men feature in famous I.R.A. escapes from the Curragh Camp', *Mayo News*, 24 January 1959; see also O'Donnell, *The Gates Flew Open*, p. 107.

7   See O'Donnell, *The Gates Flew Open*, p. 108.

8   Ibid., pp. 112–13.

9   'Mayo men feature in famous I.R.A. escapes from the Curragh Camp'.

10   See File AW/889. Court of Inquiry Escape of Internees from Tintown Internment Camp, 1 May 1923.

11   *Irish Independent*, 11 July 1923.

12   See File AW/889. Court of Inquiry Escape of Internees from Tintown Internment Camp, 1 May 1923; 'Mayo men feature in famous I.R.A. escapes from the Curragh Camp'.

13   'Mayo men feature in famous I.R.A. escapes from the Curragh Camp'.

14   See O'Donnell, *The Gates Flew Open*, p. 105; see also 'Mayo men feature in famous I.R.A. escapes from the Curragh Camp'.

15   See File AW/889. Court of Inquiry Escape of Internees from Tintown Internment Camp, 1 May 1923. John McCoy had been instrumental in springing over 100 men from Dundalk Jail in August 1922.

16 Questions on treatment of prisoners by Ailfrid O Broin. *Dáil Éireann deb.*, Vol. iv, 31 October 1923. Sourced online 8 April 2010. www.oireachtas.ie/en/debates/debate/dail/1923-10-31/3/.

17 See Durney, *Stand You Now for Ireland's Cause*, p. 368.

18 See O'Donnell, *The Gates Flew Open*, pp. 238–9.

19 Thorne, Kathleen Hegarty. *Echoes of Their Footsteps, The Irish Civil War 1922–1924* (Newberg, Oregon, 2014), p. 260.

20 www.dib.ie/biography/odonnell-peadar-a6700 (accessed 19 May 2024).

CHAPTER 13

1 MacEvilly, Michael, *A Splendid Resistance. The Life of IRA Chief of Staff Dr. Andy Cooney* (Dublin, 2011), pp. 144, 150, 157.

2 *Evening Herald*, 20 November 1925.

3 Bell, J. Bowyer. *The Secret Army. History of the IRA 1916–1970* (London, 1970), p. 53.

4 'Sensational IRA jailbreak from Mountjoy Prison (November 1925)', Military Service Pensions Collection, Military Archives, Dublin.

5 'The I.R.A. prisoners break out.' Memories of Mountjoy Prison as told by former Governor Seán Kavanagh to Liam MacGabhann, *This Week*, 1 May 1970; *The Cork Examiner*, 30 November 1925; 'Sensational IRA Jailbreak from Mountjoy Prison'.

6 *The Cork Examiner*, 30 November 1925; 'Sensational IRA Jailbreak from Mountjoy Prison'.

7 See MacEvilly, *A Splendid Resistance*, p. 161; *The Cork Examiner*, 30 November 1925.

8 *Evening Herald*, 24 January 1928.

9 'Sensational IRA Jailbreak from Mountjoy Prison'.

10 See 'The I.R.A. prisoners break out', *This Week*, 1 May 1970.

11 www.dib.ie/biography/gilmore-george-frederick-a3485 (accessed 19 May 2024).

12 *Irish Press*, 11 March 1932; *Evening Echo*, 17 August 1932; *Kerry Reporter*, 27 August 1932.

13 See MacEvilly, *A Splendid Resistance,* p. 239.

CHAPTER 14

1 Coogan, Tim Pat, *The I.R.A.* (London, 2000), pp. 124–8.

2 The life and death of Jackie Griffith (1921–1943), https://comeheretome.com/2022/02/ (accessed 19 May 2024).

3 Bell, J. Bowyer, *The Secret Army. History of the IRA 1916-1970* (London, 1970), pp. 230–1; see also Coogan, *The I.R.A.*, pp. 184–5.

4   Ibid., p. 232.
5   https://treasonfelony.wordpress.com/2020/03/20/the-derry-jail-great-escape-20th-march-1943/ (accessed 19 May 2024).
6   Ibid.; see also Bell, *The Secret Army*, p. 232.
7   https://treasonfelony.wordpress.com/2020/03/20/the-derry-jail-great-escape-20th-march-1943/
8   *Irish Press*, 22 March 1943.
9   https://treasonfelony.wordpress.com/2020/03/20/the-derry-jail-great-escape-20th-march-1943/.
10   See Bell, *The Secret Army*, p. 256.
11   https://treasonfelony.wordpress.com/2020/03/20/the-derry-jail-great-escape-20th-march-1943/.
12   Ibid.
13   *Irish Independent*, 20 May 1943.
14   *Irish Press*, 9 April 1943.
15   See Bell, *The Secret Army*, p. 234.
16   *Derry Journal*, 11 March 2016.
17   *Irish Independent*, 21 September 1943.
18   *Donegal Democrat*, 2 October 1943.
19   *Evening Herald*, 3 October 1944.
20   *Belfast News Letter*, 1 March 1944
21   https://curiousireland.ie/old-derry-jail-tower/ (accessed 19 May 2024).

CHAPTER 15

1   Durney, James, *On the One Road. Political Unrest in Kildare 1913–1994* (Naas, 2001), p. 168.
2   Bell, J. Bowyer, *The Secret Army. History of the IRA 1916–1970* (London, 1970), pp. 272–5; Murphy, Séamus, *Having it Away. A Story of Freedom, Friendship and IRA Jailbreak* (Bray, 2018), pp. 24–6.
3   Murphy, *Having it Away*, p. 103.
4   See Murphy, *Having it Away*. pp. 191–2.
5   'Irish prisoner on life sentence who escaped from Wakefield Prison', *The Irish Times*, 28 November 2015.
6   See Murphy, *Having it Away*, p. 245.
7   See Bell, *The Secret Army*, p. 335.
8   See Murphy, *Having it Away*, pp. 295–6.
9   See Bell, *The Secret Army*, pp. 262–3. In 1951 Liam Kelly, of Pomeroy, Co. Tyrone, was dismissed from the IRA for planning an operation without sanction from GHQ. He formed Saor Uladh (Free Ulster) from his own power base in Tyrone. Although there were scattered units outside Tyrone, Saor Uladh remained a local movement.
10   See Murphy, *Having it Away*, pp. 271–3.

11 See ibid., p. 306.
12 See ibid., pp. 335–6.
13 *The Irish Times*, 28 November 2015; see also Bell, *The Secret Army*, p. 317.
14 See Murphy, *Having it Away*, pp. 339–40.
15 *Irish Press*, 14 February 1959; *Leinster Leader*, 21 February 1959.
16 *Belfast News Letter*, 16 and 17 February 1959; *Leinster Leader*, 21 February 1959.
17 See Murphy, *Having it Away*, pp. 356–7.
18 *The Irish Times*, 28 November 2015. George Skotinos was also released in an amnesty in 1959.
19 *Leinster Leader*, 16 June 2018.

CHAPTER 16

1 Durney, James, *On the One Road. Political Unrest in Kildare 1913–1994* (Naas, 2001), p. 169.
2 *Evening Echo*, 8 July 1957; *The Cork Examiner*, 9 July 1957.
3 See Durney, *On the One Road*, p. 169.
4 *Irish Press*, 26 and 28 May 1958; interview with Paddy O'Neill, Kilbelin, Newbridge, 7 June 2001.
5 *Irish Press*, 7 June 1958.
6 Bell, J. Bowyer, *The Secret Army. History of the IRA 1916–1970* (London, 1970), p. 324.
7 See Durney, *On the One Road*, p. 170.
8 Maguire, John. *IRA Internments and the Irish Government. Subversives and the State 1939–1962* (Dublin, 2008), pp. 102, 139–40.
9 See Bell, *The Secret Army*, p. 324; author interview with Paddy O'Neill.
10 See Bell, *The Secret Army*, p. 323.
11 See Durney, *On the One Road*, p. 171.
12 *Irish Independent*, 3 December 1958; *Leinster Leader*, 6 December 1958; *Belfast News Letter*, 9 December 1958.
13 *Evening Echo*, 21 February 1959; *Irish Independent*, 24 February 1959.
14 *Evening Herald*, 8 June 1959.
15 See Bell, *The Secret Army*, pp. 324–5.
16 Ibid., p. 325; *The Cork Examiner*, 12 March 1959. Another reason for the closure was that there were several cases of republican detainees proceeding against the Irish government before the European Court of Human Rights.

CHAPTER 17

1 McKittrick, David and McVea, David, *Making Sense of the Troubles: A History of the Northern Ireland Conflict* (London, 2012), pp. 47, 62–4, 78.
2 Canavan, Tony, 'Crumlin Road Jail', *History Ireland*, Vol. 25, Iss. 2 (March–April 2017); crumlinroadgaol.com (accessed 20 May 2024).

3   Morrison, Danny, 'Terence "Cleaky" Clarke: Death of a Hero', 2007, www.dannymorrison.com/wp-content/dannymorrisonarchive/115.htm; crumlinroadgaol.com

4   McGuffin, John, *Internment* (Tralee, 1973), p. 101.

5   'Crumlin Kangaroos daring escape', Christy Keenan speaking to Joe Austin, 20 November 2021, www.youtube.com/watch?v=hfZYhnT01rU (accessed 20 May 2024).

6   See Keenan, 'Crumlin Kangaroos daring escape'.

7   See McGuffin, *Internment*, p. 101.

8   *Belfast News Letter*, 17 November 1971; *Irish Press*, 17 November 1971.

9   See Keenan, 'Crumlin Kangaroos daring escape.'

10   *Irish Press*, 23 and 26 November 1971.

11   See McGuffin, *Internment*, p. 102; *Irish Independent*, 23 November 1971.

12   See McGuffin, *Internment*, pp. 102–3; 'Escapes by air and by land', *An Phoblacht/ Republican News*, 31 August 2023.

CHAPTER 18

1   McGuffin, John, *Internment* (Tralee, 1973), pp. 95–6.

2   Foley, Aran, 'The "Magnificent Seven" swim to freedom' Remembering the Past: The "*Maidstone*" escape 50 years on', *An Phoblacht/Republican News*, 4, 16 January 2022.

3   'Shot on sight. Paddy Mulvanna and Jim Bryson', *Irish Republican News*, 1 September 2022.

4   See 'The "Magnificent Seven" swim to freedom'.

5   '*Maidstone* escape: swimming to freedom (Part 2)', Peter Rogers speaking to Jim Gibney, *An Phoblacht/Republican News*, 7 February 2002.

6   Jackson, Michael, 'Martin's dramatic bid for freedom from the Maidstone prison ship', BelfastMedia.com, 2 February 2022, belfastmedia.com

7   See '*Maidstone* escape: swimming to freedom (Part 2)'.

8   See McGuffin, *Internment*, p. 104.

9   See '*Maidstone* escape: swimming to freedom (Part 2)'; see also 'Martin's dramatic bid for freedom'; Browne, Vincent, 'How we beat the Maidstone. Seven tell of escape', *Irish Press*, 24 January 1972.

10   *Irish Press*, 25 January 1972.

11   De Baróid, Ciarán. *Ballymurphy and the Irish War* (London, 2000), p. 167; see also 'Shot on sight'.

12   *Belfast Telegraph*, 28 March 2004.

13   See De Baróid, *Ballymurphy and the Irish War*, pp. 210–1.

14   *Irish Independent*, 9 February 2014.

CHAPTER 19

1   Ó Faoleán, Gearóid, *A Broad Church: The Provisional IRA in the Republic of Ireland 1969-1980* (Dublin, 2019), pp. 83–4.

2   O'Brien, John, *Securing the Irish State: An Garda Síochána. A Century of Policing 1922-2022* (Carrigtwohill, 2022), p 215; *Leinster Leader*, 15 July 1972; Durney, James, *On the One Road. Political Unrest in Kildare 1913-1994* (Naas, 2001), p. 185; see also Ó Faoleán, *A Broad Church*, pp. 84–5.

3   O'Driscoll, Seán, *Heiress, Rebel, Vigilante, Bomber: The Extraordinary Life of Rose Dugdale* (London, 2022), pp. 72–4.

4   *Irish Independent*, 30 October 1972; *Leinster Leader*, 4 November 1972.

5   National Graves Association, *The Last Post: The Details and Stories of Republican dead 1913/1975* (Dublin, 1976), pp. 120–1.

6   *Leinster Leader*, 4 November 1972.

7   See O'Driscoll, *Heiress, Rebel, Vigilante, Bomber*, p. 74.

8   See Ó Faoleán, *A Broad Church*, pp. 111–12.

9   *Evening Herald*, 1 November 1973.

10   See O'Brien, *Securing the Irish State*, p. 218.

11   *Evening Herald*, 31 October 1973; *Irish Press*, 24 December 1974.

12   Trigg, Jonathan, *Death in the Fields: The IRA in East Tyrone* (Dublin, 2022), p. 33.

13   *Evening Herald*, 1 November 1973.

14   'Remembering the Past: The helicopter escape', *An Phoblacht/Republican News*, 28 October 2004.

15   See O'Brien, *Securing the Irish State*, p. 218; see also 'Remembering the Past: The helicopter escape.'

16   *Irish Independent*, 22 November 2023.

17   *Irish Press*, 15 December 1973; *Leinster Express*, 29 December 1973.

18   See O'Brien, *Securing the Irish State*, pp. 219–20.

CHAPTER 20

1   Ó Faoleán, Gearóid, *A Broad Church: The Provisional IRA in the Republic of Ireland 1969-1980* (Dublin, 2019), p. 112.

2   'Remembering the Past: 19 prisoners escape from Portlaoise', *An Phoblacht/Republican News*, 27 August 2009.

3   O'Driscoll, Seán, *Heiress, Rebel, Vigilante, Bomber: The Extraordinary Life of Rose Dugdale* (London, 2022), pp. 119–20.

4   Ibid., pp. 121–2.

5   Trigg, Jonathan, *Death in the Fields: The IRA in East Tyrone* (Dublin, 2022), p. 50.

6   '30 years on: The Great Portlaoise Escape', *An Phoblacht/Republican News*, 26 August 2004. Ian Milne was later described as one of its three 'most wanted' by the RUC, along with Francis Hughes and Dominic McGlinchey. Milne later

served fourteen years in Long Kesh, including several years 'on the blanket' protest.

7 *Belfast News Letter*, 19 August 1974.
8 Durney, James, *On the One Road. Political Unrest in Kildare 1913–1994* (Naas, 2001), p. 189.
9 *Irish Press*, 20 August 1974.
10 Fox, Mattie, 'Dermot Hegarty. From bible salesman to legendary folk performer', https://mattiefox.wordpress.com/2016/10/14/dermot-hegarty-2/ 14 October 2016.
11 *Irish Press*, 16 November and 25 December 1974.
12 See Ó Faoleán, *A Broad Church*, p. 113.
13 See Durney, *On the One Road*, pp. 189–90.
14 *The Guardian*, 18 October 2024; see also O'Driscoll, *Heiress, Rebel, Vigilante, Bomber*, pp. 142, 163.

CHAPTER 21

1 O'Donnell, Ruán, *Special Category. The IRA in English Prisons, Vol. I: 1968–1978* (Dublin, 2012), pp. 250, 319, 354, 358.
2 *Belfast Telegraph*, 16 December 1980.
3 *Irish Press*, 14 July 1982.
4 *Evening Press*, 13 July 1982; see also Bell, J. Bowyer, *The Secret Army. History of the IRA 1916–1970* (London, 1970), pp. 227–8.
5 *Irish Press*, 14 July 1982.
6 *Belfast Telegraph*, 19 December 1980.
7 O'Donnell, Ruán, *Special Category. The IRA in English Prisons, Vol. II: 1978–1985* (Dublin, 2015), p. 187.
8 *Independent*, 3 June 1993.
9 *Belfast Telegraph*, 9 June 1981.
10 See O'Donnell, *Special Category, Vol. II*, pp. 189–90.
11 Ibid., p. 193; *Belfast Telegraph*, 19 December 1980.
12 *Belfast Telegraph*, 30 June 1981.
13 See O'Donnell, *Special Category, Vol. I*, p. 138.
14 *Irish Independent*, 5 March 1982; *The Cork Examiner*, 14 August 1982.
15 *Belfast Telegraph*, 30 June 1981; *Independent*, 3 June 1993.
16 *Independent*, 7 October 1993; *Irish Daily Mirror*, 24 June 2022.

CHAPTER 22

1 Dillon, Martin, *Killer in Clowntown: Joe Doherty, the IRA and the Special Relationship* (London, 1992), pp. 82–3, 96–9, 102.
2 Ibid., pp. 41, 47, 127.
3 Ibid., p. 131
4 Ibid., pp. 133–9.

5   Ibid., pp. 140–3; *Belfast Telegraph*, 15 December 1981.
6   *An Phoblacht/Republican News*, 13 June 1981.
7   See Dillon, *Killer in Clowntown*, p. 143.
8   *The Cork Examiner*, 28 June 1981; *Irish Independent*, 19 June and 22 June 1981.
9   *Evening Press*, 23 September 1981; *Evening Press*, 3 December 1981; *Belfast Telegraph*, 4 January 1982; *Irish Press*, 26 September 1983.
10   See Dillon, *Killer in Clowntown*, pp. 166, 170, 176.
11   *Irish Independent*, 23 October 1991; *The Cork Examiner*, 13 June 1992; *The Guardian*, 9 March 2000; *Belfast Telegraph*, 19 June 2014.
12   Mullan, John, 'Great escapes of an IRA gunman', *The Guardian*, 5 January 2000.
13   Crawley, John, *The Yank: My Life as a Former US Marine in the IRA* (Dublin, 2022), pp. 207–8.

CHAPTER 23

1   'The Greatest Escape', *Iris: The Republican Magazine*, 18 (Autumn 1993), p. 3.
2   Ibid.
3   Ibid., p. 7.
4   Dunne, Derek, *Out of the Maze: The True Story of the Biggest Jail Escape Since the War* (Dublin, 1988), pp. 56, 58.
5   Ibid., p. 34.
6   Tony Kelly, Great Escape 40th anniversary presentation, Roslea, Co. Fermanagh, 14 October 2023.
7   Author interview with Tony Kelly, Roslea, Co. Fermanagh, October 2023.
8   See 'The Greatest Escape', pp. 9–10.
9   Ryder, Chris, *Inside the Maze: The Untold Story of the Northern Ireland Prison Service* (London, 2000), p. 268.
10   See 'The Greatest Escape', *Iris*, p. 11; *An Phoblacht/Republican News*, 29 September 1983.
11   See 'The Greatest Escape', pp. 12–6.
12   See author interview with Tony Kelly.
13   See 'The Greatest Escape', pp. 17–9.
14   Dermot McNally, Great Escape 40th anniversary presentation, Roslea, Co. Fermanagh, 14 October 2023.
15   See 'The Greatest Escape', pp. 20–3.
16   See author interview with Tony Kelly.
17   Jim Clarke interview, 'Escape from Long Kesh', by Tony Kelly, 25 October 2023.
18   See author interview with Tony Kelly.
19   See 'The Greatest Escape', pp. 24–5.
20   *An Phoblacht/Republican News*, 29 September 1983.
21   See 'The Greatest Escape', *Iris*, pp. 36–7.
22   See Ryder, *Inside the Maze*, pp. 274–5.

BIBLIOGRAPHY

Primary Sources

Newspapers

An Phoblacht/Republican News
Anglo-Celt
Belfast News Letter
Belfast Telegraph
Carlow Morning Post
Connaught Telegraph
Derry Journal
Donegal Democrat
Evening Echo
Evening Herald
Fermanagh Herald
Independent
Irish Daily Mirror
Irish Independent

Irish Press
Kerry Reporter
Kildare Observer
Leinster Leader
Nenagh Guardian
Roscommon Herald
The Cork Examiner
The Freeman's Journal
The Guardian
The Irish Times
The Nation
The Skibbereen Eagle
Waterford News and Star
Westmeath Independent

Witness Statements/Pension Applications, Military Archives, Dublin

Linda Kearns, Witness Statement 404
Simon Donnelly, Witness Statement 481
Martin Kealy, Witness Statement 1003
Joseph Lawless, Witness Statement 1043
Jim Dunne, Witness Statement 1571
Daniel R. Ryan, Witness Statement 1673

File AW/889. Court of Inquiry re Escape of Internees from Tintown Internment Camp, 1 May 1923. Military Archives, Dublin.
Nellie Kearns, Military Pension application MSP34REF17238, Military Services Pension Collection, Dublin.
Laurence Condon, Pension Application MSP34REF4098, Military Services Pension Collection, Dublin.

'Sensational IRA jailbreak from Mountjoy Prison (November 1925)', Military Service
Pensions Collection, Military Archives, Dublin.

Oral Interviews

Mick Sheehan interview with Ann Donohue, 1989. Copy in Kildare County Archives
& Local Studies, Naas.

Author interview with Paddy O'Neill, Kilbelin, Newbridge, 7 June 2001.

Author interview with Tony Kelly, Roslea, Co. Fermanagh, 14 October 2023.

Tony Kelly and Dermot McNally, Great Escape 40th anniversary presentation, Roslea,
Co. Fermanagh, 14 October 2023.

Jim Clarke interview, 'Escape from Long Kesh', by Tony Kelly, 25 October 2023.

Secondary Sources

Books

Andrews, C.S., *Dublin Made Me*. Dublin, 2001.

Béaslaí, Piaras, *Michael Collins and The Making of a New Ireland*. Dublin, 2008.

Bell, J. Bowyer, *The Secret Army. History of the IRA 1916-1970*. London, 1970.

Borgonovo, John, Crowley, John, Ó Drisceoil, Donal & Murphy, Mike (eds), *Atlas of
the Irish Revolution*. Cork, 2017.

Coogan, Tim Pat, *De Valera. Long Fellow, Long Shadow*. London, 1995.

Coogan, Tim Pat, *The I.R.A.* London, 2000.

Crawley, John, *The Yank: My Life as a Former US Marine in the IRA*. Dublin, 2022.

De Baróid, Ciarán, *Ballymurphy and the Irish War*. London, 2000.

Devoy, John, *Recollections of an Irish Rebel*. Shannon, 1969.

Dillon, Martin, *Killer in Clowntown: Joe Doherty, the IRA and the Special Relationship*.
London, 1992.

Dorney, John, *The Civil War in Dublin. The Fight for the Irish Capital 1922-1924*.
Dublin, 2017.

Duggan, John P., *A History of the Irish Army*. Dublin, 1991.

Dunne, Derek, *Out of the Maze: The True Story of the Biggest Jail Escape Since the War*.
Dublin, 1988.

Durney, James, *On the One Road. Political Unrest in Kildare 1913-1994*. Naas,
2001.

Durney, James, *The Civil War in Kildare*. Cork, 2011.

Durney, James, *The War of Independence in Kildare*. Cork, 2013.

Durney, James, *Interned. The Curragh Internment Camps in the War of Independence*.
Cork, 2019.

Durney, James, *Stand You Now for Ireland's Cause. A Biographical Index of Co. Kildare
Republican Activists 1913-1923*. Naas, 2023.

Dwyer, T. Ryle, *The Squad and the Operations of Michael Collins*. Cork, 2005.

Fanning, Ronan, *Éamon de Valera, A Will to Power*. London, 2015.

Golway, Terry, *Irish Rebel: John Devoy and America's Fight for Ireland's Freedom.* Dublin, 2015.

Hannigan, David, *De Valera in America. The Rebel President and the Making of Irish Independence.* New York, 2010.

Hopkinson, Michael, *Green against Green. The Irish Civil War.* Dublin, 1988.

MacEvilly, Michael, *A Splendid Resistance. The Life of IRA Chief of Staff Dr. Andy Cooney.* Dublin, 2011.

Maguire, John, *IRA Internments and the Irish Government. Subversives and the State 1939–1962.* Dublin, 2008.

Maher, Jim, *The Flying Column – West Kilkenny 1916–21.* Dublin, 1987.

Martin, Harry F. & O'Malley, Cormac K.H., *Ernie O'Malley: A Life.* Dublin, 2021.

McCullagh, David, *De Valera. Vol. I: Rise 1882–1932.* Dublin, 2017.

McGuffin, John, *Internment.* Tralee, 1973.

McKittrick, David and McVea, David, *Making Sense of the Troubles: A History of the Northern Ireland Conflict.* London, 2012.

Murphy, Seamus, *Having it Away. A Story of Freedom, Friendship and IRA Jailbreak.* Bray, 2018.

National Graves Association, *The Last Post: The Details and Stories of Republican Dead 1913/1975.* Dublin, 1976.

Neeson, Eoin, *The Civil War, 1922–23.* Dublin, 1989.

O'Brien, John, *Securing the Irish State: An Garda Síochána. A Century of Policing 1922–2022.* Carrigtwohill, 2022.

O'Callaghan, Micheál, *For Ireland and Freedom. Roscommon's Contribution to the Fight for Independence.* Cork, 2012.

O'Connor, Seamus, *Tomorrow was Another Day.* Tralee, 1970.

O'Donnell, Peadar, *The Gates Flew Open.* London, 1932.

O'Donnell, Ruán, *Special Category. The IRA in English Prisons, Vol. I: 1968–1978.* Dublin, 2012.

O'Donnell, Ruán, *Special Category. The IRA in English Prisons, Vol. II: 1978–1985.* Dublin, 2015.

O'Donoghue, Florence, *Sworn to be Free: The Complete Book of IRA Jailbreaks 1918–1921.* Tralee, 1971.

O'Driscoll, Seán, *Heiress, Rebel, Vigilante, Bomber: The Extraordinary Life of Rose Dugdale.* London, 2022.

Ó Faoleán, Gearóid, *A Broad Church: The Provisional IRA in the Republic of Ireland 1969–1980.* Dublin, 2019.

Ó Lúing, Seán, *The Catalpa Rescue.* Tralee, 1965.

O'Malley, Ernie, *On Another Man's Wound.* Dublin, 1979.

Ramón, Marta, *A Provisional Dictator. James Stephens and the Fenian Movement.* Dublin, 2007.

Ryder, Chris, *Inside the Maze: The Untold Story of the Northern Ireland Prison Service.* London, 2000.

Swithin Walsh, Eoin, *Kilkenny: In Times of Revolution 1900–1923.* Dublin, 2018.

The rescue of the military Fenians from Australia. With a Memoir of John Devoy who planned the rescue and the names and careers of the Rescued and their Rescuers. Dublin, 1929

Thorne, Kathleen Hegarty. *Echoes of Their Footsteps, The Irish Civil War 1922–1924.* Newberg, Oregon 2014.

Trigg, Jonathan, *Death in the Fields: The IRA in East Tyrone.* Dublin, 2022.

Younger, Calton, *Ireland's Civil War.* London, 1968.

Articles and Pamphlets

Browne, Vincent, 'How we beat the Maidstone. Seven tell of escape', *Irish Press*, 24 January 1972.

Byrne, Thomas, 'A tunnel to freedom. Escape from Kildare Camp', undated newspaper article, copy in author's possession.

Canavan, Tony, 'Crumlin Road Jail', *History Ireland*, Vol. 25, Iss. 2 (March–April 2017).

Conroy, John F., 'Escapes from the Rath Internment Camp, Curragh, 1921', *Western People*, 6 June 1964.

Donoghue, Fergal, *Kilkenny Jail, 22 November 1921*, Kilkenny Co. Library, 2021.

Dorney, John, 'Today in Irish History, August 14, 1922, The anti-Treaty IRA attack on Dundalk', www.theirishstory.com

'Escapes by air and by land', *An Phoblacht/Republican News*, 31 August 2023.

Foley, Aran, 'The "Magnificent Seven" swim to freedom. Remembering the Past: The "*Maidstone*" escape 50 years on,' *An Phoblacht/Republican News*, 4, 16 January 2022.

Fox, Mattie, 'Dermot Hegarty. From bible salesman to legendary folk performer', https://mattiefox.wordpress.com/2016/10/14/dermot-hegarty-2/ 14 October 2016.

Gillis, Liz, 'The Great Escape', *Kilmainham Tales – remembering for the future.* Kilmainhamtales.ie

'Irish prisoner on life sentence who escaped from Wakefield Prison', *The Irish Times*, 28 November 2015.

Jackson, Michael, 'Martin's dramatic bid for freedom from the Maidstone prison ship', BelfastMedia.com, 2 February 2022, https://belfastmedia.com/maidstone#:~:text=The%20plan%20to%20escape%20the,into%20the%20piercingly%20cold%20water.

'*Maidstone* escape: swimming to freedom (Part 2)', Peter Rogers speaking to Jim Gibney, *An Phoblacht/Republican News*, 7 February 2002.

'Mayo men feature in famous I.R.A. escapes from the Curragh Camp', *Mayo News*, 24 January 1959.

McLoughlin, Pat, 'Clara and Ballycumber men among twenty that went over the wall at Mountjoy in 1919', *Offaly History Blog*, 21 January 2023.

Mullan, John, 'Great escapes of an IRA gunman', *The Guardian*, 5 January 2000.

O'Keefe, Patrick, 'My reminiscences of 1914–1923', *Oughterany. Journal of the Donadea Local History Group.* Donadea, 1993.

Ó Maoláin, Tomás, 'The inside story of famous I.R.A. escape from the Curragh Camp', *Mayo News*, 17 May 1959.

'Remembering the Past: 19 prisoners escape from Portlaoise', *An Phoblacht/Republican News*, 27 August 2009.

'Remembering the Past: The helicopter escape', *An Phoblacht/Republican News*, 28 October 2004.

'Shot on sight. Paddy Mulvanna and Jim Bryson', *Irish Republican News*, 1 September 2022.

'The escape from Newbridge Barracks', *Leinster Leader*, 31 December 1927.

'The Greatest Escape', *Iris, the republican magazine*, 18, Autumn 1993.

'The I.R.A. prisoners break out.' Memories of Mountjoy Prison as told by former Governor Seán Kavanagh to Liam MacGabhann, *This Week*, 1 May 1970.

'30 years on: The Great Portlaoise Escape', *An Phoblacht/Republican News*, 26 August 2004.

Online Sources

crumlinroadgaol.com (accessed 20 May 2024).

'Crumlin Kangaroos daring escape', Christy Keenan speaking to Joe Austin, 20 November 2021, www.youtube.com/watch?v=hfZYhnT01rU (accessed 20 May 2024).

Durney, James, 'The Greatest Escape. Newbridge Barracks 14/15 October 1922', https://kildare.ie/ehistory/index.php/the-greatest-escape-newbridge-barracks-14-15-october-1922/.

Howard, Marcus, 'Dundalk Gaol 1922. The Great Escape', www.youtube.com/watch?v=OXm7-LdO6W4 (accessed 11 May 2024).

https://treasonfelony.wordpress.com/2020/03/20/the-derry-jail-great-escape-20th-march-1943/ (accessed 19 May 2024).

https://curiousireland.ie/old-derry-jail-tower/ (accessed 19 May 2024).

McCann, Lorraine, 'Dundalk Jail during the Civil War', Louth County Archives, www.www.youtube.com/watch?v=9gc9qKsCcSk.

Morrison, Danny, 'Terence "Cleaky" Clarke: Death of a Hero', 2007. www.https://www.dannymorrison.com/wp-content/dannymorrisonarchive/115.htm.

Ó Ríordáin, Aodhán, 'The story of my grandfather's escape from Dundalk Jail 100 years ago today', 27 July 2022, https://m.facebook.com/AodhanORiordain.

Questions on treatment of prisoners by Ailfrid O'Broin. *Dáil Éireann deb.*, Vol. iv, 31 October 1923. Sourced online 8 April 2010. www.oireachtas.ie.

The life and death of Jackie Griffith (1921–1943) https://comeheretome.com/2022/02/ (accessed 19 May 2024).

www.dib.ie/biography/duggan-eamonn-john-edmund-a2820 (accessed 9 May 2024).

www.dib.ie/biography/omalley-ernest-bernard-ernie-a6885 (accessed 9 May 2024).

www.dib.ie/biography/coyle-eithne-anne-a2132 (accessed 9 May 2024).

www.dib.ie/biography/aiken-francis-thomas-frank-a0070 (accessed 11 May 2024).

www.dib.ie/biography/odonnell-peadar-a6700 (accessed 19 May 2024).

www.dib.ie/biography/gilmore-george-frederick-a3485 (accessed 19 May 2024).

INDEX